KU-845-105

Some Comparative Aspects
of
Irish Law

Alfred Gaston Donaldson

PUBLISHED FOR THE

Duke University Commonwealth-Studies Center

DUKE UNIVERSITY PRESS, DURHAM, N. C.
CAMBRIDGE UNIVERSITY PRESS, LONDON
1957

UNIVERSITY LIBRARY NOTTINGHAM

© 1957, DUKE UNIVERSITY PRESS

Library of Congress Catalogue Card number 57-8815

Second Printing, 1967

Printed in the United States of America

PUBLICATION NUMBER 3
Duke University Commonwealth-Studies Center

*Some Comparative Aspects
of Irish Law*

Duke University Commonwealth-Studies Center Publications

1. *The British Commonwealth: An Experiment in Co-operation among Nations*, by Frank H. Underhill

2. *South Africa: Economic and Political Aspects*, by Hector Menteith Robertson

3. *Some Comparative Aspects of Irish Law*, by Alfred Gaston Donaldson

In
Maiorem Honorem
Ulidiae Hiberniaeque

BS8-00293

INTRODUCTORY NOTE

In a series of monographs on the British Commonwealth it is fitting that there should be some study of the part which Ireland has had. Of the various aspects of Ireland's relationship to the general subject, the development of Irish law, viewed both historically and comparatively, has special fascination. To present an account of the development in this field, the Commonwealth-Studies Committee of Duke University has been much pleased to have a scholar of great learning in the law of his native island and of the Commonwealth in general, who has in the present volume demonstrated his insight into the relationship between the legal and the political.

Three of the chapters in the book comprise the substance of lectures which the author delivered at Duke University in 1955. The three additional chapters have been combined with the lecture material to constitute an illuminating and imaginative account. In it the author has of course expressed his own views, which are not to be ascribed to the Commonwealth-Studies Center or to the Carnegie Corporation, which has through a grant made possible the enterprise which the Center represents.

Mr. A. G. Donaldson, a native of Belfast, received the LL.B. degree and the Ph.D. degree from Queen's University in that city, and has been a lecturer in the Law Faculty of the same institution. Since 1948 he has been connected with the Office of Parliamentary Draftsmen to the Government of Northern Ireland. A member of the Inn of Court of Northern Ireland and of the Bar of Northern Ireland, he has been active in the work of the International Law Association. He has contributed to various Irish, British, and Canadian legal and historical journals.

Robert R. Wilson
Member, Duke University
Commonwealth-Studies Committee

PREFACE

AMERICAN readers may well ask themselves why a book on aspects of Irish law should be of particular interest to them today. For most Americans, apart from Great Britain itself, it is the other present or past parts or members of the British Empire or Commonwealth which seem of far more vital concern in contemporary international crises. The Far East—India, Hong Kong, and Malaya—Africa—the Union of South Africa and Kenya—the Middle East and the Mediterranean—Cyprus, the Suez, and Palestine—and Canada, Australia, and New Zealand all figure prominently in American foreign policies during and since the Second World War. Not so Ireland—neither the Irish Republic nor Northern Ireland is apt to be present in the thoughts of Americans who are striving to master the intricacies of current world politics.

Apart from the sheer pleasure to be derived from the clarity and wit of Mr. Donaldson's text—for he exhibits that mastery of English prose which so many Irishmen have had—Americans will, I venture to believe, find much in his comments on Irish law of both interest and value to them. Many of the most troublesome and apparently unsolvable issues in international affairs which threaten world peace today result from the transformation of the British Empire of the nineteenth century into the British Commonwealth of the middle of the twentieth century. In that transformation Ireland has played a prominent, often a leading role, far transcending its relative size in area or population. On the one hand, the Irish Free State or Eire while a member of the Commonwealth took the lead in seeking ever-increasing amounts of freedom of action and self-government and ultimately even complete independence. On the other hand, Northern Ireland has followed quite the contrary course. We cannot hope to understand the British Commonwealth today and the problems arising out of its existence without a grasp of the Irish developments in the twentieth century. It is these aspects of Irish law which Mr. Don-aldson has so skilfully and vividly portrayed in the six chapters of this book. Indeed, throughout the book Mr. Donaldson has chosen, most wisely it seems to me, to emphasize at every opportunity the comparative phase of his primary topics—the surprising (to me) extent to which developments in Irish constitutional history, in Irish land law and policies, in Irish administrative law, have been paralleled and often deliberately imitated in other parts of the British Commonwealth. Of course, such comparisons must not be pushed too far—there are peculiar conditions in Ireland not duplicated elsewhere which must always be kept in mind. Yet even when these differences found in Ireland are given full weight, one is still impressed by the striking similarities between the attitudes and laws of a nation emerging into freedom and independence, whether it be Ireland, India, Pakistan, or South Africa. We can, perhaps, find much that will explain otherwise incomprehensible aspects of the laws and policies of India or South Africa if we are familiar with the events of the last few decades in Ireland which are so well described by Mr. Donaldson.

There are, moreover, not a few direct ties between the history and laws of Ireland and those of the United States. As Mr. Donaldson tactfully reminds us, many ideas which did much to shape American constitutional and legal history developed from proposals originating, in part at least, in Ireland which often came to naught there because of adverse conditions but which when transplanted to the United States, sometimes by Irish emigrants, flourished rapidly. This is a debt which it behooves us to acknowledge freely, just as, in turn, our constitution and laws have left their imprint on many aspects of those of the Irish Republic and even of Northern Ireland.

ROBERT KRAMER

ACKNOWLEDGMENT

My SINCERE thanks are due to Duke University and the Committee of the Commonwealth-Studies Center for inviting me to deliver the lectures on which Chapters III, IV, and VI of this work are based. I was both honored by that invitation and glad to be able to present to those interested in Commonwealth affairs some reflections on Ireland and the Commonwealth, Constitutional Developments in Ireland since 1920, and Irish Land Law. (The remaining three chapters have been added to sketch in the background of Irish legal and constitutional history, and to outline the working of the administrative systems in present-day Ireland.) I trust that this work will repay in some small measure the pleasure which I had in delivering the lectures and the benefit which I derived from seeing something of the work of the Commonwealth-Studies Center. I am particularly glad to have the opportunity of referring to both the Irish jurisdictions, those of Northern Ireland and of the Irish Republic, and I trust my Dublin friends will forgive the presumption of a member of the Bar of Northern Ireland in writing of the legal position in the Republic.

I must acknowledge my debt to the books and articles mentioned in the Bibliography, which were of great assistance in the preparation of this work. Generally, I owe much to my former teachers in the Faculty of Law at the Queen's University of Belfast, Professor J. L. Montrose (Dean of the Faculty) and especially Professor F. H. Newark, who has both brought light to the dark places of Irish legal history and commented on the operation of the Constitution of Northern Ireland. Mr. Vincent Grogan, Barrister-at-Law, of the Parliamentary Draftsman's Office, Dublin, kindly obtained for me some information about affairs there, as did Dr. V. T. H. Delany, Barrister-at-Law, Lecturer in Law at Queen's University, Belfast. Dr. E. R. R. Green, of Manchester University, was good enough to allow me to read his informative essay on "The Place of Ireland in the Evolution of the British Empire," for which I thank him. I am also obliged to the University of Toronto Press for permission to use, in an abridged form, some material from an article on The Constitution of Northern Ireland which appeared in the 1955 volume of the *University of Toronto Law Journal*. My colleagues in the Office of the Parliamentary Draftsmen, Belfast, gave me every encouragement and much assistance, and my wife gave me considerable help in preparing the text for publication. I wish to reiterate my thanks to Professor R. Taylor Cole and the Committee of the Commonwealth-Studies Center, to Professor Robert Kramer for his extremely helpful editorial advice and care, and especially to Professor Robert R. Wilson, who may well be described as the "onlie begetter" of this work.

Finally, I wish to stress that this work is written in my personal capacity, not in my official one of Second Parliamentary Draftsman to the Government of Northern Ireland.

A. G. DONALDSON

CONTENTS

Introductory Note
vii

Preface
ix

Acknowledgments
xi

1. Legal History and Present-Day Legal Systems
3

2. Constitutional History
37

3. Ireland and the Commonwealth: Dominion Status
and International Law
77

4. Constitutional Developments since 1920
123

5. Administrative Law
181

6. Land Law
229

Bibliography
270

Index
283

Some Comparative Aspects
of Irish Law

Legal History and Present-Day Legal Systems

IN THE WORDS of a Dublin judge noted both for legal learning and historical scholarship, Ireland was the country of "the first adventure of the common law." Because of this, Irish legal history is worthy of study not only by Irish lawyers but also by all those with an interest in the legal heritage which emanated from Westminster Hall and spread throughout the English-speaking world. Therefore it is doubly a matter for regret that so little has yet been written on the history of Irish law; as one commentator has remarked, "Ireland not only still awaits its Reeves or Holdsworth; it even lacks an elementary textbook on Irish legal history."[1] Still more does Ireland lack its Maitland, but then there are no laws of genetics to ensure that there is a scholar of Maitland's caliber to deal with each legal system in the world. In the circumstances, this chapter does little more than refer to some of the main features of the development of the common law in Ireland, suggesting that these might be studied in comparison with the development of the common law elsewhere in the Commonwealth. In contrast with other areas where the common law and other legal systems continue to exist side by side, Ireland provides a somewhat protracted example of the displacement of a native legal system by the common law.

EARLY IRISH LAW

In the nineteenth century Sir Henry Maine drew on Victorian translations of the seventh and eighth century Irish law tracts for his descriptions of the legal systems governing the early Celtic communities. More recently the late Professor Eoin MacNeill, in his

---

[1] Francis Headon Newark, "Notes on Irish Legal History," *Northern Ireland Legal Quarterly*, VII (1947), 121.

Early Irish Laws and Institutions,[2] countered Maine's view of the primitive, customary nature of early Irish law and stressed the important part played by the local kings as well as by the professional jurists, the *brehons*. Still more recently, Professor D. A. Binchy (now of the Dublin Institute for Advanced Studies), lecturing on "The Linguistic and Historical Value of the Irish Law Tracts,"[3] pointed out that the manuscripts of these documents were written eight hundred years after the compilation of the tracts in the seventh and eighth centuries. Although there are considerable linguistic problems, and original text has to be distinguished from subsequent gloss and later commentary, Professor Binchy demonstrated the value of these documents in placing Celtic Ireland and her legal institutions in the Indo-European tradition, and in tracing the influence of Christianity on Irish law. Further, he showed that development was possible in such matters as the legal status of women, despite the conservatism of the jurists. As he later remarked:

. . . the main interest of Irish law for the student of early institutions is that it shows how a legal system based, not on State sanctions but on the power of traditional custom, formulated and applied by a learned professional caste, could function and command obedience.[4]

It is not suggested that the legal systems of the Indian, the Australian aborigine and the Maori, the South African native and the North American Indian will necessarily be close, or even parallel, to the system which developed in Celtic Ireland; but the historian of comparative law and the anthropologist cannot afford to neglect the Irish evidence in any study of the legal systems displaced by the common law. A difficulty is that the value of the edition of the *Ancient Laws of Ireland*, published in the second half of the nineteenth century by the authority of a Commission specially appointed for the purpose in 1852, is doubted by modern scholars on linguistic grounds. As Gavan Duffy P. put it in *Foyle and Bann Fisheries Ltd. v. Attorney General*, (1949) 83 I.L.T.R. 29, at p. 41:

The law still has to be deduced from elliptical, incomplete and often corrupt texts, which appear to be copies of copies of archaic manuscripts, reproduced by much later hereditary scholars, to the accompaniment of

[2] Dublin, 1935.
[3] *Proceedings of the British Academy*, XXIX (1943), 195-227.
[4] "Secular Institutions" in *Early Irish Society* (Dublin, 1954), 52, 62-63.

unreliable and often unskilled and sometimes unscrupulous interpretations. The study of Irish law, seriously undertaken only in recent times, is still in its infancy and the conclusions of the most experienced scholars are tentative, and seem at best generally to represent plausible historical speculation. Dr. Dillon's view is that law texts cannot be used as a solid basis for any conclusion at all until they are edited and examined.

The combined linguistic and legal learning displayed in Professor Binchy's work leads one to hope for the eventual production by him of a definitive work on early Irish law. Such a work would not be of purely antiquarian interest, for in three cases heard in the Dublin courts during the past thirty years questions have been raised of rights under the *brehon* law, as the early Irish legal system has been called. These cases were *R. (Moore) v. O'Hanrahan,* [1927] I. R. 406; *Little v. Cooper,* [1937] I. R. 1, and the *Foyle and Bann Fisheries* case just mentioned. Although, as Gavan Duffy P. pointed out, the exact position of older rights in a modern legal system is necessarily somewhat speculative, the evidence given in these three cases provides important material for both lawyers and historians.

THE INTRODUCTION OF THE COMMON LAW

The story of the coming of the common law to Ireland may be said to have begun with the visits of Henry II in 1171-1172, when he established his lordship over Ireland, confirmed Strongbow, the Earl of Pembroke, as Earl of Leinster, and received the recognition of certain Irish kings. Almost four centuries later this lordship of Ireland became a kingdom attached to the English crown, but even by that time the common law had not spread throughout the whole island. Ireland's link with the common law is certainly an ancient one, but it was also one which varied very much in strength during the first four and a half centuries of its existence.

Towards the end of the twelfth century evidence begins to appear of the existence in Ireland of the common law and its institutions. The county court began to exercise jurisdiction in Dublin and the surrounding districts, writs were issued, particularly in real property actions, and the justiciar who acted as the royal representative sat to hear disputed cases. In the first quarter of the thirteenth century the limitation of writs in real actions was a frequent subject of royal instructions, and the justiciar was given power both to issue writs and to hear "pleas of the crown" either personally or by deputy. In 1227 there was transmitted to Ireland a copy of the Register of Writs, which as Maitland pointed out is of value in showing the state of English law at that time as well as the intention to apply it in Ireland.[5]

The idea that the law used in Ireland should be the same as that in England was not only acted upon but was also declared in express terms. In the descriptions of John's visit to Ireland in 1210 it was stated that he ordered the laws and customs of England to be observed in Ireland. This general theme became particularly apparent in the period 1226-1237, when various points of English law were set out in a series of directions on such matters as tenancy by the curtsey, the right of co-parceners, the jurisdiction of the ecclesiastical courts to deal with advowsons, and legitimacy disputes. Clearly the common law would not fail to take root in Ireland because of lack of information about its substance or procedure.[6]

There were, however, two limitations on the operation of the common law, the one territorial and the other personal. The territorial restriction lay in the fact, mentioned in the chapter on Constitutional History (infra), that the area of Anglo-Norman influence in Ireland waxed and waned considerably until the beginning of the seventeenth century. As a result, the king's writ could not run in areas where there was no machinery to enforce it, and where indeed the king's name might not be held in very high esteem. The personal restriction on the operation of the common law stemmed from the fact that the native Irish living in the jurisdiction of the royal courts did not always have direct access to these courts.

It is an indication of the time at which English institutions were transplanted to Ireland that there were restrictions on the right to use the common law. In the early thirteenth century the practice became common of granting to individual Irishmen or groups of them the right to use English law. Thus it came about that members of the five principal Irish septs had access to the king's courts, and a plea that he was "of the five bloods" gave this right to an O'Neill

[5] Frederic William Maitland, "The History of the Register of Original Writs," *Harvard Law Review*, III (1889), 97, 110; "The Introduction of English Law into Ireland," *Collected Papers* (3 vols.; Cambridge, 1911), II, 81-83.

[6] The documents on which these paragraphs are based are calendared or printed in the works of H. S. Sweetman and H. F. Berry referred to in the Bibliography: for comment, see the articles of W. J. Johnston and F. H. Newark there mentioned.

of Ulster, an O'Melachlin of Meath, an O'Connor of Connaught, an O'Brien of Thomond, or a MacMurrough of Leinster. Recent research has shown that an Irishman living in the Anglo-Norman area was not, however, automatically deprived of all rights. In an age when the substance of the law was "secreted in the interstices of procedure," it is not surprising that legal ingenuity contrived to evade restrictions of this kind. A free Irishman, a *hibernicus*, could obtain a hearing in the royal courts by joining his lord as co-plaintiff or by alleging that crown rights were affected. Alternatively, the Irishman might have unfree status, being called a *betagh*, a *nativus*, or (ambiguously) a *hibernicus*. In Anglo-Norman eyes he was the equivalent of a villein, although the status was known to Irish law long before the Normans set foot on Ireland. A *betagh* had the right to sue in his lord's court, and if he were injured his lord might sue in the king's court for injuries to him. During the period 1277-1280 there were negotiations for a general grant of English law to the Irish, but these did not come to fruition. It was not until 1331 that the Irish, other than the *betaghs*, became entitled to the use of English law, and even after this date the practice continued of making grants of the right to use English law to individual Irishmen. As for the *betaghs*, presumably their decline was parallel to that of the English villein.[7]

Outside the Anglo-Norman pale the *brehon* law continued to flourish. Indeed, the famous Statutes of Kilkenny, passed by the Irish parliament in 1366, can be regarded as a triumph for the native Irish institutions over those imported from England, because it was necessary to legislate to prevent the Anglo-Norman lords from becoming *Hibernis ipsis hiberniores*. But the relations between the Anglo-Norman and Irish jurisdictions have not yet been worked out, and would undoubtedly prove fruitful for some comparative legal historian with the patience necessary to quarry the fragmentary material. For example, despite the wide cleavage between the two systems, it appears that as late as 1558 the Privy Council of Ireland ordered a dispute between certain of the O'Carrolls of Tipperary to be settled by *brehons*.[8] It would be interesting to

[7] Annette Jocelyn Otway-Ruthven, "The Request of the Irish for English Law, 1277-80," *Irish Historical Studies*, VI (1949), 261-270; "The Native Irish and English Law in Medieval Ireland," *Irish Historical Studies*, VII (1950), 1-16.

[8] *Charles Haliday Manuscripts, Historical Manuscripts Commission, 15th Report* (London, 1897), No. 40, Appendix, Part III, 63.

see how far, if at all, the system of arbitration which was the core of the *brehon* law influenced the use of English law in such matters as disputes about land.   Yet such a study would have to stop in the first decade of the seventeenth century, when Sir John Davies, lawyer and poet, historian and politician, progressed through those parts of Ireland which had not been subject to English law.   Counties which formerly had no sheriff were "shired" so that the machinery of English law could operate, and Davies and his fellow judge of assize inaugurated the use of English law in these areas.   In the result, as the Irish parliament put it in an Act passed in 1612 (11, 12 & 13 Jac. 1, c. 5):

. . . all the natives and inhabitants of this kingdom, without difference and distinction, are taken into his Majestie's gratious protection, and doe now live under one law as dutiful subjects of our Soveraigne Lord and Monarch.

The legal problem confronting the Anglo-Normans in Ireland was solved by overriding the legal system in existence when the Normans arrived there.   There was no question of fusing two systems of law and of courts, such as took place in India during the nineteenth century; or of the continuation of local systems of law, subject to the gradual encroachment of the English system, such as has taken place in Ceylon; or of setting up special courts to protect the rights of the original inhabitants as in New Zealand.   But it must be remembered that the common law was a comparatively young plant when it was first put into Irish soil; and the very fact that it took so long to root in the whole island is itself an explanation of the reluctance to compromise, for the "first adventure of the common law" was not only lengthy, it was also hazardous.

THE SYSTEM OF COURTS

Some mention has already been made of the English legal institutions which began to flourish in Ireland at the end of the twelfth century.   In the succeeding centuries the judicial system was settled on English lines, thus providing yet another source of comparison for the Commonwealth legal historian.   The stages in the setting up of the system of courts have been skilfully traced by Professor F. H. Newark in his "Notes on Irish Legal History" (*supra* note 1). As in England the main source was the royal court, represented in Ireland by the justiciar.   On his journeys throughout the country he was accompanied first by one justice and later by more. After Richard II's visit to Ireland in 1394-1395 this court became the Irish court of King's Bench, and the justiciar ceased to sit in it. In the sixteenth century the King's Bench ceased to itinerate and sat in Dublin, exercising original civil and criminal jurisdiction, and an appellate jurisdiction over the court of Common Pleas and the lower and ecclesiastical courts.

The court of Common Pleas developed in the thirteenth century from the practice of sending itinerant justices throughout the country; when in Dublin they sat to hear common pleas and came to have a fixed seat like their Westminster counterparts. The jurisdiction of this court lay in purely civil matters in which no Crown interest was involved. Also in the thirteenth century there was established an Exchequer, which towards the end of that century was to exercise judicial functions, and these expanded into a triple jurisdiction in revenue matters, common pleas, and equity. Apparently it was much later that the Chancery developed jurisdictions in both equity and common law matters.

It is fortunate that we possess a collection of the records of the justiciar's court in the two-volume *Calendar of the Justiciary Rolls, Ireland, 1295-1307,*[9] which gives a fascinating picture of judicial activity in Ireland at the turn of the thirteenth century, and provides useful material for comparison with the situation in England. Similarly, such information as now remains and relates to the activities of the Irish county court, the seignorial jurisdictions, and the ecclesiastical courts would be of value in comparing developments on either side of the Irish Sea. The Court of Castle Chamber in Ireland corresponded to the Court of Star Chamber in England, and there were Irish equivalents of the Court of High Commission and the Court of Wards. Again, the palatinate jurisdiction belonging to the Ormonds in Tipperary showed a microcosm of the Anglo-Irish system at work within a limited area until its eventual abolition in 1715.

From this brief glimpse it will be apparent that the Irish courts developed more or less concurrently with their English counterparts. The judicial system was not imported, as happened later in other parts of the Commonwealth, when the differences between

---

[9] Dublin, 1905, 1914. A third volume, covering the period 1308-1314, was published in Dublin in 1956.

the various jurisdictions had crystallized. The officials round whom the courts grew were appointed for Ireland as they were in England, and the jurisdictions increased and diminished accordingly. Much of the outline of this period of Irish legal history requires to be filled in, and while the most obvious comparisons are with the English judicial system, future research in the field of comparative legal history may well reveal contrasts with a similar, but somewhat later, development in the history of the common law—the introduction of legal institutions in the North American colonies.[10]

THE JUDICIARY

If the general pattern of Irish legal history has not yet been fully documented, one aspect of it has been very thoroughly investigated. In his two-volume history of *The Judges in Ireland, 1221-1921*,[11] F. E. Ball compiled and catalogued from many sources a mass of minute information about the occupants of the Irish bench during a period of seven centuries. (As the author himself remarked, it was fitting that his researches ended with considerable changes in the judicial regime which had flourished in Dublin since the Norman occupation.) From this study emerged certain salient facts as to the policy adopted in Whitehall in the making of Irish judicial appointments. As was perhaps to be expected, during the first century or so of its existence the Irish bench was recruited mainly from England. Then, towards the end of the fourteenth century, when the Anglo-Norman community had become settled in Ireland, men of Irish birth (though not belonging to the native race) were appointed to the Irish bench, and in the following century the proportion of such appointments increased. The proportions of Irish and English judges varied during the Tudor period and at the beginning of the Stuart era, as Ball puts it:

. . . the new members of the bench were all drawn from the English bar. Apart from the desire to obtain men of large professional experience, such a course had to become necessary owing to the extent that recusancy permeated the legal profession in Ireland.[12]

[10] Cf. Paul Samuel Reinsch, "The English Common Law in the Early American Colonies," *Select Essays in Anglo-American Legal History* (3 vols.; Boston, 1907), I, 367-415.

[11] New York, 1927.

[12] Ball, *op. cit. supra* note 11 at I, 233-234.

During the Cromwellian period English appointments predominated, but it is noteworthy that when a reorganization of the Dublin courts was carried out in 1655 the historic pattern of the "Four Courts" was followed; the courts of Chancery and Exchequer retained their former names, while the King's Bench and the Common Pleas were renamed the Upper Bench and Lower Bench. This system was fated to be short-lived, and at the restoration of Charles II the courts resumed their old titles and jurisdictions. An interesting feature of the Restoration bench was that it included no fewer than three judges of Celtic origin, though of course the remainder included a number of English appointees. With the rise of the party system in the politics of the eighteenth century, the pattern of appointments becomes familiar to a modern eye. The Irish House of Commons was frequently an antechamber to the Four Courts. While there were appointments from the English bar, Ball noted that in 1770 the bench was, with two exceptions, Irish, and commented:

> Henceforth, as a rule, an English element is alone visible in legal education, and the Irish element is dominant alike in family, in birth, in general education and in influence. At the same time the professional element begins to overshadow the extraneous attributes.[13]

During the brief period of freedom from the domination of the English House of Lords (from 1782 until 1801, mentioned in the next section of this chapter), the bench was wholly Irish. The Union gave different colors to the appointments to the Irish bench, but the pattern did not change greatly. Since the Lord Chancellorship of Ireland was a political office, there were a number of English appointments to it, and the Great Seal of Ireland was held for a brief space by Lord Campbell, the author of the *Lives of the Lord Chancellors* and the *Lives of the Chief Justices*. For a longer period the post was filled by Sir Edward Sugden, later Lord St. Leonards, who, fittingly, was the last and one of the most distinguished members of the English bar to grace the Irish bench. Also, as befitted the century in which Catholic emancipation changed from a political aim to a definite fact, a number of Catholic members of the Irish bar ascended the bench.

[13] Ball, *op. cit. supra* note 11 at II, 155.

Two points which Ball made are relevant in considering his compilation of biographical details concerning the Irish judges. The first is that the Irish element must not be overstressed, because of the requirement that members of the Irish bar must keep terms at one of the inns of court in London. This stemmed from the medieval practice, and the requirement was not removed until the passing of the Barristers Admission (Ireland) Act, 1885 (48 & 49 Vict. c. 20). Therefore, whatever their background, the members of the Irish bench had some contact with the English nurseries of the common law, although if they were members of the Irish bar they would also have attended the King's Inns in Dublin. A second point worthy of note is the influence which Trinity College, Dublin, must have had indirectly on the course of Irish law during the latter part of the eighteenth century, the nineteenth century, and the early part of the present one. According to Ball's calculations:

Between the accession of George the Third in 1760 and the last appointment by England in 1921 a hundred and forty-five men were raised to the bench. Of these Dublin University claimed as alumni as many as a hundred and eleven.[14]

It would be interesting to trace the university education which these men received during the century and a half to which Ball refers, as the legal, philosophical, and historical doctrines which they read must have had some ultimate reflection in their pronouncements from the bench.

In his voluminous and detailed work Ball provided an illuminating description of the progress of the Irish bench from a stepping-stone to English promotion to a judicial body with an inherent strength and a recognizable prestige. Here also the material exists for the comparison of the position of Ireland with other parts of the Commonwealth. The emergence of a local bar, and the appointment of its members to the bench, must be a recognizable feature of the different Commonwealth legal systems; and a comparison of judicial backgrounds would provide a valuable commentary on the way in which the common law was disseminated through the agency of men's minds.

[14] Ball, *op. cit. supra* note 11 at I, xvii.

THE SYSTEM OF APPEALS

Closely allied to the jurisdiction of the Irish courts and the personnel of the Irish bench was the matter of appellate jurisdiction. As is mentioned in the chapter on Ireland and the Commonwealth *(infra)*, appeals from Dublin to London were much discussed during the 1920's and 1930's, and the Privy Council still exercises jurisdiction over different parts of the Commonwealth. It is, therefore, trebly relevant in discussing Irish legal history to touch on the question of appeals. In the first place, it unfolds an important part of Irish legal development; secondly, disputes about the ultimate appeal tribunal for Ireland were, as will be seen in the chapter on Constitutional History *(infra)*, closely linked with disputes about the exercise of legislative power over Ireland; and thirdly, this aspect of appellate jurisdiction gives part of the background to more recent controversies.

The story commences with the constitution of the Irish courts in the thirteenth century. The reason why in the medieval period appeals lay by writ of error from the Irish King's Bench and other courts to the English King's Bench has been put thus by Mr. Richardson and Professor Sayles:

It must be remembered that, among the outlying dominions of the English Crown, Ireland stood in an exceptional relation. Alone it was subject to the English common law and to English legislation. Consequently the king's bench was in every way qualified to hear appeals from Irish courts and being, moreover, the court held technically *coram rege* and exercising its appellate jurisdiction by direct delegation from the king, it was the appropriate tribunal to which to refer appeals of a strictly judicial character.[15]

Johnston J. drew attention to a successful appeal of this kind as early as 1223, when a decision given by the justiciar in 1217 was overruled when the case was taken to England. The same learned author also pointed out that four centuries later in the case of *Mulcarry and ——v. Eyres*, (K. B. 1638) Cro. Car. 511, 79 Eng. Rep. 1041, an attempt was made to persuade the English King's Bench that because the word "bog" appearing in a grant of Irish land was unknown in England it was not known to the common

---

[15] *The Irish Parliament in the Middle Ages* (Philadelphia, 1952), 252.

law.[16] This argument was not successful, but it is indicative of the way in which Irish appeals might be treated when they were brought to England.

It was in the seventeenth century that the first assertion was made of the independence of the Irish judicial system. In 1641 the Irish House of Commons resolved that the "court of parliament" was the supreme court of judicature in Ireland; in effect, this would have made the Irish House of Lords the final appeal court. However, towards the end of the century appeals in chancery cases were taken directly to the English House of Lords, bypassing the Irish House, and on at least one occasion the former court overruled a decision of the latter. The Patriot Parliament which James II held in Dublin in 1689 sought to establish the supremacy of the Irish courts, but this gesture was speedily nullified by English legislation. In the second decade of the eighteenth century protracted litigation in the case of *Annesley v. Sherlock* led to open conflict between the two Houses on a judicial matter. The result was the passing by the Westminster parliament in 1720 of the Declaratory Act, the "Sixth of George the First" as it became known because of its regnal year citation—6 Geo.1, c. 5. This not only asserted the legislative supremacy of the British parliament over Ireland, but also deprived the Irish House of Lords of all judicial power and nullified its previous judgments.

For over sixty years the British House of Lords held sway over Irish case law. (In passing, it is of interest to note that the confirmation of this jurisdiction followed closely on the jurisdiction which the House of Lords took to hear appeals in civil cases from Scotland after the Union of 1707.) However, the recrudescence of the demand for legislative independence was coupled with a claim for judicial independence; and when the Repealing Act (22 Geo. 3, c. 53) was passed by the Westminster parliament in 1782, it removed both kinds of restriction imposed on Ireland in 1720. But it was not until the following year that the Renunciation Act (23 Geo. 3, c. 28) set all legal doubts at rest by declaring that no writ of error was to lie from the Irish courts to the English courts and that the right to have Irish actions and suits finally determined by the

[16] "The First Adventure of the Common Law," *Law Quarterly Review*, XXXVI (1920), 9, 24.

Irish courts was established and unquestionable. This jurisdiction of the Irish House of Lords did not last long, for eighteen years later, when the Act of Union came into force in 1801, both the legislative and the judicial functions of the Irish House of Lords were merged with those of its British counterpart in the new parliament of the United Kingdom.

From what has been said of Irish appellate jurisdiction it will be apparent that there is a major distinction between the early methods used for the decision of Irish appeals and for those from parts of the royal dominions outside the British Isles. Whereas appeals from overseas were brought by way of petition and referred to the Privy Council, Irish litigants invoking the aid of the English courts came to present their appeals to the House of Lords. This appears to be a natural development of the proximity of Ireland and the parallel development of the common law on either side of the Irish Sea. The remedy by way of writ of error remained open to the overseas appellant until the nineteenth century, but the method of petition was the one which was used; in Ireland, on the other hand, the use of the writ of error to the King's Bench in London flourished until the inauguration of appeals to the British House of Lords. In both cases, however, it is possible to see a centralizing influence at work in the insistence on the decision of appeals in London, by whatever tribunal or procedure. Not until the twentieth century was it possible for a member of the Commonwealth to obtain that judicial self-sufficiency which had been the claim of Ireland three centuries before.

THE NINETEENTH CENTURY

The turn of the eighteenth century is a convenient point from which to look back on the development of the common law in Ireland. It was the nineteenth century which saw considerable reforms in the judicial system in England, the fusion of courts in India, the setting up of the Supreme Court of Canada, and the decision of many Privy Council cases which are still of considerable importance today. It will be seen that Ireland was affected by the atmosphere of judicial reform and change, and might have been further affected had certain constitutional proposals for the government of the island come to maturity. But before looking at these the development of the institutions which were changed may be briefly summarized.

During the first four centuries of its existence in Ireland the common law had to contend with the problems of fluctuating territorial jurisdiction, a matter which was not finally settled until the commencement of the seventeenth century. But the institutions of the common law were implanted at an early date, and the development of these on lines similar to those of England was insured by the appointment of English judges or of Anglo-Irish judges trained in the common law. Then, just as the Privy Council supervised the development of the common law in other parts of the world, so the English House of Lords was given jurisdiction over Ireland when the upper House there showed signs of divergent opinion. Unfortunately, a lack of legal literature and the paucity of research into such sources as are still available make it difficult to say precisely how far Irish law differed from English law in these centuries. For instance, with the exception of the reports which Sir John Davies compiled at the beginning of the seventeenth century, reports of Irish decisions do not appear until the end of the following century. Yet material does exist for the investigation of many problems of Irish legal history, and a comparative study of these might well throw light on the development of the common law in different parts of the world.

Thus, for example, the researches of Professor F. H. Newark have disclosed the origins of a jurisdiction which is still extant in Northern Ireland and which stems from the medieval English "bill in eyre." This informal alternative to procedure by writ appears to have died out in England in the fifteenth century, but it survived in Ireland. Professor Newark suggests that what happened was that litigation commenced in a county was stayed when the judges of assize came on circuit, and that they would be the appropriate persons to hear the cases commenced by bill; the recognition of the bill procedure would naturally follow. In the eighteenth century the procedure was recognized by the Irish parliament, and at the end of that century barristers were appointed to assist the justices of quarter sessions who heard civil bills. These assistant barristers were the forerunners of the county court judges who today exercise jurisdiction in Northern Ireland, and the judges going circuit there still hear appeals from the decisions of county court judges in civil bill cases. This is a good example of the kind of discovery which may be made as a result of research in a comparative perspective.

Again, the recent decision in *Terrell v. Secretary of State for the Colonies*, [1953] 2 Q. B. 482 showed that colonial judges do not enjoy the independence possessed by the English judiciary. In this connection the struggle for the independence of Irish judges is relevant. Throughout the eighteenth century numerous attempts were made by the Irish parliament to secure the passing of a Judges Tenure Bill, which would have made Irish judges removable only for misconduct, thus placing them in the same position as their Westminster counterparts under the Act of Settlement, 1701 (12 & 13 Will. 3, c. 2). Not until 1782 was the Irish request finally acceded to, when the Irish statute 21 & 22 Geo. 3, c. 50 was passed. Similarly, the numerous attempts to secure an Irish Habeas Corpus Act, which also came to fruition in 1782 (21 & 22 Geo. 3, c. 11), form part of the movement towards the assertion of common law liberties.

Turning to the question of judicial organization and reform, in its last session in 1800 the Irish parliament set up a Court of Exchequer Chamber to act as an appeal tribunal in common law matters, and in its first session in 1801 the new parliament of the United Kingdom gave the Irish Master of the Rolls judicial functions in chancery matters. Later in the century, particularly in the 1850's, there were considerable alterations in the judicial system, several new courts being set up to deal with different matters at first instance while a Court of Appeal in Chancery was also constituted. In the result there were no less than nine courts of first instance. The reorganization of the English system of courts and the common administration of law and equity achieved by the Supreme Court of Judicature Act, 1875 (36 & 37 Vict. c. 66) were reproduced in Ireland by the Supreme Court of Judicature Act (Ireland), 1877 (40 & 41 Vict. c. 57). Under the 1877 Act seven of the nine courts of first instance were amalgamated to form five divisions of the High Court, subject to a Court of Appeal, from which in turn appeals lay to the House of Lords. In the succeeding two decades further changes reduced the divisions of the High Court to two, bearing the historic names of Queen's Bench and Chancery. Nineteenth-century reforms were not, however, confined to the superior courts, for the jurisdiction of the lower courts—the county courts and the quarter and petty sessions—was also altered in Ireland. The English changes in court procedure were also followed on the other side of the Irish Sea, so that once again the principle of parallel development was given general effect.

In addition to the changes which were made in the Irish judicial system in the nineteenth century a number of alterations were proposed but did not take effect because of the failure of larger schemes for the settlement of "the Irish question." These schemes will be discussed in the chapter on Constitutional History *(infra)*; but for the present purpose the effect which they would have had on the legal system in Ireland may be noted. For example, under the first Home Rule Bill introduced by Gladstone in 1886 the Irish courts of first instance (other than the Exchequer division) were to continue to be subject to the Irish Court of Appeal and the Irish judges would have been removable only on an address to both orders of the projected Irish legislative body; the ultimate appeal to the House of Lords in Irish cases was preserved. Because of the proposed financial relationships between Ireland and Great Britain the Exchequer division was to try revenue cases, with a direct appeal to the House of Lords, and its judges were to be appointed by the Lord Lieutenant of Ireland and the Lord Chancellor of England. This innovation was also contained in the second Home Rule Bill introduced in 1893. Under the later Bill, Irish appeals would have gone to the Judicial Committee of the Privy Council, an express application of the method used for the determination of cases from Canada and those jurisdictions then regarded as colonial. Both the 1886 and 1893 Bills contained provisions whereby the validity of enactments of the proposed Irish legislatures could have been tested either by appeal to the Privy Council if the constitutional point arose in the course of litigation, or by reference to the Privy Council if the point arose otherwise; here also the obvious intention was to place Irish legislation in the same position as that of other British legislatures with limited powers.

However, as events happened the alterations in the system of Irish courts did not follow any strict pattern but were made to deal with the unique situation which developed in Ireland.

THE GOVERNMENT OF IRELAND ACT, 1920 AND THE LEGAL SYSTEM
IN NORTHERN IRELAND

When the Government of Ireland Act, 1914 (4 & 5 Geo. 5, c. 90) became law, it contained provisions, similar to those in the 1886 and 1893 Home Rule Bills, for testing the validity of Irish legislation, but the proposal for a distinct jurisdiction in revenue cases was dropped, possibly because by that time the Irish Exchequer division had been merged in the King's Bench division. However, the operation of the 1914 Act was suspended as soon as it received the royal assent and it never took effect. To take its place the Government of Ireland Act, 1920 (10 & 11 Geo. 5, c. 67) was passed. The federal structure of the 1920 Act necessitated the provision of separate Supreme Courts for Northern and Southern Ireland, each consisting of a High Court and a Court of Appeal. In addition, a new court, the High Court of Appeal for Ireland, was to act as an appellate court common to both jurisdictions; it was to consist of the Lord Chancellor of Ireland and the Lord Chief Justices of Northern and Southern Ireland, together with additional judges in important cases. Appeals were to lie from the High Court of Appeal to the House of Lords both in ordinary litigation and in cases involving the validity of legislation passed by either the parliament of Northern Ireland or the parliament of Southern Ireland. The power to refer constitutional questions to the Privy Council was also repeated. Matters relating to the new Supreme Courts were to be reserved to the United Kingdom parliament and would not fall within the local powers until "the date of Irish union." These provisions form the basis of the legal system at present in Northern Ireland, though as will be seen the courts of the Irish Republic are governed by different provisions.

The High Court of Appeal for Ireland had a very brief life, as it commenced to sit in 1921 and last sat a year later. It heard a number of appeals from both Northern and Southern Ireland and in one case, Cooper v. General Accident, Fire and Life Assurance Corporation Limited, [1922] 2 I. R. 214, its decision was upheld by the House of Lords. It resembled the Supreme Court of Canada and the High Court of Australia, and in different circumstances might well have played a part in the development of Irish law similar to the roles of these courts in their respective jurisdictions. Indeed, the presiding judge of the Irish court, Sir John Ross (the last Lord Chancellor of Ireland) drew the comparison specifically in *Leyburn v. Armagh County Council*, [1922] 2 I.R. 15 when he said at pp. 18-19 that

. . . this central Court is absolutely necessary for the determination of the mutual rights and obligations of the component parts of the federation. In every federal system, such as the United States, the Australian Commonwealth, a court of this kind is absolutely essential. It is the supreme guardian of the constitution, and the pivot upon which all the constitutional machinery turns. . . . In view of the ultimate unity of the country, as contemplated by the Act, uniformity of the law is of the first importance in all matters of this kind, and that could only be secured by the action of the High Court of Appeal exercising jurisdiction over all Ireland.

However, with the coming into operation of the Irish Free State Constitution in December 1922 the High Court of Appeal ceased to function, and it was abolished by paragraph 6 of the First Schedule to the Irish Free State (Consequential Provisions) Act, 1922 (13 Geo. 5, Sess. 2, c. 2).

In the result, the sole survivor of the judicial system contemplated by the Government of Ireland Act, 1920 is the Supreme Court of Northern Ireland, just as the parliament of Northern Ireland is the sole survivor of the legislative provisions of that Act. Because the Supreme Court remains a matter reserved to the Westminster parliament, and has not been transferred to the jurisdiction of the Northern Ireland parliament, the judges are appointed by the Crown, on the advice of the Lord Chancellor of England. The Lord Chief Justice of Northern Ireland is a member of both the High Court and the Court of Appeal, and he is assisted in the former by two puisne judges and in the latter by two Lords Justices of Appeal. The High Court judges may sit as members of the Court of Appeal and the Lords Justices of Appeal may assist in the work of the High Court. Although there are no formal divisions in the High Court, the previous distinctions are preserved under a procedure whereby the Lord Chief Justice assigns a particular judge to deal with certain kinds of work; in this way the puisne judges act as Queen's Bench and Chancery judges. Under the Criminal Appeal (Northern Ireland) Act, 1930 (20 & 21 Geo. 5, c. 45) the Westminster parliament established a Northern Ireland Court of Criminal Appeal of which all the judges of the Supreme Court are members.

The original and appellate jurisdictions of the superior courts at present operating in Northern Ireland are in the direct line of descent from those of the courts first established over seven centuries ago, and likewise the system of inferior courts also stems from the establishment of Anglo-Norman institutions in Ireland. The jurisdiction and procedure of the county courts, quarter sessions, and courts of summary jurisdiction are contained in a series of statutes passed by the parliaments at Dublin (before 1801), Westminster, and Belfast, since these are matters within the powers of the Northern Ireland parliament; this legislation still awaits consolidation such as has taken place at Westminster in relation to the corresponding English institutions.

In setting up the judicial system in Northern Ireland the Westminster parliament was confronted with the problem, which had arisen in other parts of the Commonwealth, of fitting an existing set of courts into a new scheme. Here, as elsewhere in the Commonwealth, continuity was of the essence of the solution.

THE DÁIL COURTS

Before considering the judicial systems of the Irish Free State and the Irish Republic mention may be made of the creation of what were popularly known as the Sinn Féin courts but are more correctly termed the Dáil courts. When the first Dáil Eireann was constituted in 1919 it set up a system of courts to oust the jurisdiction of the ordinary courts. For this purpose parish courts were constituted to deal with petty sessions cases, district courts were set up to deal with county court matters, and provision was made for a Supreme Court. These were to function in place of the institutions which were regarded as having been forced on Ireland by British rule. The ordinary courts refused to recognise the existence of the Dáil courts, and in *R. (Kelly) v. Maguire and O'Sheil*, [1923] 2 I. R. 58 certiorari to quash a decision of a Dáil court was refused on the ground that it was an illegal tribunal to which the prerogative writs would not issue. Yet apparently over nine hundred parish courts and over seventy district courts came into operation; a rules committee was set up and it was provided that the early Irish law tracts, decisions of continental courts, and Roman law could be cited as persuasive authorities but that British works were not to be used in argument. This system of courts was suspended in 1922 and brought to an end by the Irish Free State parliament when it passed the Dáil Eireann Courts (Winding-Up) Act, 1923 (No. 36 of 1923) to protect the rights of litigants in these courts, and the Dáil Eireann Courts (Winding-Up) Amendment Act, 1924 (No. 32 of 1924) to convert decrees in land cases into arbitration awards. A study of the work of the Dáil courts would not only throw some light on the period euphemistically referred to in Ireland as "the Troubles"; it would also show the relative success of an attempt to supplant the ordinary legal system by one based on vastly different principles.

THE LEGAL SYSTEM OF THE IRISH FREE STATE

Under Art. 64 of the 1922 Constitution of the Irish Free State the judicial power was to be exercised and justice administered in courts established by the Oireachtas. The High Court was given original jurisdiction and, by Art. 65, a special jurisdiction in relation to "the validity of any law having regard to the provisions of the Constitution." Under Art. 66 the Supreme Court was to have appellate jurisdiction "with such exceptions . . . and subject to such regulations as may be prescribed by law," but no exception could be made to prevent appeals on questions relating to the validity of legislation. While the decision of the Supreme Court in all cases was to be final, conclusive, and incapable of review, there was added to Art. 66 a proviso preserving the right to appeal with special leave to the Privy Council; the difficulties arising from this provision are mentioned in the chapter *(infra)* on Ireland and the Commonwealth. Under Art. 68 judges were to be appointed by the Governor-General on the advice of the Executive Council, and were not to be removed except "for stated misbehaviour or incapacity, and then only by resolutions passed by both Dáil Eireann and Seanad Eireann." Added to this was a specific declaration, in Art. 69, that judges were to be independent, subject only to the Constitution and the law, ineligible to sit in the Oireachtas, and incapable of holding any other office or position of emolument. Having dealt with the judicial power and its exercise the 1922 Constitution proceeded in Art. 70

to authorize the establishment of tribunals for the trial of offences against military law; these were to have jurisdiction " in accordance with the regulations to be prescribed by law" over the civil population in time of war or armed rebellion. In addition, as is mentioned in the chapter on Constitutional Developments since 1920 *(infra)*, the Constitution (Amendment No. 17) Act, 1931 (No. 37 of 1931) authorized the setting up of special tribunals.

Perhaps the closest parallel to the provisions in the 1922 Constitution relating to the judicial power is to be found in Chapter III of the Australian Constitution. This also provided for the vesting of judicial power in the High Court of Australia, for the appointment and removal of judges, for the hearing of appeals from state courts, and for the limitation of the right of appeal to the Privy Council to *"inter se"* questions and appeals by special leave. But the Australian Parliament was, by s. 76, to confer jurisdiction on the High Court in constitutional matters and questions arising under legislation, while in the Irish Free State the power of judicial review was expressly embodied in the fundamental law. Again, the independent position of Irish Free State judges was not insured, as in the older Dominions, only by providing for a particular method of removal; there was an express declaration that they were to be independent, subject only to the Constitution and the law. Evidently the long eighteenth-century struggle for judicial independence was not forgotten when the 1922 Constitution was drafted.

The power to constitute courts conferred by Art. 64 of the 1922 Constitution was exercised by the passing of the Courts of Justice Act, 1924 (No. 10 of 1924). This Act was based on the report of a committee set up in the preceding year, and an extract from a letter written to its members by the then President of the Executive Council, Mr. W. T. Cosgrave, shows the general aim:

In the long struggle for the right to rule in our own country there has been no sphere of the administration lately ended which impressed itself on the minds of our people as a standing monument of alien government more than the system, the machinery, and the administration of law and justice, which supplanted in comparatively modern times the laws and institutions till then a part of the living national organism. The body of laws and the system of judicature so imposed upon this Nation were English (not even British) in their seed, English in their growth,

English in their vitality. Their ritual, their nomenclature, were only to be understood by the student of the history of the people of Southern Britain. A remarkable and characteristic product of the genius of that people, the manner of their administration prevented them from striking root in the fertile soil of this Nation.[17]

The Courts of Justice Act, 1924 accordingly reconstituted the judicial system, although there are some resemblances to the previous pattern. A Supreme Court was set up, presided over by the Chief Justice, while the senior judge of the new High Court was given the title of President. The Chief Justice and two judges of the High Court formed the Court of Criminal Appeal. (In setting up such a court Dublin preceded Belfast by some seven years, for it was not until 1931 that the corresponding Northern Ireland court was constituted.) As for the inferior courts, the district courts replaced the former system whereby justices and resident magistrates sat in petty sessions, while the circuit courts replaced the former county courts and courts of quarter sessions; in both cases the new courts were given wider jurisdiction than their predecessors, while the area of a circuit court judge's jurisdiction was much wider than that of a county court judge. When the 1924 system was inaugurated, no provision was made for High Court judges to go on circuit, but this was reintroduced by the Courts of Justice Act, 1936 (No. 48 of 1936), forming yet another link with the system previously in force. Subsequent amendments of the 1924 Act have not altered the main outline, although the details of the scheme have been varied.

THE LEGAL SYSTEM OF THE IRISH REPUBLIC

The 1937 Constitution followed that of 1922 in providing specifically that Dublin judges are to be independent and removable for misconduct only on resolutions of both Dáil and Seanad (Art. 35). Original jurisdiction and the power of judicial review are by Art. 34 conferred specifically on the High Court, subject to an appeal to the Supreme Court, whose decision is final. The power given to the Oireachtas in 1922 to establish courts is repeated while Art. 37 allows "the exercise of limited functions and powers of a judical

[17] Quoted by Hanna J. in "Review of Legislation, 1924: the Irish Free State," *Journal of Comparative Legislation and International Law*, (3d Series) **VIII**, Part II (1926), 38.

nature, in matters other than criminal matters" by persons or bodies other than judges or courts; this latter provision is discussed in the chapter *(infra)* on Administrative Law. Art. 38 provides for the establishment of military tribunals "for the trial of offences against military law alleged to have been committed by persons while subject to military law" and also to deal with a state of war or armed rebellion. This provision is similar to Art. 70 of the 1922 Constitution, but in addition special courts can be established by law "for the trial of offences in cases where it may be determined . . . that the ordinary courts are inadequate to secure the effective administration of justice, and the preservation of public peace and order." This authorizes in general terms the setting up of tribunals similar to that constituted by Art. 2A of the 1922 Constitution, inserted in 1931 by Constitution (Amendment No. 17) Act, 1931 (No. 37 of 1931). The 1937 power was exercised by Part III of the Offences against the State Act, 1939 (No. 13 of 1939); it was challenged in *In re MacCurtain,* [1941] I. R. 83 but upheld by the Supreme Court. Another provision of Art. 38 of the 1937 Constitution specifically authorizes the trial of minor offenses by courts of summary jurisdiction.

Here it may be noted that the provisions of the Irish Constitution relating to the judicial power and its exercise are much more general and less elaborate than those relating to the Union Judiciary in Chapter IV of Part V of the 1950 Constitution of India, or those contained in Part IX of the 1956 Pakistan Constitution. In the Irish Republic the details are left to ordinary legislation. Another point of difference is that both Art. 132 of the Indian Constitution and Art. 157 of the Pakistan Constitution give an appellate jurisdiction in cases involving a substantial question of law as to the interpretation of the respective Constitutions. The power conferred on the Dublin courts is much more pragmatic, for instead of interpreting the 1937 Constitution the Irish judges have to determine the validity of laws having regard to the provisions of that document. This aspect of the judicial function is emphasized by Art. 26 of the 1937 Constitution under which the President may, after consultation with the Council of State, refer a bill (other than a money bill, a constitutional amendment, or an emergency measure) to the Supreme Court for a decision on its repugnancy to or compliance with the provisions of the Constitution. With this power may be contrasted the wide powers conferred by Art. 143 of the Indian Constitution and Art. 162 of the Pakistan Constitution, both of which authorize presidential references to the respective Supreme Courts for advisory opinions on questions of public importance.

In the Irish Republic no steps have yet been taken to set up the courts authorized by Art. 34 of the 1937 Constitution. Art. 58 provided that the pre-1937 courts were to continue in existence with similar jurisdictions but "subject to the provisions of this Constitution relating to the determination of questions as to the validity of any law." In 1951 in *The State (Killian) v. The Minister for Justice*, [1954] I. R. 207 it was contended that a circuit court judge had not been validly appointed because he was sworn in after the coming into operation of the 1937 Constitution but not in accordance with it. However, the Supreme Court held that the pre-1937 courts were still functioning by virtue of Art. 58 of the Constitution and that judicial appointments were validly made by the President on the advice of the Government in accordance with Art. 49 of the Constitution. Again, in *Sullivan v. Robinson*, [1954] I. R. 161, it was argued that an appeal did not lie from the High Court to the Supreme Court, notwithstanding Art. 34, 4, (3), of the Constitution, since such an appeal could not have been brought in the circumstances before 1937. The Supreme Court upheld this contention, pointing out at p. 173 that "the courts mentioned in Article 34 are the courts to be established under the Constitution and no such courts have yet been established"; the court also pointed out that the power of judicial review and of determining presidential references on repugnancy points had been specifically preserved so that the courts could determine such questions although they were operating only under the transitory provisions of the 1937 Constitution.

In the result, the Courts of Justice Act, 1924 (No. 10 of 1924), as amended, is the basis for the legal structure in the Irish Republic. The Supreme Court consists of the Chief Justice and four ordinary judges, the High Court of the President and six ordinary judges; there are ten circuit court judges and over forty district justices. The 1924 Act has been amended by post-1937 legislation but the general pattern remains. A final illustration of the continuity of the Irish Free State courts is provided by the case of *O'Byrne v. Minister for Finance and Attorney General* (1955, unreported), in which the question for decision was whether the deduction of income tax from a judge's salary contravened the prohibition against diminution of remuneration contained in Art. 68 of the 1922 Constitution. In the High Court Dixon J. rejected this contention, thereby implying that Dublin judges are in no better position in this respect than their brethren in the Commonwealth or the United States.

THE DOCTRINE OF PRECEDENT

The doctrine of precedent formed a special part of the common law as it was exported from the courts in London to different parts of the world. In the older jurisdictions in the Commonwealth it is now implicit, having been introduced by English-trained judges. Thus, for example, the doctrine is now applied in those systems of law in use in Ceylon which were formerly innocent of any such principles. But s. 212 of the Government of India Act, 1935 (26 Geo. 5, c. 42) provided that decisions of the Federal Court were to be binding on all Indian courts, and in Art. 141 of the 1950 Indian Constitution and Art. 163 of the 1956 Pakistan Constitution a similar provision appears, so that the doctrine is now part of the fundamental law of those countries: it is noteworthy, however, that Art. 137 of the former document and Art. 161 of the latter authorized the respective Supreme Courts to review their judgments. The doctrine of precedent was not expressed in the Government of Ireland Act, 1920 and it does not appear in either the 1922 Constitution of the Irish Free State or the 1937 Constitution of the Irish Republic. But some reference to the application of the docrine in Ireland will show how judges in Belfast and Dublin have handled problems of precedent following the setting up of new jurisdictions.

The application of the doctrine of precedent in Irish case law has not been investigated as fully as, for example, the part it plays in Scots law has been examined by Professor T. B. Smith of Aberdeen in his work on *The Doctrines of Judicial Precedent in Scots Law*.[18] In any comparison of the application of the doctrine in Irish law and and Scots law a factor of importance would be that the English and Irish systems had a common origin, while in Scotland the legal system had a different source; the growth of the doctrine of precedent in Scots law was not a natural development but an in-

[18] Edinburgh, 1952.

filtration from English law which, in the words of a former Lord President of the Court of Session, the late Lord Cooper of Culross, leaves the Scots lawyer "helpless in its suffocating grip." The doctrine came more naturally to the Irish legal system.

As has been seen earlier in this chapter, during the greater part of the eighteenth century, the whole of the nineteenth, and the first two decades of the present century the judicial systems operating in the British Isles had a common apex; this continues to be the case for the United Kingdom including Northern Ireland, but for the courts of the Irish Republic recent decisions of the House of Lords have ceased to be binding authorities. In view of the lengthy period during which the House of Lords has been the ultimate appellate tribunal for three different systems of law it is surprising that its precise function has never been specifically formulated. According to one view, their Lordships sit as the highest court of each system; on the other hand, they may be regarded as sitting as a United Kingdom court, but applying the law used in the jurisdiction from which each appeal comes. But the difference between the United Kingdom constitution and that of the United States prevents the House of Lords from giving to the law of England or Scotland or Northern Ireland the supremacy which the United States Supreme Court gave to state law in *Erie Railroad Co. v. Tompkins*, 304 U. S. 64 (1938).

Yet whatever view is taken of the functions of the House of Lords, it is clear that the courts of Northern Ireland are bound by the decisions of the House of Lords on appeals from Northern Ireland; and while it might be possible to argue that, strictly, decisions in other cases are not binding, a clear divergence of Northern Ireland law from English law would have to be adduced to make such an argument successful. It has already been indicated that there are not such compelling reasons for such a course in Northern Ireland as there are in Scotland. The similarity of the English and Irish systems led to the emergence of a practice in the former Irish Court of Appeal which Holmes L. J. described in *McCartan v. Belfast Harbour Commissioners*, [1910] 2 I. R. 470, at pp. 494-495, as follows:

It is true that, although we are not technically bound by decisions in the co-ordinate English Court, we have been in the habit, in adjudicating on questions as to which the law of the two countries is identical, to follow them. We hold that uniformity of decision is so desirable that it is better, even when we think the matter doubtful, to accept the authority of the English Court and leave error, if there be error, to be corrected by the Tribunal whose judgment is the same on both sides of the Channel.

In view of this declaration it is especially interesting to note that in *McCartan's* case the Irish Court of Appeal exercised an independent judgment by distinguishing a decision of its English counterpart, and that it was upheld in this course by the House of Lords. As for its own decisions, the Irish Court of Appeal adopted the practice of assembling a full court to override a previous decision, and the ordinary court overruled itself as late as 1920 in *Milligan v. Mayor of Londonderry*, [1920] 2 I. R. 1.

The setting-up of new judicial systems in Northern Ireland and the Irish Free State raised fresh problems in relation to the doctrine of precedent, but their solution lies in the realm of tacit assumption rather than that of specific statement. In passing it may be noted that the short-lived High Court of Appeal for Ireland which functioned briefly in 1922 did not regard itself as bound by decisions of the former Irish Court of Appeal. In the case of *Leyburn v. Armagh County Council (No. 2)*, [1922] 2 I. R. 58 Sir John Ross L. C. repeated at p. 62 his view that the Court must be "the pivot upon which all the constitutional machinery was intended to turn." Unfortunately the pivot disappeared with the greater part of the machinery, and with them went the prospect of an appellate court exercising jurisdiction over both parts of Ireland but untrammeled by previous decisions. Had it survived it might well have developed a uniform common law for the two new jurisdictions.

In Northern Ireland the force of decisions of the former Irish courts was first raised in the Court of Appeal in *R. (Greenaway) v. Justices of Armagh*, [1924] 2 I. R. 55 where the court refused to follow a decision of the Irish Court of Appeal. On the other hand, in *Walsh v. Wightman*, [1927] N. I. 1 the Northern Ireland court followed a decision of the Irish Court of Appeal in preference to that of an English judge of first instance. Again, in *Collier v. Down County Council*, [1941] N. I. 113 Babington L. J. declared, at p. 120:

Strictly speaking, the decisions of the Court of Appeal in Ireland are not binding on us but we follow them as a matter of course unless there are very strong reasons to the contrary and more especially in cases in which the law as declared has been accepted as the law of the land for any considerable time.

In *Ministry of Agriculture v. Turtle*, [1946] N. I. 63, Black J. (as he then was) opined at pp. 78-79 that the King's Bench division should follow the practice of the Court of Appeal and "while holding ourselves entitled to reconsider decisions of the former Irish King's Bench division should ordinarily follow such decisions unless clearly persuaded that they are wrong." As for English decisions, in *In the Matter of the Northern Ireland Road Transport Board*, [1941] N. I. 77 Murphy L. J. cited with approval the principle laid down thirty years earlier by Holmes L. J. in *McCartan's* case. In *Parkinson v. Watson*, [1956] N. I. 1 the Northern Ireland Court of Appeal followed *Young v. Bristol Aeroplane Co.*, [1944] K. B. 718 in holding that, like its English counterpart, it is bound by its own decisions (with certain limited exceptions) and Porter L. J. expressed the view that *Milligan's* case had been wrongly decided.

Thus it appears that the tacit acceptance of the doctrine of precedent by the Northern Ireland courts has left them in a favorable position. The judges are free to depart from former Irish decisions but will not always do so; they can follow the English Court of Appeal but will not necessarily accept these decisions. In this respect the position of the Northern Ireland courts is rather similar to that of the High Court of Australia, which aims at the development of the common law without committing itself to following English decisions of which it disapproves. But so far as the legal systems operating in the British Isles are concerned, the law courts in Belfast are placed half-way between the Four Courts in Dublin and the law courts in the Strand.

It might have been expected that the setting up of a new judicial system in Dublin in 1924 would have resulted in a complete break with previous doctrines, but such did not prove to be the case. Both Art. 73 of the 1922 Constitution and Art. 50 of the 1937 Constitution continued the laws in force, and earlier in this chapter an indication was given of the continuity of judicial organization. Perhaps the most extreme exponent of the view that Irish law should be self-sufficient was the late Gavan Duffy, judge and later President of the Dublin High Court. On the application of this view to the doctrine of precedent he remarked in *Exham v. Beamish*, [1939] I.R. 336 at pp. 348-349:

As a matter of practice, we constantly refer to judgments in the English Courts, and such judgments, as every lawyer will recognise, have often proved to be of great service to us; but let us be clear. In my opinion, when Saorstát Eireann, and afterwards Eire, continued the laws in force, they did not make binding on their Courts anything short of law. In my opinion, judicial decisions in Ireland before the Treaty, and English decisions which were followed here, are binding on this Court only when they represent a law so well settled or pronounced by so weighty a juristic authority that they may fairly be regarded, in a system built up upon the principle of *stare decisis*, as having become established as part of the law of the land before the Treaty; and to bind, of course, they must not be inconsistent with the Constitution. . . . In my opinion, this Court cannot be fettered in the exercise of the judicial power by opinions of very different Courts under the old régime, unless those opinions must reasonably be considered to have had the force of law in Ireland, so that they formed part of the code expressly retained. For the rest, we must give to Irish judicial views and to judgments in England and elsewhere interpreting a similar jurisprudence, that respect which their intrinsic worth may entitle them to claim, though here, too, in many a case of doubt one may reasonably incline to follow precedent to avoid unsettling a law in the course of becoming established. . . . Our new High Court must mould its own *cursus curiae*; in so doing I hold that it is free, indeed bound, to treat any such absurdity in the machinery of administration as having been imposed on it as part of the law of the land; nothing is law here which is inconsistent with derivation from the People.

The tendency of this passage is clear—that the nature of the 1937 Constitution is such that only certain elements of the pre-1922 law can be retained; and that the application of the doctrine of precedent must be sufficiently flexible to permit the selection of those rules of law which should be retained and the rejection of those which should not. With considerable skill Gavan Duffy P. put his principles into practice, particularly in dealing with the doctrines of equity, but it would be wrong to give the impression that all his brethren on the Dublin bench concurred. On the contrary, what the learned judge himself referred to as "the traditionalism of lawyers practising under a law of precedent" triumphed over his application of the novel views which he propounded.

For example, in *Boylan v. Dublin Corporation*, [1949] I. R. 60 the Dublin Supreme Court had to consider the effect of *Fairman v. Perpetual Investment Building Society*, [1923] A. C. 74 (1922), which was decided a month before the Irish Free State Constitution came into operation in December 1922. Both Maguire C. J., who dissented in *Boylan's* case, and Black J., who sided with the majority of the court, took the view that the Supreme Court was bound by *Fairman's* case though they differed in their interpretation of the decision. Again, in *Minister for Finance and Attorney General v. O'Brien*, [1949] I. R. 91 a question arose as to the effect of the Privy Council decision in *British Columbia Electric Railway Co. Ltd. v. Loach*, [1916] 1 A. C. 719 (1915). Gavan Duffy P. described it as "an advisory opinion of the Judicial Committee that, as I apprehend it, formed no part of the law in force, effective here under the new regime that followed the Treaty," and he refused to follow the case because it had not been applied by any Dublin court since 1922. In the Supreme Court the majority approved of the reasoning in *Loach's* case, but statements made by the two dissenting judges are of particular interest for the present purpose. Murnaghan J. stated at p. 116:

> Decisions—or, rather, the advice—of the Privy Council are not of binding authority here, but as I understand the position, decisions of the House of Lords upon law common to England and Ireland given before the coming into operation of the Constitution of 1922 are of binding force in the Courts until their effect has been altered by the Legislature.

Black J., at p. 150, drew attention to the relevance of another House of Lords decision, *Admiralty Commissioners v. S. S. Volute*, [1922] 1 A. C. 129 (1921), saying that "since *S. S. Volute* was decided on 15th December, 1921, as I understand our Constitution, we have made it as binding on this Court as it is on the Courts of Great Britain." Thus it is evident that, despite the doctrine which Gavan Duffy P. advocated, pre-1922 cases still have an important part to play in the decision of issues in the Dublin courts, as indeed the reports of the arguments and judgments there amply demonstrate.

Two further points may be made about the application of the doctrine of precedent by the Dublin courts. The first is that the much discussed Privy Council practice of delivering a single opinion has been adopted for a limited type of case. Art. 34, 4, (5), of the 1937 Constitution (as amended by the Second Amendment of the Constitution Act, 1941, pp. viii, xxx) provides that where the Supreme Court decides a question involving the constitutional validity of a law the decision

shall be pronounced by such one of the judges of that Court as that Court shall direct, and no other opinion on such question, whether assenting or dissenting, shall be pronounced, nor shall the existence of any such other opinion be disclosed.

Art. 26, 2, (2), (as amended by the Second Amendment of the Constitution Act, 1941, pp. viii, xxii) contains a similar rule relating to decisions on a presidential reference on a repugnancy point. These provisions embody the Privy Council practice in specific terms, but they do not extend to private law cases, nor do they preclude the expression of dissenting opinions on questions of constitutional interpretation which do not relate to the validity of a law.[19]

A second point is that by Art. 34, 4, (6) (as amended by the Second Amendment of the Constitution Act, 1941, pp. viii, xxx) of the 1937 Constitution the Supreme Court's decisions are to be final and conclusive. The High Court of Australia has interpreted a similar provision in s. 73 of the Australian Constitution to permit the overruling of its own decisions, so that the Australian court is in the same position as that in which the Supreme Courts of India and Pakistan are placed by their respective Constitutions. As yet the Irish court has not made any move similar to the Australian one, but should it decide to do so Dublin may well witness a court revolution such as took place in Washington in 1937, or as might happen if the Canadian Supreme Court broke away from the trend of Privy Council decisions.

In sum, in both Northern Ireland and the Irish Republic the

---

[19] Professor Edward McWhinney, in his article on "Judicial Concurrences and Dissents—A Comparative View of Opinion Writing in Final Appellate Tribunals," *Canadian Bar Review*, XXXI (1953), 596, suggests at p. 607 that the unanimity of the Dublin Supreme Court's decisions on constitutional questions can be explained in terms of judicial personalities. Where, however, the cases concern the validity of legislation, the provisions of the constitution make unanimity inevitable.

judicial techniques of the common law have been continued in use, as they have elsewhere in the Commonwealth; but the judges of both jurisdictions have held themselves free to exercise a certain choice in the matter of the previous cases which they will follow, thus insuring some flexibility in the application of the common law in fresh circumstances.

SUMMARY

This chapter has sought to give a sketch of the transplanting of the common law to Ireland and of the development of the institutions of the common law there. It has also shown something of the systems of courts at present operating in Northern Ireland and the Irish Republic, and of the way in which the judges in Belfast and Dublin regard the decisions of their predecessors in the Four Courts and their counterparts on the other side of the Irish Sea. The chapter has glanced briefly at the Irish law tracts of the eighth century and the decisions of judges twelve centuries later.

Turning this bird's-eye glance to other parts of the common law world, the first point which appears is that the former Irish law is now mainly a matter for speculation, though from time to time it has become of practical interest in modern litigation. But there is no Irish counterpart of those systems of native law which survive in certain parts of the Commonwealth; the common law does not have to co-exist with or encroach upon any other system, for in Ireland it now reigns supreme.

Next, the physical proximity of Ireland to England led to parallel developments of the two judicial systems. The English model was imported into Ireland when it was still an organic nucleus rather than a completely elaborated system, so that the time of the reception of the common law facilitated its growth. In Ireland as elsewhere the process was aided by the appointment of English or English-trained judges, though by the end of the eighteenth century the Irish bench had acquired distinctive characteristics which it has never entirely lost.

Thirdly, the similarity of judicial systems and the use of the common law did not prevent the emergence of differences, such as that relating to civil bill procedure which has been described. Here there is room for comparative research, to discover how far the

varying conditions in different common law jurisdictions have resulted in the emergence of modified common law procedures.

Coming to the modern period, we find the legislative introduction
of two systems where one had previously flourished. The links between Northern Ireland and the rest of the United Kingdom provide reasons for the continued uniformity of legal development,
though this is by no means automatic. In this Northern Ireland is
perhaps more akin to the legal systems of Australia and New Zealand than it is to the judicial attitudes in the newer members of the
Commonwealth. In the Irish Republic, on the other hand, the
avowed aim was the creation of a completely new system, though
the application of the doctrine of precedent and the citation of
United Kingdom cases has so far prevented any radical alteration.
When further cases have accumulated some future researcher will
doubtless find interesting comparisons between the development of
the legal system of the Irish Republic and the evolution of the
corresponding institutions and doctrines under the constitutions of
India and Pakistan.

It is appropriate that the final words of the summary should have
referred to the possibility of future research, for throughout this
chapter emphasis has been laid on the possibilities for further study.
Irish legal history is a relatively untilled field, made all the stonier
by the fate of Irish records. The Introduction to Herbert Wood's
work, *A Guide to the Records Deposited in the Public Record Office
of Ireland*,[20] tells a sorry story of the hapless fate of the Irish records
almost from the time of their inauguration, and indeed the contents of
Wood's book make melancholy reading, for almost all the records
there mentioned perished in the four courts in Dublin in 1922. Yet
it is possible to reconstruct the history of Irish institutions from other
sources, as Mr. Richardson and Professor Sayles have shown in their
volume on *The Irish Parliament in the Middle Ages* (*supra* note 15).
This is an example which could profitably be followed.

On the substance of Irish law little has been written in a comparative strain,[21] but there is abundance of material. Both the history

---

[20] Dublin, 1919.

[21] A notable exception is Vincent Thomas Hyginus Delany, *The Law relating to
Charities in Ireland* (Dublin, 1956), which treats this specialized branch of the law
in a comparative way. Cf. also Dr. Delany's article "The Development of the Law
of Charities in Ireland,"*International and Comparative Law Quarterly*, (New Series)

and the substance of Irish law are eminently suited to further investigation against the background of the development of the common law throughout the Commonwealth. This chapter will not have failed in its object if it helps to point the way to sources and subjects which others may study, in the hope that the "first adventure of the common law" and its subsequent development may yet yield rich harvests of research.

IV (1955), 30-45; Lionel Astor Sheridan, "Irish Private Law and the English Lawyer," *International and Comparative Law Quarterly*, (New Series) I (1952), 196-212.

2

Constitutional History

JUST AS the common law developed in Ireland so did the institutions and practice of parliamentary government; both originated in the Anglo-Norman system of administration and both separated and evolved as they did in England. In the chapter on Legal History (*supra*) it has been shown that the Irish courts were subject to appeals to the English courts; in the same way Ireland was subject to both executive and legislative control from Westminster. Again, the territorial jurisdiction of both the Dublin courts and the Dublin parliament was restricted until the seventeenth century; the native Irish and the Anglo-Irish living close to them did not need to pay any undue respect to the authorities in Dublin, whether they were judges or legislators.

The historical and geographical links between the Dublin and Westminster parliaments distinguish the history of the Irish institution from that of its counterparts elsewhere in the Commonwealth, but it will be seen that the relations between the Irish and English parliaments were relevant to the relations between Westminster and other legislatures, and that in the nineteenth century the process was reversed, for the colonial and Dominion precedents were relevant to the proposals for constitutional alterations in the government of Ireland. But before discussing the growth of parliamentary government in Ireland it is necessary to say something of the institutions which existed in Ireland when the Anglo-Normans arrived there, and which continued in use for over four centuries.

NATIVE IRISH INSTITUTIONS

Here, as with the early Irish law, the Irish sources have produced considerable controversy. Goddard Orpen, in his *Ireland under the Normans, 1169-1216,*[1] emphasized the loose, tribal structure of Irish government and argued that the organization of the country into five provinces under the supreme authority of the *ard-ri* or high king was not to be found in any historical period. Professor Eoin MacNeill took exception to the description of the historic Irish political community as tribal, and he asserted that the Irish kingships were arranged in a fixed hierarchy and subject to the authority of the *ard-ri* and a national assembly. The most accurate diagnosis of this controversy is that of Professor D. A. Binchy, who pointed out that both these scholars assessed the evidence available to them of early Irish communities according to the conception of the State held at the turn of the nineteenth century. In Professor Binchy's view, early Irish society was based on the tribe, which was made up of small landholders. The king was the head of the tribe, but he was not all-powerful since the powers and status of the various ranks of society were fixed, and the membership of the tribe was determined by kinship. The king represented the tribe and the kings of other tribes might owe him fealty; in the same way the provincial king was recognized by the tribal kings in the province, but the *ard-ri's* claim to the overlordship of Ireland was a late one, apparently de facto rather than de jure.[2]

On this view of early Irish society it is not surprising that the Anglo-Norman system of government, stemming from a single royal source, should have conflicted with the Irish conception, yet when the Normans came to Ireland some of the Irish subkingdoms were continued subject to the lordship of Henry II. This lordship was conferred on John in 1177, and when John became king the lordship was attached to the English crown. Various Irish kings acknowledged John's lordship and almost two centuries later others similarly recognized the position of Richard II when he visited Ireland in 1394, but such acknowledgments did not insure the continuity of English influence. On the contrary, the actual area of English domination fluctuated greatly. It was greatest under Edward I, but outside what became known as the Pale there were the earldoms of the Anglo-Irish who were virtually independent, as well as the areas occupied by the native Irish under their kings. In the fifteenth

---

[1] Oxford, 1911.
[2] "Secular Institutions" in *Early Irish Society* (Dublin, 1954), 52.

century the Pale had dwindled to a small area outside Dublin, but after that period it began to increase. As mentioned in the chapter on Land Law *(infra)*, in the sixteenth century the policy of "Surrender and Re-grant" enabled the Irish to hold their land under a common law title rather than a native one. The settlement of various areas further increased the scope of the Dublin government's authority, and when the O'Neill of Tyrone and the O'Donnell of Donegal left Ireland in the "Flight of the Earls" in 1607 the subsequent plantation of Ulster finally brought the whole of Ireland under Dublin rule. In discussing the growth of the Irish parliament it is essential to remember that it did not emerge fully fledged until the commencement of the seventeenth century, when the last of the native Irish institutions of government passed into the realms of academic speculation.

THE FIRST THREE CENTURIES OF THE IRISH PARLIAMENT

For an authoritative summary of the material relating to the medieval Irish parliament we are indebted to Mr. Richardson and Professor Sayles, whose work on *The Irish Parliament in the Middle Ages*[3] collects and interprets the evidence now remaining about this episode in the history of parliamentary government. From this work it is possible to see how the Irish parliament evolved from the justiciar's court in the same way as the English parliament sprang from the court of the king whom the justiciar represented in Ireland. In the often-quoted phrase of Fleta "the king has his court in his council in his parliament," and a similar pattern can be traced in the work of the justiciar. He was aided by a common council of the magnates from the innermost circle of which developed the Irish privy council on which the ministers sat. When the council sat in the Irish parliament it formed the nucleus, the remaining members being specially summoned and under a duty to attend. It was not until the middle of the thirteenth century that the practice developed of summoning parliaments regularly, and it was at the end of that century, somewhat later than in England, that elected representatives of counties and liberties, and subsequently those of cities and boroughs, were first summoned. In addition to legislation, judicial work, the hearing of petitions, administrative business, and

[3] Philadelphia, 1952.

taxation all formed part of the proceedings at such gatherings, but the idea of regular representation was absent. Formerly the term "model parliament," meaning a legislative body composed of elected representatives, was used to describe the parliament which sat in London in 1295 and one which was held in Dublin in 1310; now the search for such precedents has been abandoned and the development of parliamentary institutions is thought to have been more gradual.

In the fourteenth century the House of Lords began to emerge in England. In the same way the concept of peerage commenced to grow in Ireland; and the magnates and judges formed an upper chamber, in distinction to the knights of the shire and burgesses, who were summoned to deal with the imposition of special taxes and the presentation of messages to the king. Like the commons in England, the Irish presented petitions for the remedying of grievances, but the learned authors of the work just mentioned have pointed out a significant difference between the subjects dealt with in the Irish and English parliaments. In the fifteenth century the English chancery jurisdiction reduced the bulk of private business at Westminster; in Ireland there was no equivalent jurisdiction and the common law courts were still struggling to assert themselves, so that petitions on legal points continued to come before the Dublin parliament. This was one of the ways in which the Irish institution differed from the London model because of local circumstances.

During the first three centuries of its existence the evolving Irish parliament did not grow in isolation from the activities of the Westminster parliament. In a variety of ways the English statute law and ordinances were applied in Ireland, paralleling the introduction and development of the common law. The process began in the thirteenth century when several different methods were used to insure that Westminster legislation was used on both sides of the Irish Sea. Mandates were sent to the justiciar ordering the observance of English statutes, the state of the English law was certified to the justiciar, replies were given to petitions from Ireland, and enactments were transmitted to Ireland with a writ ordering their observance there. The Statute of Merton, 1236 (20 Hen. 3) was sent to Dublin, as were the Statutes of Westminster the First (3 Edw.1) and the Second (13 Edw. 1) which were transmitted to

Ireland in 1285, the year in which the latter enactment was made. The last-mentioned statute also contained references indicating that it was meant to apply in Ireland as well as in England. On the other hand, towards the end of the thirteenth century there is evidence that English enactments such as the Statute of Mortmain, 1279 (7 Edw. 1) were used in the Irish courts without any apparent formal authority for this practice. In the succeeding century the various methods which have been mentioned were used to secure the observance of Westminster enactments in Ireland, and in addition the Irish parliament confirmed and extended to Ireland various English statutes. At the beginning of the fifteenth century the practice of extending English enactments to Ireland by writ ceased, but Ireland was included with England and Wales in the scope of Westminster statutes dealing with trade.

The legal basis of the English parliament's power to legislate for Ireland was discussed in two fifteenth-century cases which were to be the subject of much subsequent argument. In *Pilkyngton's* case in the Exchequer Chamber in 1441 (Y. B. 20 Hen. 6, f. 8) it was contended that English statutes applied in Ireland only if the Irish parliament confirmed them, an assertion which is not borne out by the events of the two previous centuries.[4] The case was not specifically decided, but in the seventeenth century in Ireland and in the eighteenth century in America it was cited in support of independence from Westminster, although it was not a conclusive authority. Again, in 1483-1484, in the case of the *Merchants of Waterford* (Y. B. 2 Ric. 3, f. 12; 1 Hen. 7, f. 2) the English judges were first of opinion that Ireland was not bound by an English statute, but later held that English statutes bound persons living in Ireland.[5] Against these English judicial declarations may be set an Irish parliamentary one, for in 1460 the Irish parliament asserted that although Ireland was subject to the same "obedience" as England, nevertheless it was bound only by statutes made by Irish parliaments or great councils. The current interpretation of this incident is that it was an attempt by Richard, Duke of York, to enlist the Irish against the Lancastrians, but the independent sentiment which was

[4] M. Hemmant, ed., *Select Cases in the Exchequer Chamber, 1377-1461* (Selden Society, London, 1933, LI), 81.

[5] M. Hemmant, ed., *Select Cases in the Exchequer Chamber, 1461-1509* (Selden Society, London, 1945, LXIV), 94.

expressed by the Irish parliament in this fifteenth-century meeting at Drogheda was one which found an echo on the other side of the Atlantic three centuries afterwards.

POYNINGS' LAW

In the constitutional history of Ireland the parliament held by Sir Edward Poynings at Drogheda in 1494-1495 is a landmark. For the historian, this parliament marked the assertion by the Tudors of their authority over the great Irish earls; for the constitutional lawyer it consolidated the position of the English statute law in Ireland, and provided a means of exercising executive control over Dublin legislation.

The phrase "Poynings' Law" is used to describe the Irish statute 10 Hen. 7, c. 22, as it is cited in the printed versions of the Irish statutes, though it was originally c. 39. This declared that

. . . all estatutes, late made within the said realm of England, concerning or belonging to the common and publique weal of the same, from henceforth be deemed good and effectuall in the law, and over that be acceptyd, used, and executed in this land of Ireland in all points at all times requisite according to the tenor and effect of the same. . . .

In effect, this constituted a general confirmation by the Irish parliament of the English statute law as it stood at the end of the fifteenth century, with the exception of what would now be regarded as temporary or local or personal. As has been noted, English enactments were extended to Ireland in a variety of ways; by Poynings' Law they were either confirmed if they had been applicable, or extended if they had not. It is noteworthy that Ireland was not concerned, as other parts of the common law world were later to be, with the problem of statutes declaratory of the common law at a specific time.[6] Instead, the operation of the common law in Ireland was reinforced by the specific application of the statute law.

"Poynings' Law" has, however, another meaning, for in a historical context it is used to describe the Irish statute 10 Hen. 7, c. 4, originally c. 9. This statute provided that no parliament was to be held in Ireland until the Lord Lieutenant (as the justiciar had become known) and the Irish council had certified to the king under

[6] Cf. St. George Leakin Sioussat, "The Theory of the Extension of English Statutes to the Plantations," *Select Essays in Anglo-American Legal History* (3 vols.; Boston, 1907) I, 416-430.

the great seal of Ireland "the causes and considerations, and all such acts as them seemeth should pass. . . ." Such of the proposals as the English council approved were to be returned to Ireland, together with a license to hold a parliament. At the time, the object of this provision was probably to give London some control over the activities of Irish nobles whose influence loomed large in Dublin; it would also prevent the Irish parliament from giving support to a pretender to the English crown, in which connection it is important to remember that Lambert Simnel had been crowned as Edward VI in Dublin in 1487. But perhaps the best summary of the effect of this part of the legislation of Poynings' parliament is that of two English humorists who stated that by Poynings' Law "The Irish could have a Parliament of their own, but the English were to pass all the Acts in it."

The way in which Poynings' Law regulated the activities of the Irish parliament was used as a precedent in dealing with the Jamaican legislature in 1678-1680, but the attempt to fetter the activities of this colonial body failed and a similar attempt about the same time to impose the Poynings' Law system on Virginia did not get further than the proposal stage.[7] Whereas in the colonies reservation or disallowance might follow the enactment of legislation, in Ireland the process of scrutiny and rejection took place at an earlier stage, though as will be seen there were later modifications in the way in which Poynings' Law was applied.

Summing up developments at the end of the fifteenth century we see that the Irish parliament had progressed towards the emergence of a representative assembly, in so far as any pre-Union Irish parliament could be described as representative; that it had accepted the corpus of English statute law, part of which had previously become applicable in Ireland by a variety of means; and that its relations with the administration in London gave the English government control over affairs in Dublin, just as it was later to exercise control over colonial affairs.

THE IRISH PARLIAMENT IN THE SIXTEENTH AND SEVENTEENTH CENTURIES

The period from 1495 to 1720, from Poynings' parliament to

[7] Arthur Berriedale Keith, *Constitutional History of the First British Empire* (Oxford, 1930), 12, 82.

the passing of the Irish Declaratory Act, contained many historic events—the Reformation, the Cromwellian interlude and the Restoration, the Bloodless Revolution, and the accession of the Hanoverians. It saw the growth of the overseas possessions of the Crown and in Ireland it saw the extension of English administration throughout the country, the settlement of English and Scottish planters in Ulster, the 1641 rising, and the Williamite wars. For the present purpose the most significant constitutional developments were the growth of the Irish parliament, the authority which England exercised over Ireland, and the arguments about the nature of that authority.

On the development of the Irish parliament, it is noteworthy that not until the opening of the eighteenth century did it become the practice to hold biennial parliaments. The unsettled state of Ireland during the sixteenth and seventeenth centuries and the method of governing the country by deputies under instruction from London were doubtless responsible for this. As for the composition of the parliament, in 1542 the basis of the county franchise was fixed, as in England, at forty shillings freehold, and in 1612 James I greatly increased the number of boroughs, which used a variety of tenures for the election of their representatives. This produced a House of Commons of some two hundred and thirty members. By the end of the seventeenth century the number had increased to three hundred, composed of two hundred and thirty-four borough members, sixty-four knights of the shire (two from each county), and two representatives of Trinity College, Dublin. In procedure and in the relations between the two houses the Irish parliament followed the Westminster model, and the same is true of the methods used to secure representation. When seats in the Irish House of Commons were sought, the influencing of votes, both in boroughs and counties, proceeded much as it did in England, and Ireland had her equivalents of Old Sarum and the rotten boroughs. A point of difference was that not until 1692 was the oath of supremacy used to exclude Roman Catholics from membership of the Irish House of Commons whereas they had been prevented from attending as representatives at Westminster since the middle of the preceeding century.

As regards Poynings' Law, the restrictions which it imposed on the passage of Irish legislation were suspended on two occasions in the Tudor period, and in 1557 it was amended by the Irish statute 3 & 4 Philip and Mary c. 4 to permit the Lord Lieutenant, during a session of the Irish parliament, to propose matters to the English Privy Council for enactment in Dublin. In 1612, in the case of *Parliament in Ireland*, (K. B.) 12 Co. Rep. 110, 77 Eng. Rep. 1386 the English Chief Justices, the Chief Baron, and the law officers gave their opinion on the procedure to be followed under Poynings' Law, and affirmed the right of the English Privy Council to make alterations or amendments in the Irish proposals. But the Irish legislators were not without ingenuity, and in the seventeenth century the practice developed of proposing and debating "heads of bills" which were forwarded through the Lord Lieutenant to London; if approved by the Privy Council there they were returned to Dublin and could be passed in the Irish parliament. It was, of course, open to the Lord Lieutenant to "cushion" the heads of a bill by refusing to forward them, and even if they were forwarded they might not be returned, or might be sent back with material alterations. Despite the strong resemblances between the parliaments of Ireland and England, legislative activities in Dublin were as securely under control from London as those of the legislatures on the eastern seaboard of America.

Here it may be noted that a nominal change took place in Ireland's constitutional position in 1541, when the Irish parliament passed an act which has since become known as the Crown of Ireland Act (33 Hen. 8, c. 1). This declared that the Lord of Ireland, a title dating from the Norman occupation, was to be known as King of Ireland, to have that style and title, and to enjoy the privileges of that office "as united and knit to the imperial crown of the realm of England." This recognition of the link between the two countries raised Ireland from a lordship to a kingdom, and at the same time cleared Henry VIII's title to Ireland of any trace of the Papal authority conferred on Henry II. The English parliament confirmed the new royal title by the statute 35 Hen. 8, c. 1, but the link between the ancient Crown of England and the newly constituted (but merely notional) Irish Crown was not regarded by the English courts as placing Ireland in the same position as Scotland after the union of the Crowns in 1603. Thus in the classic case on the effect of that union, *Calvin's Case*, (K. B. 1608) 7 Co. Rep. 1a, 77 Eng. Rep.

377, Scotland was described as a dominion of the king but Ireland was regarded as a conquered country and therefore a dominion of the Crown and subject to the English parliament. Again, in *Craw v. Ramsey*, (C. P. 1670) Vaughan 274, 124 Eng. Rep. 1072 the doctrine of conquest was applied to Ireland, which was thus regarded as being in the same position as colonial territories.

In the chapter on Legal History *(supra)* an indication was given of the circumstances which led to the passing in 1720 of the Irish Declaratory Act (6 Geo. 1, c. 5). Although the immediate dispute concerned appellate tribunals, the "Sixth of George the First" is an important factor in Irish constitutional history, not only because of its contents but also because it became the focal point of subsequent Irish protests. In addition, it formed the precedent for the similar act passed in 1766 (6 Geo. 3, c. 12) in relation to the American colonies.

That the Irish act was declaratory in form was due to the fact that the Westminster parliament continued on occasion to legislate for Ireland after the passing of Poynings' Law as it had done before. In the Tudor and early Stuart periods the power was used, for example, to insure that certain portions of the reformation legislation applied in Ireland, although the Irish parliament was the chief means used to extend these English statutes to Ireland or to re-enact their provisions so that they had effect there. After the 1641 rising the English parliament passed acts for the settlement of Ireland and the redistribution of Irish land, and the Cromwellian parliament took similar steps, though it was not until 1654 that Irish representatives were admitted to that parliament. At the Restoration some of the English accession legislation applied in Ireland, and later in Charles II's reign the Navigation Act restrictions had the same hampering effect on Irish trade as they had on the trade of the colonies. On the accession of William and Mary, Ireland was included in the scope of English statutes relating to the succession to the crown, the nullification of the proceedings of James II's Patriot Parliament, the oath of supremacy, and, later, the Williamite settlement of Irish land. From the British viewpoint, therefore, the statement of Westminster's parliamentary supremacy over Ireland contained in the Declaratory Act was nothing more than a recognition of what had happened in practice.

However, the subordinate position which Ireland occupied in English constitutional theory did not always commend itself to those in Ireland, any more than similar statements were accepted without dissent in other areas. In 1641 the Irish House of Commons claimed that Ireland was governed only by the common law and by statutes made by the Irish parliament; in the same decade the Catholic Confederation of Kilkenny sought a similar declaration from Charles I; and at the Patriot Parliament which James II held in Dublin in 1689 after he had fled from England there was a definite enactment of Irish legislative independence. But the proceedings of this assembly were nullified by both the Westminster and Dublin parliaments: the Patriot Parliament was far from being even a modified version of the Continental Congress.

From the comparative standpoint the most important facet of Irish constitutional development during this period was the argument which developed about the basis of English authority to legislate for Ireland. When the Irish parliament made its protest in 1641 the leading figure was Patrick Darcy, a lawyer who argued in favour of Irish independence. To him has been attributed the work entitled *A Declaration setting forth how, and by what Means, the Laws and Statutes of England, from Time to Time came to be of force in Ireland*; this adduced historical and constitutional reasons for Ireland's independence. In reply there appeared *The Answer of Sir Samuel Mayart*, who was a judge of the Court of Common Pleas in Dublin and who sought to refute the arguments in the *Declaration*. These works were not, however, referred to in the next controversy to be mentioned and they were not published until Walter Harris, the Irish antiquarian, published his *Hibernica*[8] in the middle of the following century.

A considerable controversy developed at the end of the seventeenth century when the English parliament imposed restrictions on the Irish woolen trade. This was part of a deliberate policy of repression, for as has been mentioned the Navigation Acts restricted Ireland and the American colonies equally. In protest William Molyneux published in 1698 *The Case of Ireland's being bound by Acts of Parliament in England, Stated*.[9] Molyneux sided with Darcy in marshaling a variety or arguments, legal and historical, constitutional

[8] Dublin, 1750.   [9] Dublin, 1698.

and philosophical, in support of the claim for Irish independence. The work was condemned by the Irish parliament and a reply was made by an English barrister, William Atwood (later Chief Justice of New York), who published *The History and Reasons of the Dependency of Ireland upon the Imperial Crown of the Kingdom of England.*[10] While Atwood's book seemed, in retrospect, to express views more consonant with legal and constitutional history than Molyneux's work, it is not surprising that the latter was subsequently acclaimed by those asserting Irish independence. Moreover, the influence of Molyneux's work spread to the American colonies, where it served to strengthen the independent views held on that side of the Atlantic.

Looking back on these two centuries of Irish constitutional history we see the gradual growth of a parliament closely following the Westminster pattern. The expansion of its membership in James I's reign was indicative of the way in which it was used for the purposes of government from London, and the unsettled state of Ireland in the seventeenth century was such that not until the end of that century did it begin to function in the way which was to become normal during the following century as, for instance, in the holding of biennial sessions to vote supplies. Over all its proceedings hung the shadow of Poynings' Law, whether in its original or its modified form.

A second feature of the period was the emergence of a definitive declaration of the doctrine of conquest, which was later to be elaborated in the classic case of *Campbell v. Hall*, (K. B. 1774) 1 Cowp. 204, 98 Eng. Rep. 1045. A third significant fact was that strong protests were made against the English exercise of legislative jurisdiction over Ireland, although these were overruled by the passing of the Declaratory Act. Finally, the disputes in the 1640's and 1690's showed that the basis of English power was subject to scrutiny both by those who denied its efficacy and those who argued in favor of its potency. Both in Ireland and in America in the eighteenth century speculation of this kind was rife and challenge was inevitable.

THE EIGHTEENTH CENTURY—DEPENDENCE, INDEPENDENCE, AND UNION

For over six decades the Irish Declaratory Act remained on the

[10] London, 1698.

British statute-book, where, as has been mentioned, it served as the precedent for the Declaratory Act (6 Geo. 3, c. 12) passed in 1766 to remind the American colonists of their dependence on the imperial crown and the Westminster parliament. Just as the common law arguments adduced by the judges pointed to the subordinate position of both Ireland and the colonies, so the London legislators asserted their claims over both the nearby island and the far-away continent. There was, however, the difference that in Ireland's case the opposition was delayed and the constitutional change was partial, while in the case of America the opposition was immediate and the constitutional change complete and final.

The assertion of legislative authority over Ireland did not lead to the integration of that country in the United Kingdom of Great Britain which had come into existence in 1707. The Irish parliament continued to operate, though of course British influence predominated, but not, as will appear, to the complete exclusion of Irish interests. Of the special legislation which the British parliament passed for Ireland during the period from 1720 to 1782 the bulk was concerned with commercial matters. The same was true of those statutes in which both Great Britain and Ireland were included, though the two series of acts which dealt with mutiny and marine mutiny were also to become the subject of controversy.

While the cabinet system was developing at Westminster in the eighteenth century there was no corresponding evolution in the Dublin legislature. Indeed, the transfer of power in London from king to cabinet prevented any such development, for the Lord Lieutenant of Ireland became a servant of the British government rather than of the Crown and he was responsible to the executive in London, not to the legislature in Dublin. Another factor was the Poynings' Law procedure which imposed restrictions on the course of Irish legislation. Two examples of such restrictive practices, relating to judicial independence and habeas corpus, were given in the chapter on Legal History (*supra*), and a third is provided by the eighteenth-century proposals for limiting the life of the Irish parliament to seven years. These proposals were not accepted at first, and when the Irish statute 7 Geo. 3, c. 2 was allowed to pass in 1768 it was an octennial one and not a septennial one as was the British statute 1 Geo. 1, St. 2, c. 38. While the "heads of bills" procedure gave the Irish parliament some initiative in the matter of legislation, the ultimate control lay outside that body. Conversely, to secure the passage of financial legislation, or of some measure which the British government desired the Irish parliament to enact, the Lord Lieutenant had to rely on such inducements as he could offer to members of parliament to secure their vote. From this practice stemmed the system of government by "undertakers," who undertook to see that the requisite number of votes was available to pass the necessary measures. Such a system was naturally a fluctuating one, by no means certain in its operation, and it is not surprising that the principles of cabinet responsibility and party government did not develop in conditions of this kind. The House of Commons had no quarrel with the House of Lords, in which episcopal influence predominated, underlining the Protestant nature of the Anglo-Irish ascendancy; but it suffered from the fact that the executive was not, and even during the period of Irish legislative independence did not become, responsible to parliament. In other ways, however, the organization of parliamentary strength was effective, the most notable example being the growth of the Patriot party, which was determined to secure legislative and judicial independence for the country.

Here it is relevant to mention the resemblances between the American Declaration of Independence and the securing of independence for Ireland in 1782. The ideas of William Molyneux had traveled across the Atlantic and had landed on fertile intellectual ground. The Irish precedent was used in argument by such persons as James Wilson, John Adams, and Benjamin Franklin, and those engaged in the two independence movements were in communication.[11] But the resemblence did not lie only in the realm of ideas and argument. The Navigation Acts bore hardly on Irish trade as they did on that of the colonies; the Continental Congress protested against standing armies, and the Irish parliament was concerned that the army in Ireland was governed by an English Mutiny Act; and the spirit which produced the Minute Men was closely akin to that which caused the organization of the Irish Volunteers. Taking into account the names of Irishmen who figured prominently

[11] Arthur Berriedale Keith, *Constitutional History of the First British Empire* (Oxford, 1930), 374; Reginald Coupland, *The American Revolution and the British Empire* (London, 1930), 102.

in the movement for American independence, it is clear that the two movements had personal links as well as similarities of outlook.

Two years after the American Declaration of Independence the Irish Volunteers were formed as a voluntary militia to protect the country against a possible invasion from France, but they rapidly developed into a powerful pressure group whose opinion could not be ignored, whatever the constitutional system. Also at this time the restrictions on native Irish industries, such as those which had been imposed on the export of wool and glass from Ireland, were removed, and Ireland was placed in the same position as Great Britain under the Navigation Acts. By 1780 resentment against the English Mutiny Act had reached such a pitch that Irish magistrates were refusing to convict deserters who were charged under the British legislation. The Irish parliament passed a Mutiny Bill which was duly sent to London; but there the Poynings' Law powers were used; and when the Irish statute 19 & 20 Geo. 3, c. 16 became law it was a perpetual, not an annual, enactment, though it was later replaced by an annual series of Irish acts similar to those passed in England. Another source of Irish discontent was the corresponding provision for the Navy, the Marine Mutiny Act. In 1782 the British government, recognizing the state of Irish opinion, deleted the reference to Ireland from the annual bill at Westminster, the Irish parliament proceeded to pass a similar act, and another proof of Ireland's subordinate position was removed.

The year 1782 is, however, more noted for the culmination of a series of events which led to the repeal of the "Sixth of George the First." In 1780 Henry Grattan moved a series of resolutions in the Irish House of Commons asserting that while the Crown of Ireland was inseparably annexed to the Crown of Great Britain, only the king and the Lords and Commons of Ireland could make laws to bind Ireland. The American precedent was frequently cited and although the motion was defeated the stage had been set for the controversy of the succeeding years. There were three main issues in the constitutional dispute—the validity of certain Westminster enactments, the Poynings' Law procedure, and the subordination of Ireland to Great Britain in legislative and judicial matters.

On the first point, in 1782 Barry Yelverton, later Chief Baron of the Exchequer and Viscount Avonmore, sponsored legislation to clarify the position of certain Westminster statutes. After considerable debate on the advisability of passing such an act without obtaining a declaration of Irish legislative independence, this bill reached the Irish statute-book as 21 & 22 Geo. 3, c. 48. This Act was similar to that of Poynings' parliament (10 Hen. 7, c. 22) which both extended and confirmed Westminster legislation. But while the 1494 statute was general, the 1782 Act was much more particular, dealing only with statutes on such subjects as the settlement of Irish lands, commercial acts affecting both Great Britain and Ireland equally, and the demise of the Crown. In this way doubts about the effect of this Westminster legislation were set at rest.

Yelverton's name is also linked with the second constitutional issue, for in 1780 and 1781 he sought leave to bring in heads of a bill to alter the Poynings' Law procedure, and in 1782 the Irish statute 21 & 22 Geo. 3, c. 47 was passed. This provided that only bills approved by both houses of the Irish parliament were to be sent, unaltered, by the Irish privy council to London, and those returned from London were to be given the royal assent; in addition, it was no longer necessary to put forward proposed legislation in order to obtain permission to hold an Irish parliament. Thus the power of the Irish privy council to "cushion" bills was removed, though that of the Privy Council in London to disapprove Irish legislation was retained. From 1782 Ireland was in a position similar to that of the colonies in that her legislation was subject to reservation and possible disapproval.

The third issue, that of Irish constitutional independence, dominated and was closely connected with the other matters just mentioned, for it occurred perpetually in the debates in the Irish parliament. Outside that body, one of the most important expressions of public opinion was contained in a resolution passed at the convention of the Irish Volunteers held at Dungannon, in county Tyrone, in February 1782. This declared that "a claim of any body of men, other than the king, lords and commons of Ireland, to make laws to bind this kingdom is unconstitutional, illegal and a grievance." This was followed by further parliamentary debate, both in Dublin and London, and eventually the Repealing Act (22 Geo. 3, c. 53) received the Royal assent in Westminster in June 1782 and the "Sixth of George the First" was removed from the Westminster statute-book. The declared constitutional domination of Great Britain over Ireland was at an end.

However, the constitutional dispute was not finally settled. The embers of controversy were stirred by incidental references to Ireland in Westminster legislation and by the decision by the English King's Bench of an Irish appeal which had gone to London before the passing of the Repealing Act. Arguments were again put forward in favor of the contention that the mere repeal of a declaratory statute did not alter the law, and in the result the Renunciation Act (23 Geo. 3, c. 28) was passed. Under this statute the Westminster parliament renounced its claim to legislate for Ireland by declaring that

. . . the said right claimed by the people of Ireland to be bound only by laws enacted by his Majesty and the Parliament of that kingdom, in all cases whatever, and to have all actions and suits at law or in equity, which may be instituted in that kingdom, decided in his Majesty's courts therein finally, and without any appeal from thence, shall be, and it is hereby declared to be established and ascertained for ever, and shall, at no time hereafter, be questioned or questionable.

Yet the independence which Ireland obtained in 1783 was in no way comparable to that which the American colonies had achieved. There was no breach of the relationship with the British Crown; the modification of the Poynings' Law procedure left the British Privy Council with a measure of control and in fact a number of bills were "detained" in London and not returned to Dublin; and conditions in the Irish House of Commons did not conduce to the emergence of cabinet government after the Repeal and Renunciation Acts any more than they had done so before.

The constitutional relations between Dublin and London came under strain in 1789. At Westminster Pitt and the Tories contended that legislation was necessary to set up a regency during George III's mental illness, while Fox and the Whigs contended that the proper procedure was by way of address of both Houses of Parliament. In the Irish parliament Grattan adopted the Whig argument, but he was opposed by John Fitzgibbon, then Attorney General and later Lord Chancellor and Earl of Clare, who argued that the regent should first be appointed in Great Britain and then confirmed by Irish legislation. Grattan's views prevailed, and after the Lord Lieutenant had refused to present the Irish address to the Prince of Wales, a committee of the Irish Lords and Commons did so. The Prince deferred replying, and the constitutional crisis was solved by George III's recovering his senses. The link with the British Crown was undenied, but the exact interpretation of the relationship showed a wide cleavage of opinion between those who thought that Ireland could and should act independently, and those who favored following the British lead.

Two of the main issues confronting the Irish parliament during its brief period of legislative independence were parliamentary reform and Catholic emancipation. In 1793 a measure of both these aims was achieved when the Irish parliament provided that Roman Catholics could exercise the franchise in counties, and could be admitted as freemen in boroughs, so that they would be entitled to vote (33 Geo. 3, c. 21); but while most of the penal code was repealed at this time, the ban on Roman Catholics' sitting in parliament was not lifted and remained until the movement led by Daniel O'Connell came to fruition in 1829. Another Irish act of 1793 (33 Geo. 3, c. 41) excluded the holders of newly created offices and Crown pensioners from sitting in the Irish House of Commons. Provisions such as these did not, however, prevent the distribution of lavish favors to secure the union.

While Ireland in the last two decades of the eighteenth century was concerned with these internal constitutional and political changes she did not remain unaffected by events elsewhere. The republicanism which had manifested itself in America and in the French Revolution led to the rising of the United Irishmen in 1798, which was both a protest against the political, economic, and social conditions prevailing in Ireland and an attempt to replace the constitution by one based on the ideas prevailing in France and America. But the rising was suppressed and the British government, unwilling that the sister island should remain in a state of unrest while the war with France was proceeding, determined on legislative union.

At the beginning of the eighteenth century, when plans were being prepared for the union between Scotland and England, the idea of Ireland's uniting with Great Britain had been mooted, but these proposals had not come to fruition. At the end of the century, the project was carried into effect, but the procedure was different from that used for the Scottish union. A plan to appoint commissioners, as had been done in Scotland, was approved by the Irish House of Lords in 1799 but was rejected by the House of Commons. The plan was then altered to state the details of the scheme, which involved a reduction in the number of borough constituencies, the payment of compensation to borough owners, and the introduction of a system of electing representative members of the Irish peerage to sit in the new House of Lords. The details were settled by the British government and the Irish executive and presented to the Irish parliament. To ensure acceptance of the union, bribes of various kinds were freely used so that the majority who were opposed to union in 1799 became a minority in the following year. The articles of union passed by the Dublin parliament were submitted to the British parliament and approved after unsuccessful attempts by the exponents of parliamentary reform to have them altered. Identical Acts of Union were passed by the parliaments at Dublin (40 Geo. 3, c. 38) and at Westminster (39 & 40 Geo. 3, c. 67), and on January 1, 1801, the new United Kingdom of Great Britain and Ireland came into existence. The inalienable right of self-government recognized by the Renunciation Act in 1783 was itself renounced, in legal form, less than two decades later. At the end of the eighteenth century the movement for independence in the colonies had placed America even farther away from Westminster, while that for Irish independence had the eventual result of bringing Dublin even nearer to London.

THE NINETEENTH CENTURY—UNION AND HOME RULE

As with legal history, the turn of the century provides a convenient point from which to look back over constitutional developments in Ireland during the six centuries following the establishment of the Anglo-Norman administration.

The early part of the period saw the slow emergence of the Irish parliament from the justiciar's equivalent of the *curia regis*. The summoning of knights of the shire and burgesses became a regular feature, and the development of an Irish peerage led to the division into two houses, as in England, though the Irish House of Commons did not have the same struggle as its English counterpart against the influence of the upper chamber. But the English parliament not only provided a model for Dublin, it was also an active participant in legislation for Ireland, and the English judges supported this legislative action. In Poynings' parliament the Irish legislature not only applied the then existing English statute law in Ireland, it also provided a method of English executive control of Irish legislation. Thus what might have developed into an independent institution remained under restrictions imposed by London, as did the constitutional systems developed for the colonies. While the Irish parliament extended the area of its jurisdiction, the variations of its composition never rendered it representative of anyone other than members of the ascendancy. Yet despite the continuance of English control and the declaration of legislative subordination the spirit of liberty flourished and was expressed in both parliamentary protests and philosophical treatises. There was a two-way traffic in ideas across the Atlantic; and, although the Irish parliament took no official move in support of American independence, this served as a spur, so that Irish independence flourished rapidly and flowered briefly before it wilted before the pressure for legislative union. Over a century after its demise an echo of the parliament in College Green was heard in London, for in *Swifte v. Attorney General for Ireland*, [1912] A.C. 276 the House of Lords had to consider the effect of an eighteenth-century marriage statute and it held that legislation of the pre-union Irish parliament could not have extraterritorial effect.

However, during the nineteenth century there were stronger voices with Irish accents than that of a defunct legislature, though there was no major constitutional change in Ireland during the century that produced the Durham Report, saw Canada become a Dominion, gave New Zealand a constitution, and watched the Australian colonies federate. The Irish Exchequer was amalgamated with that of Great Britain in 1817; in 1838 a poor-law system on the English model was introduced; the various changes described in the chapter on Legal History (*supra*), were made; and in 1898 the system of local government was reorganized. Throughout the nineteenth century Ireland was represented in the House of Lords by twenty-eight members of the Irish peerage elected for life, and by one hundred (and, after 1832, one hundred and five) members of the House of Commons. The country was represented in the British government by the Lord Lieutenant, the Chief Secretary for Ireland, and the Irish Attorney-General and Solicitor-General. The Irish franchise was also extended. In form, the integration of Ireland into the United Kingdom was complete.

In practice, the references to Ireland in the pages of the Westminister statute-book and of Hansard show that conditions in the country were by no means satisfactory and that opinion was far from being peaceful. In the opening decades of the nineteenth century a major issue was that of Catholic emancipation, which was eventually secured by the passing of the Roman Catholic Relief Act, 1829 (10 Geo. 4, c. 7) after Daniel O'Connell had fought the famous election for county Clare. As mentioned in the chapter on Land Law (*infra*), in the 1840's famine exacerbated the land question, which was to dominate much of Irish affairs. This decade also saw the foundation of the Young Ireland movement, and its unsuccessful contribution to the series of European revolutions in 1848, a contribution which also led to the creation of an offense new to British criminal law, that of treason felony (11 & 12 Vict. c. 12). Ten years later the Irish Republican Brotherhood was formed and in 1867 it inspired the Fenian Rising, which was also unsuccessful. Through this movement there descended the republican, anti-constitutional tradition which was to play an important part in affairs in Ireland in the present century. From the viewpoint of the British government, such activities, and those of the Land League, necessitated a series of special measures for the preservation of law and order. There was also, however, considerable constitutional activity for the alteration of the union of Ireland with England.

Agitation for the repeal of the union began in the first decade of the nineteenth century and continued, in varying forms, until the second decade of the present century. As early as 1810 a movement for repeal was supported by both Daniel O'Connell and Henry Grattan. The latter was then M.P. for Dublin in the Westminster House of Commons, and his support for repeal was based on his desire for harmony between the two islands; the former was already deeply immersed in the cause of Catholic emancipation. Once this had been achieved he threw himself into the repeal movement, conducting a parliamentary campaign against the union in the course of his activities in the House of Commons during the

1830's. In 1840 there was formed the Loyal National Repeal Association aimed at the repeal of the union by constitutional means. This was organized on a nation-wide basis, with "repeal wardens" collecting a "repeal rent" to provide the association with funds. The year 1843 saw the climax of this movement's activities, and one of the highlights was a debate on the question of repeal in the Dublin Corporation, when O'Connell's arguments in favor of repeal were answered by Isaac Butt, who thirty years later was the leader of another Home Rule movement. One of the methods used by the Repeal Association was that of mass meetings, which were held with greater numbers and increasing fervor. It was at one of these that O'Connell put forward his scheme for a "Council of Three Hundred" which was to meet, apparently fortuitously, in Dublin, and which could be made into an Irish parliament by the simple expedient of the Crown issuing writs; the number of delegates was obviously related to the membership of the former Irish House of Commons.[12] O'Connell based his plan on the view that though the union may have been legally valid, the Irish parliament had not the right to attempt to renounce the Irish constitution. As will be seen in the chapter on Constitutional Developments since 1920 *(infra)*, this appeal to a popular basis for the constitution was to be repeated in Ireland in another context. Another interesting feature of the Repeal Association's activities was its organization of repeal arbitration courts which would provide litigants with an alternative to the ordinary courts;[13] this scheme resembles that of the Dáil courts mentioned in the chapter on Legal History *(supra)*.

However, this movement petered out after the proscription of a mass meeting which was to be held at Clontarf in October 1843; and in any event the scheme for the Council of Three Hundred would have encountered difficulties, since it was clearly contrary to legislation which the Irish parliament had passed in 1793 (33 Geo. 3, c. 29) to prevent the emergence of a rival representative assembly. O'Connell was tried with others for seditious conspiracy, convicted, and imprisoned, but the conviction was quashed on appeal to the House of Lords, (*O'Connell v. R.*, (1844) 11 Cl. & Fin.

[12] Patrick Sarsfield O'Hegarty, *A History of Ireland under the Union 1801 to 1922* (London, 1952), 159.

[13] William Edmund Hartpole Lecky, *Leaders of Public Opinion in Ireland* (new ed.; 2 vols.; London, 1912), II, 257.

155, 8 Eng. Rep. 1061.). The movement for outright repeal began to weaken, partly because a suggestion for a federal scheme was introduced and partly because of the growth of more militant opinion which led eventually to the formation of the Young Ireland movement. With the death of O'Connell this phase of the movement for constitutional reform ended.

In view of developments elsewhere during the nineteenth century, it is interesting that a federal scheme was suggested to solve the Irish problem. In the 1830's the idea was current when O'Connell was considering the possibility of a subordinate Irish legislature. During the repeal debate in the Dublin Corporation in 1843 O'Connell contrasted the lack of an Irish legislature with the growth of local self-government in other parts of the Empire. The following year saw the idea of a federal scheme becoming even more prevalent, and the proposal for an Imperial Congress and federal parliament commended itself to the *Times*, which pointed out that while Lord Lieutenants of Ireland "are called to speedy account Governor-Generals quietly accumulate transgression," and continued:

> There are other difficulties which the idea of a Congress promises to meet. How else are we to give our colonies that voice both in their internal affairs, and also in the internal concerns of the Empire, which is the inalienable birthright of British blood, and without which it has never flowed in quietness? In fact, how else to retain our colonies? [14]

For a time it seemed that O'Connell was prepared to support some kind of federal scheme, but he made his position clear by saying that his first aim was full repeal of the union, though he would not refuse additional benefits which might come from Irish participation in a federal scheme. Another federal proposal planned to retain Irish representation in the Westminster parliament with, at the same time, a subordinate Irish parliament with powers similar to those then possessed by Canada under the British North America Act, 1840 (3 & 4 Vict. c. 35).[15] In the event, however, neither the devolutionary project nor the wider plan for an imperial federa-

[14] O'Hegarty, *op. cit. supra* note 12 at 194. In chap. xix O'Hegarty discusses the federal episode; cf. Robert Brendan McDowell, *Public Opinion and Government Policy in Ireland 1801-46* (London, 1952), 157, 236.

[15] Brian Aloysius Kennedy, "Sharman Crawford's Federal Scheme for Ireland" in *Essays in British and Irish History in Honour of James Eadie Todd* (London, 1949), 235.

tion materialized, so that there was no reflection in Ireland of any of the constitutional changes which occurred during the nineteenth century in the overseas dominions.

The next phase of the movement for constitutional reform in Ireland was inaugurated by Isaac Butt, whose views had developed considerably from the stand he took in opposing O'Connell during the 1843 debate. In the intervening years the famine, the Young Ireland rising in 1848, the Fenian rising in 1867, the disestablishment effected by the Irish Church Act, 1869 (32 & 33 Vic. c. 42), and the passing of the Landlord and Tenant Act, 1870 (33 & 34 Vict. c. 46) had all made alterations of varying kinds in the state of Ireland. At Butt's instigation, in 1870 the Home Government Association was formed in Ireland and in 1873 it was reconstituted as the Irish Home Rule League. A corresponding organization, the Home Rule Confederation of Great Britain, was formed in 1871 to bring Irish affairs to the attention of parliamentary candidates for British constituencies in which an Irish vote might be important. The aim of these groups was the creation of a bicameral Irish parliament with power to legislate on Irish affairs and control Irish revenue; the new parliament was to contribute to imperial expenditure and the Westminster parliament was to deal with the Crown, the colonies, "the relations of the United Empire with foreign states, and all matters relating to the defence and stability of the Empire at large."[16] Despite Butt's interest in federalism, the rallying cry of this movement was neither "Repeal" nor "Federalism" but "Home Rule."

At Westminster Butt led the Irish party, which after the general election of 1874 contained fifty-nine members pledged to the support of Home Rule. Although Butt disapproved, the emphasis of the party's tactics changed from parliamentary activity to parliamentary obstruction, a campaign which was to bring Irish affairs before the House of Commons at all possible times and if necessary impede the course of business in order to do so. The activities of the parliamentary party (of which Charles Stewart Parnell became leader in 1880) and the agitation on the land question, referred to in the chapter on Land Law *(infra)*, kept the twin issues of land reform and Home Rule before the public. By the middle of the 1880's it

[16] O'Hegarty, *op. cit. supra* note 12 at 467.

was clear even in London that some move in the direction of Irish self-government would have to be made. In 1884 and 1885 Joseph Chamberlain discussed various schemes for the setting up in Ireland of boards with either legislative or administrative functions, but the plan was not adopted by the Liberal cabinet.[17] The Liberals went out of office in 1885, and when they returned to power in 1886 Gladstone brought forward the first Home Rule Bill, a landmark in the parliamentary campaign.

Looking back from 1886 to the union, three salient facts emerge. One was the early appearance of constitutional agitation for repeal. The second was the undercurrent of direct action, an undercurrent which came to the surface from time to time in the 1848 and 1867 risings. Finally, the variety of proposals for changes in the constitutional position of Ireland ranged from Imperial federation through a local legislature with limited powers to bodies charged solely with administrative functions. Despite the colonial precedents which were adduced, none of these schemes were ever carried into effect. As will appear from the measures about to be discussed, this was also to be the fate of subsequent official proposals for dealing with the Irish question.

THE FIRST TWO HOME RULE BILLS

In comparison with its successors, the first Government of Ireland Bill introduced by Gladstone in 1886 was a short and simple measure. Under it, Ireland would have had an Irish legislature composed of the Queen and two "orders" of an Irish legislative body. The first order was to consist of a hundred and three members, seventy-five of them elected from different districts for a ten-year period and the twenty-eight Irish representative peers, who would have been replaced after thirty years by elected members. The second order was to be wholly elected for a maximum period of five years from the then existing Irish constituencies. The two orders of the legislative body were to sit together but vote separately; if there were a dispute between the two orders, followed by a dissolution or a three year interval, the two orders were to vote together and the majority decision was to prevail.

The Bill planned to delegate to the legislative body power to

[17] C. H. D. Howard, "Joseph Chamberlain, Parnell and the Irish 'Central Board' Scheme, 1884-5," *Irish Historical Studies,* VIII (1953), 324-361.

make laws for the "peace, order and good government" of Ireland, subject to such exceptions as matters relating to the Crown, peace and war, the armed services and defense, treaties and foreign and dominion relations, and trade and navigation. Specific restrictions were imposed on the endowment of religion and religious discrimination, compulsory religious instruction in public schools, the imposition of customs and excise duties, and the alteration of the 1886 Bill itself. There was to be an Irish executive, the power being vested in the Crown but exercised by the Lord Lieutenant "with the aid of such officers and such council as to Her Majesty may from time to time seem fit." An Irish Consolidated Fund was to be set up, and Ireland was to make contributions to the United Kingdom Consolidated Fund to defray Ireland's share of the National Debt and the cost of defense, civil, and police services. As mentioned in the chapter on Legal History (*supra*), the Privy Council was to determine constitutional questions, such as the validity of Irish legislation. A final feature of the 1886 Bill was the method of amendment, which was to be undertaken either by the Westminster parliament (in which the Irish members would have ceased to sit) on an address from the Irish legislative body, or by a special meeting of the Westminster parliament at which the House of Lords would contain the Irish representative peers and the House of Commons representatives of the Irish constituencies. In addition, the sovereignty of the imperial parliament was specifically preserved.

From this summary of the provisions of the first Home Rule Bill it will be seen that Ireland was to have a subordinate legislature with powers wider than those of a Canadian province but not so wide as those of the Dominion of Canada; that provision was made for the development of a responsible executive, though the Lord Lieutenant was given the power of disallowance; that the colonial precedent was also to be used for the determination of constitutional issues; and that a special procedure was devised for constitutional amendment.

Not unnaturally, the novelty of some of these provisions caused some comment, and Albert Venn Dicey published his *England's Case against Home Rule*,[18] a strenuous argument against the measure, based on a variety of grounds. In particular he contended that the

[18] London, 1886.

sovereignty of the British parliament was impaired by the introduction of a specially constituted imperial parliament, and he foresaw difficulties in the use of the Lord Lieutenant's veto and in the powers of judicial review. Sir William Anson was of the same opinion as Dicey on the point about the sovereignty of parliament, and he remarked that "There would be some novelty in the spectacle of an English Court considering an Act of Parliament, not as regarded its construction, but as regarded its validity. . . ."[19] What was good enough for the colonies would not do nearer home, at least on this view, though James Bryce contended, both in parliament and out of it, that the Bill did not affect its sovereignty.[20]

However, these arguments about parliamentary sovereignty and speculations about the application of modified colonial systems to Irish affairs were academic. The Bill failed to get a second reading in the House of Commons because of the secession of a section of the Liberals led by Joseph Chamberlain, and the Irish question was relegated to the realm of political controversy instead of that of constitutional possibility. At this point it must be noted that Unionist opinion against Home Rule had crystallized and become extremely vocal, especially in the North of Ireland, a fact which was to have a considerable bearing on subsequent events.

After their defeat in 1886, the Liberals gradually won their way back into favor, and they were returned to power at the general election of 1892. In this interval the Parnellite split had occurred in the Irish Nationalist party; nevertheless, all the Irish Nationalists supported Gladstone when he introduced the second Government of Ireland Bill in 1893.

The legislature proposed in 1893 was to consist of a Legislative Council and a Legislative Assembly. The former was to consist of forty-eight members elected for eight years by the counties and county boroughs; the latter, like its 1886 predecessor, was to consist of one hundred and three elected members. In cases of disagreement, the period to elapse before a joint session was reduced to two years. There was to be a full delegation of legislative power "in respect of matters exclusively relating to Ireland or some part thereof," subject to specified exceptions which were similar to those in the 1886

[19] "The Government of Ireland Bill and the Sovereignty of Parliament," *Law Quarterly Review*, II (1886), 423, 432.

[20] *Studies in History and Jurisprudence* (2 vols.; Oxford, 1901), I, 207.

Bill. There were, however, added such subjects as "matters arising out of a state of war," "the use of arms for military purposes," and extradition, while the restriction on legislation about trade was confined to "trade with any place outside Ireland." There was a considerable difference in the specific restrictions imposed by the later Bill, and one of these appears to be attributable to the fact that James Bryce was a member of the cabinet subcommittee responsible for the drafting of the Bill. This was the inclusion of a provision that the Irish legislature could not make any law "whereby any person may be deprived of life, liberty or property without due process of law in accordance with settled principles and precedents, or whereby private property may be taken without just compensation." The reference to settled principles and precedents may be regarded as an attempt to marry the general words of the United States Constitution to the common law doctrine of precedent. The 1893 Bill also expanded the 1886 prohibitions on religious discrimination and added a ban on discriminating against British subjects on the ground of parentage or place of birth or business.

As for the executive, the 1893 Bill proposed that the Lord Lieutenant should be aided by a special executive committee of the Irish Privy Council, though the veto power was retained. The financial arrangements involved the imposition of customs and excise duties by the Westminster parliament, the reservation to the Westminster parliament of the power to levy existing taxes for a six-year period, the conferring of power to levy new taxes on the Irish legislature, and the payment of a contribution from Irish revenues to the United Kingdom Consolidated Fund. One of the clauses in the 1893 Bill as originally introduced had proposed a reduction in the number of Irish members in the Westminster House of Commons, and would have prevented those members and Irish representative peers from discussing British affairs. This "in-and-out" proposal was dropped at the committee stage, and there was added a declaration of the supremacy of the Westminster parliament. The power of the Irish legislature to alter the Bill was confined to such topics as election laws.

Once again the indefatigable Dicey put his views in print, this time under the title *A Leap in the Dark, or Our New Constitution*.[21]

----

[21] London, 1893.

He contended that the "in-and-out" scheme would effect a major alteration in the British constitution by introducing a semi-federal element; he argued that Westminster would be hampered in the exercise of its power over Ireland just as it was limited by convention in its relations with the State of Victoria; and he prophesied that the restrictions on Irish activities imposed by the Bill were inadequate in that they did not apply to executive action nor prevent the passing of indemnity acts or ex post facto laws. This marshaling of the arguments against the Bill by a distinguished constitutional lawyer was another example of the reluctance to introduce novel elements into the British constitution, even though similar expedients had been adopted in other parts of the Empire as it then existed. The 1893 Bill was more detailed than the 1886 measure and the amendments made by the Commons clarified some points and cleared away others, yet it was still unpalatable to the members of the House of Lords. The defeat of the Liberals at the general election in 1895 was regarded as a justification of the rejection of the Home Rule Bill two years earlier.

This précis of the provisions of the first two Home Rule Bills has done little more than outline the main features of the proposals and indicate points of comparison with other nineteenth century constitutions. Because of the special nature of the Irish problem these Bills had to be eclectic, drawing from the colonies and Canada and (in the case of the 1893 legislative restrictions) from the United States. The much-discussed question of continued Irish representation in the Westminster parliament and the special arrangements for financial contributions from Ireland are two examples of the exceptional provisions put forward as a solution. In addition to the details of the proposed constitutional changes, the principles to be applied were considerably discussed both in and out of parliament. Thus federalism, devolution, and the nature of colonial government were very much in the Irish air at the end of the nineteenth century, though that air was clouded by political prejudices. There were almost as many differing views as there were persons holding them, but one common feature was the limit placed on the application of these theories; there was no question of putting them into practice. When the century closed Canada was a Dominion, Australia was about to become a Commonwealth, New Zealand's Constitution had been in operation for five decades, but all that Ireland had obtained was a reorganization of the local government system by the Local Government (Ireland) Act, 1898 (61 & 62 Vict. c. 37). As an Irish historian commented recently:

> Throughout the nineteenth century Englishmen were always ready to encourage and support demands for self-government put forward by Greeks, Serbs, Italians, Magyars, Poles; and they considered it quite reasonable that British colonists in Australia, South Africa and Canada should manage their own affairs. Yet hostility to Ireland persisted; and this hostility was peculiarly English. . . . To some extent the English attitude was dictated by obviously selfish motives: Ireland was valuable both as a market and as a source of food supply and her position made her of vital strategic importance to Britain. The various home rule bills contained safeguards on these heads, which might have satisfied legitimate anxiety; but English public opinion was opposed to the essential principle of any sort of self-government for Ireland, no matter how hedged about with conditions, and no matter how costly and inconvenient the task of keeping an unwilling partner within the union.[22]

The outlook for Ireland at the beginning of the new century was not particularly bright. It was certain that Irish affairs would continue to occupy a considerable portion of the time of the Westminster parliament and a prominent place in the minds of the people of the United Kingdom, but it did not look as if the aims of O'Connell and Butt, of Parnell and Gladstone, would easily be achieved, and such proved to be the case.

THE TWENTIETH CENTURY TO THE GOVERNMENT OF IRELAND ACT, 1914

Mention has been made of the emergence in the north of Ireland of strong Unionist opposition, based on social, economic and religious grounds, to the idea of Home Rule. This opposition was also manifest when the 1893 Home Rule Bill was introduced, and it continued throughout the first two decades of the twentieth century.

The organization of the other main element in Irish political affairs may also be traced back to the 1880's. The foundation of the Gaelic Athletic Association in 1884 and of the Gaelic League in 1893 gave impetus to national feeling in the diverse fields of sport and literature, while in the 1890's Sir Horace Plunkett's work in the establishment of co-operative agricultural societies fostered the notion

[22] James Camlin Beckett, *A Short History of Ireland* (London, 1952), 168.

of economic self-sufficiency. Another event symptomatic of later developments was the formation of Irish brigades to fight with the Boers in the South African War.[23] Then in 1890 Arthur Griffith (later to become leader of Dáil Eireann and President of the Provisional Government of Ireland in 1922) founded Cumman na nGaedheal, one of the precursors of Sinn Féin, to co-ordinate separatist activities. Griffith was an outstanding thinker in the movement for Irish independence, and one of the schemes he propounded involved the withdrawal of the Irish parliamentary representatives from Westminster. Taking as his model events in Hungary in the mid-nineteenth century, Griffith argued that the 1782 Constitution and the Renunciation Act of 1783 should be treated as if they were still in force, and he suggested a plan similar to that which O'Connell had for the formation of a Council of Three Hundred. However, on the formation of Sinn Féin in 1908 this "dual monarchy" plan was abandoned in favor of a movement for complete independence, to be achieved by a long-term program of internal reforms. The nineteenth century was too great a gap to bridge by reverting to a system which had flourished during the last twenty years of the eighteenth century.

Another proposal for Ireland, but of a very different character, was put forward in 1904 by the Irish Reform Association under the Earl of Dunraven. Their scheme would have involved the setting up of two new bodies, a Financial Council and a "Statutory Body." The former would have been partly nominated by the Crown, and partly elected for parliamentary and local government constituencies, while the latter was to consist of the Irish representative peers and the Westminster M.P.s for Irish constituencies. The Council was to exercise control over Irish revenues and expenditures, while the Statutory Body was to have power to deal with Irish legislation by private bill and with such other legislative work as might be delegated to it. Associated with this scheme was Sir Anthony McDonnell, then Under-Secretary for Ireland and head of the Irish civil service; in the course of the protest made against permanent officials interfering in political matters the Chief Secretary, George Wyndham (the sponsor of an important

[23] In *Rex. v. Lynch*, [1903] 1 K. B. 444, a leading case in the law of treason, the accused was the commander of the 2nd Irish Brigade.

measure referred to in the chapter on Land Law *infra*) was forced to resign, and the scheme itself perished.[24]

The idea of devolution was, however, not entirely eclipsed, and when the Liberals returned to power in 1906 it was taken up again. A full-scale Home Rule measure would have brought forward the inevitable constitutional conflict between the Lords and the Commons, so in 1907 an Irish Council Bill was introduced. This is comparable in very few respects with the Home Rule Bills of 1886 and 1893. Under it, there would have been constituted an Irish Council consisting of eighty-two members elected for boroughs and counties, twenty-four nominated by the Crown or later by the Lord Lieutenant, and the Under-Secretary ex-officio. Unlike the body contemplated by the Irish Reform Association, this Council would have had no legislative powers, but would have controlled local administration in Ireland, defraying the cost from a specially constituted Irish Fund. Even in such a measure it was considered necessary to insert a prohibition against the showing of preference to any religious denominations, and any alleged breach of this provision could have been challenged before the Judicial Committee of the Privy Council. But administrative devolution would, at most, have gone only part of the way towards Home Rule; the solution of the Irish problem was not to be found in this direction.

Another solution proposed was that of "Home Rule all round," which would have entailed the setting up of subordinate legislatures in England, Scotland, Wales, and Ireland. In 1910 an unofficial suggestion for a federal arrangement on these lines was again put forward, but was rejected by the Irish Unionists,[25] and there was no federal element in the third Home Rule Bill which the Liberals launched in 1912. In the interval since the 1907 plan for administrative devolution, the powers of the House of Lords had been restricted by the Parliament Act, 1911 (1 & 2 Geo. 5, c. 13), and as events happened it was necessary to make use of that Act to ensure that the Home Rule Bill became law. In the Government of Ireland Bill, 1912, the projected Irish legislature was given the title of

[24] Francis Stewart Leland Lyons, "The Irish Unionist Party and the Devolution Crisis of 1904-5," *Irish Historical Studies*, VI (1948), 1-22.

[25] Harford Montgomery Hyde, *Carson: The Life of Sir Edward Carson, Lord Carson of Duncairn* (London, 1953), 278; cf. also J. A. Murray Macdonald and Lord Charnwood, *The Federal Solution* (London, 1914).

"Irish Parliament." This was to consist of a Senate whose forty members (at first nominated by the Lord Lieutenant but for second and subsequent Senates to be elected by the four Irish provinces as separate constituencies) were to hold office for a five-year term, and a House of Commons of one hundred and sixty-four members. There was no time limit for the settlement of disputes between the two Houses, but if both Houses failed to agree on a measure in two consecutive sessions, a joint session was to be held. The delegation of executive power was subject to exceptions similar to those in the 1893 Bill, with the addition of postal services outside Ireland, and the term "reserved matter" was introduced to describe subjects on which the Irish parliament was not to have power to legislate until a later date; of these, the most important were the land purchase schemes and the national insurance scheme, which at that time was a comparative novelty. The 1893 restrictions on the exercise of legislative power were compressed into a general provision against religious discrimination.

The executive power was to be exercised by the Lord Lieutenant, on the advice of the ministerial heads of the Irish administrative departments, who were to form the executive committee of the Privy Council. As for financial powers, the new legislature would have been able to vary Westminster taxes in certain respects and could have levied independent taxes; these revenues were to be paid into the United Kingdom Exchequer, from which a "transferred sum" was to be paid out for the administration of Irish services. The amount of this sum was to be determined by a Joint Exchequer Board representing the British and Irish treasuries. The relationship between Ireland and the Westminster parliament was continued not only by the Irish representative peers and the Irish M.P.s in the Westminster House of Commons but also by a provision which stated that "the supreme power and authority of the Parliament of the United Kingdom shall remain unaffected and undiminished over all persons, matters, and things in Ireland and every part thereof."

That the 1912 Bill followed the pattern of its Victorian predecessors may be seen from the general scheme for the delegation of legislative power, the more detailed provisions for the Irish executive, and the proposals (mentioned in the chapter on Legal History *supra*) for the determination of constitutional questions. The new scheme for financial relations between the two countries was further evidence of the extreme complexity of this problem, and the supremacy of the Westminster parliament was not only specifically declared but reinforced by a provision (similar to that in the 1893 Bill) invalidating any law of the Irish parliament conflicting with a Westminster enactment passed after the new Constitution came into force and extending to Ireland. This would have placed Ireland in a position similar to that of Dominion and Colonial governments subject to the restriction of s. 2 of the Colonial Laws Validity Act, 1865 (28 & 29 Vict. c. 63). The idea of an elective upper chamber had been put into practice in Australia, but the Irish expedient was fated never to be carried out. In the academic field Dicey returned to the fray by republishing *A Leap in the Dark*,[26] though in view of developments in Australia he had to substitute references to New Zealand for those in the earlier edition to the State of Victoria. Two years later he denounced Home Rule again in *A Fool's Paradise*[27] reiterating his arguments that Home Rule would weaken the British constitution, would not relieve the Westminster parliament of the burden of dealing with Irish affairs, and would not satisfy Irish demands. He also deprecated the notion of a federal solution and feared the effect of a possible extension of the federal idea to the Empire itself. However, events in Ireland up to the outbreak of the First World War were such that arguments as to principles were outweighed by the exigencies of a mounting crisis.

It was during the debates on the 1912 Bill that a parliamentary proposal was made for the exclusion of Ulster, the northeast province of Ireland, or of some of its counties, from the provisions of the Bill. As far back as 1886 Gladstone had referred to this possibility, and to the alternative of setting up some kind of separate autonomy. In the interval, however, the Unionist opposition in the north of Ireland had become organized, outspoken, and determined. Nor was this opposition confined to political and parliamentary activity, for a movement began to oppose Home Rule by force if necessary. The 1912 Bill was passed by the Commons but rejected by the Lords early in 1913. It achieved the same fate at another session of parliament held in the same year. Meantime the Ulster Volunteer Force had been organized (thus setting a precedent for the formation of

---

[26] 2d ed.; London, 1911.   [27] London, 1913.

the Irish Volunteers in Dublin later in the same year) and a provisional government was planned. When the Government of Ireland Bill was introduced for a third time (in the same terms, to comply with the provisions of the Parliament Act) in 1914 it was clear that a major political and constitutional crisis existed. After the Bill had passed its third reading in the Commons, but before it received the Royal Assent, the government introduced in the Lords a Government of Ireland (Amendment) Bill which would have instituted a system of "county option" in the nine counties of Ulster, so that electors could decide whether or not they were in favor of the exclusion of their counties from the Home Rule measure for a six-year period. Counties with a majority in favor of this exclusion were to be administered by the Lord Lieutenant, but the judicial system of the 1914 measure was to extend to the excluded counties. However, a scheme on these lines had been rejected earlier in the year by Sir Edward Carson (as he then was) on the ground that it was a "sentence of death with a stay of execution for six years," and in the course of its passage through the Lords the Bill was altered to exclude Ulster permanently from the operation of the 1914 measure. This Bill was not proceeded with in the Commons, and representatives of the opposing parties met at a conference held in Buckingham Palace under the chairmanship of the Speaker of the House of Commons, but they failed to reach any agreement. Events outside Ireland determined the next step for on the outbreak of the First World War the operation of the Government of Ireland Act was suspended for a six-year period. In fact, the Suspensory Act, 1914 (4 & 5 Geo. 5, c. 88) was placed on the statute-book before the 1914 Act itself (4 & 5 Geo. 5, c. 90).

In retrospect, the variety of proposals put forward for the constitutional solution of the Irish question never attained their common objective of providing a scheme which would have been acceptable both in Ireland and in Great Britain because the different aims of the opposing factions prevented any facile solution. The proposals which were worked out in the greatest detail in the 1912 and 1913 Bills and the 1914 Act were regarded on the one hand as but the first step to eventual independence and on the other as a concession which must be resisted, if necessary, by the use of force. This tendency to extraconstitutional activity is one which appeared before and which was to recur. Indeed, the core of the Irish question was not the difficulty of devising a form of constitution, a problem which had been successfully solved in Australia and South Africa in the previous decade; the chief difficulty was to discover a basis on which any constitutional system could be founded.

FROM THE FIRST WORLD WAR TO THE GOVERNMENT OF IRELAND ACT, 1920

The next six years of Ireland's history also exhibited these twin trends of varied constitutional proposals and extraconstitutional activity. The most significant example of the latter was, of course, the rising in Dublin in 1916. In 1914 the Irish Volunteer movement had divided on the question of participation in the war against Germany; the National Volunteers under John Redmond, the leader of the Irish Nationalist party, supported this policy while the Irish Volunteers under Eoin McNeill, the Gaelic scholar and historian, opposed it. The combined forces of the Irish Volunteers and James Connolly's Irish Citizen Army, together with the Sinn Féin and Irish Republican Brotherhood organizations, led to the declaration of the Republic. Later in 1916 the Government produced "Headings of a Settlement as to the Government of Ireland" based on the exclusion of six of Ulster's nine counties from the operation of the 1914 Act, but this movement was frustrated between the desire of the Ulster Unionists for permanent exclusion and the aim of the Irish Nationalists that Ulster should be eventually included in the whole of Ireland. Another attempt to deal with the question was made in 1917 when the Irish Convention was set up, representing the parliamentary parties, local government and other public bodies, the churches and labor organizations, but not including any representative of the Sinn Féin movement. When the Convention reported the following year[28] it revealed as wide a divergence as ever of Irish opinion on the constitutional question. A majority of the members agreed to a proposal which would have given Ireland a constitution on the lines of the 1914 Act, with a representative Senate of forty-eight members and a House of Commons of one hundred and sixty members. This parliament would not have been given immediate power to deal with customs and excise, but otherwise would have been able to levy taxes; Irish representation at Westminster would

[28] (1918) Cmd. 9019.

have been retained with a reduced number of M.P.s, and the overall supremacy of the Westminster parliament would have been expressly declared, as in the 1914 Act. However, this piece of constitution-making by modifying the 1914 proposals was completely nullified by the opinion expressed in the various minority reports. The Ulster Unionists desired the exclusion of Ulster, a majority of the Nationalists were prepared to postpone fiscal autonomy if an Irish parliament and responsible executive were constituted, a minority of the Nationalists sought full power of legislation, while the Earl of Dunraven, the Provost of Trinity College, Dublin, and the protestant Archbishop of Armagh pressed for a federal scheme. In short, the diversity of opinion was such that no legislation could have been based on the report. Meantime, the Sinn Féin movement was growing in strength, and it ousted the Nationalist party in the elections for the Westminster parliament held in December 1918. These Sinn Féin representatives in 1919 set up Dáil Eireann as a representative assembly, elected Mr. de Valera as President of the Irish Republic, and inaugurated an administration. A plan on the lines of O'Connell's Council of Three Hundred had been put into operation, and a constitutional form had been given to the movement for complete Irish independence. The only moves made by the British government in 1919 to alter the pattern of Irish government were to provide that local government elections were to be conducted on the principle of proportional representation, and to introduce a Private Legislation Procedure (Ireland) Bill under which the provisional order procedure would have been applied to Irish private legislation. The latter proposal was dismissed as a form of "gas and water Home Rule" and it was not proceeded with. It was not until the following year that the last of the series of Home Rule measures was brought before the Westminster parliament. This was the Bill for the Government of Ireland Act, 1920 (10 & 11 Geo. 5, c. 67).

If the Government of Ireland Act, 1920 had come into full force there would have been two parliaments in Ireland, that for Northern Ireland having jurisdiction over six of the nine counties of Ulster, and that for Southern Ireland legislating for the remainder of the island. Both would have been bicameral, the Senate of Southern Ireland consisting of three ex officio members, seventeen nominated members, and forty-four elected to represent the Roman Catholic Church, the Church of Ireland, the peerage, the Privy Council, and the county councils, while the Senate of Northern Ireland was to have two ex-officio and twenty-four elected members. The Southern Ireland House of Commons was to have one hundred and twenty-eight members and that for Northern Ireland fifty-two. The legislative powers, restrictions, executive authority, and financial provisions for the two bodies were the same, and are discussed in relation to the present parliament of Northern Ireland in the chapter on Constitutional Developments since 1920 *(infra)*. For the present purpose it will suffice to say that they were broadly similar to, but differed in detail from, the 1914 Act. The most interesting feature of the 1920 Act was the provision it made for co-operation between the parliaments. A Council of Ireland was to be constituted with a President nominated by the Lord Lieutenant and twenty representatives of each of the new parliaments, seven from each Senate and thirteen from each House of Commons. The Council was to have power to deal with private bill legislation and it could also legislate with respect to such matters concerning the two areas as railways, fisheries, and diseases of animals. Both parliaments were empowered by identical acts to delegate to the Council of Ireland their legislative or executive functions. The Council was to cease to exist if both parliaments agreed by identical acts to establish a parliament for the whole of Ireland; "the date of Irish union" was the focal point of this constitutional scheme. As has been mentioned in the chapter on Legal History *(supra)*, the legislative and executive provisions were paralleled by the establishment of a High Court of Appeal for Ireland with jurisdiction to hear cases coming from both Northern and Southern Ireland.

From this outline of its provisions it will be seen that the 1920 Act contained something of federalism, something of devolution, and a great deal of previous Home Rule measures. It was accepted by the Ulster Unionists because it appeared to be the only alternative to the 1914 Act, but it involved the separation of three counties of Ulster from the rest of the province; it was not welcomed by the Southern Unionists, and it was, of course, ignored by Sinn Féin. It must be remembered that events in Ireland at this time were such that the Restoration of Order in Ireland Act, 1920 (10 & 11 Geo.

5, c. 31) was passed to give additional powers to the authorities, and towards the end of the year martial law was declared in certain areas. Thus the constitutional scheme embodied in the 1920 Act did not fall on the most fertile ground. On the contrary, as will be seen in the chapter on Constitutional Developments since 1920 *(infra)*, the seed failed to germinate in southern Ireland, though it has continued to flourish in the north. Perhaps it is fitting that the last of the Home Rule measures should have had this result in achieving only a partial solution to an almost completely insoluble problem.

CONCLUSION

It is difficult to compress the constitutional history of a country into small compass, but this chapter has sought to show briefly how Anglo-Norman institutions took root in Ireland and flourished.

In the formative period of parliamentary development the Irish legislature, unlike its Westminster counterpart, did not have a fixed area of jurisdiction, but it nevertheless proceeded along the lines laid down by London. By virtue of the provisions of Poynings' Law the Irish parliament was subject to closer control than colonial legislatures, and perhaps because of this there came from Dublin both parliamentary protests and legal and philosophical argument. These ideas were used on both sides of the Atlantic to combat the idea of imperial legislative supremacy, and they flowered in both America and Ireland in the eighteenth century, though the Irish bloom soon faded.[29] For only eighteen years Ireland was outside the scope of Westminster legislation, which has been extended to Ireland in a variety of ways since the thirteenth century.

After the union, when Ireland was represented in both Houses of the Westminster parliament, statutes in general terms applied automatically in Ireland, for which there was also much specific legislation. The variety of nineteenth-century proposals for constitutional alteration has been mentioned, but none of these were put into effect, despite the numerous constitutional changes in other

[29] A good example of this trans-Atlantic traffic in ideas is given by Caroline Robbins, " 'When It Is That Colonies May Turn Independent': An Analysis of the Environment and Politics of Francis Hutcheson (1694-1746)," *William and Mary College Quarterly*, XI (1954), 214-251. (Hutcheson was an Irishman who taught philosophy at Glasgow.) For a particular link between Ireland and America, see Edward Rodney Richey Green, "The Scotch-Irish and the Coming of the Revolution in North Carolina," *Irish Historical Studies*, VII (1950), 77-86.

parts of the Empire at this time. As well as constitutional proposals, there were separatist plans based on physical force, and an equally determined movement for the retention of the union. The impasse reached in 1914 was ended by the outbreak of the First World War, but the problem was no nearer solution. The mainstream divided into two channels, the one leading to the 1916 rising and the formation of Dáil Eireann and the other to the Government of Ireland Act, 1920 and the operation of the devolutionary system of government in Northern Ireland. When at last the federal solution, which had helped to bring other countries in the Commonwealth to virtual co-equality with the United Kingdom, was applied in Ireland, it was destined not to operate there. The peculiarities of the Irish situation demanded novel treatments and fresh devices and, as the succeeding chapters indicate, it was in new fields that Ireland was to make her contribution to Commonwealth affairs, international law, and constitutional law.

3

Ireland and the Commonwealth: Dominion Status and International Law

DURING THE PAST thirty-five years, Ireland has had a contribution to make in the field of Commonwealth relations, in the practice of international law, and in the application of the rules of private international law. The period is limited, for it was only in 1920 that the term "Northern Ireland" first appeared in the Government of Ireland Act of that year (10 & 11 Geo. 5, c. 67) and in 1921 that the phrase "Irish Free State" (Saorstát Eireann) was introduced in the Anglo-Irish agreement. The emergence of these two entities in Ireland regulated the contribution by Ireland to the three topics which have been mentioned. Northern Ireland remains part of the United Kingdom, and its subordinate parliament has no power to legislate on foreign affairs; its main contribution therefore lies in the field of conflict of laws. On the other hand, the Irish Free State was granted dominion status when it came into existence, played a considerable part in the development of that status in the 1920's and 1930's, entered the international arena, and ultimately left the Commonwealth. The starting-point of this process is the Anglo-Irish agreement of 1921.

I. DOMINION STATUS

THE ANGLO-IRISH AGREEMENT, 1921

The state of war in Ireland was called to a truce on July 11, 1921. For the next five months protracted negotiations resulted in the signing, on December 6, of what were entitled "Articles of Agreement for a Treaty between Great Britain and Ireland." These were signed by a British delegation and an Irish delegation, though the latter had been authorized as "Envoys Plenipotentiaries from the

Government of Ireland" by Mr. de Valera, President of Dáil Eireann, the legislative assembly which had first been constituted by Sinn Féin in 1919; but the Irish delegation were not recognized as diplomatic representatives. From these negotiations there emerged the twin ideas of "external association" and reciprocal citizenship between members of the Commonwealth which were later elaborated by Mr. de Valera, and which might have transformed the conception of the Commonwealth. But the pragmatic view of the nature of Commonwealth relations was nowhere shown more clearly than in the different ideas held on the nature of the agreement.

On this point both official and academic opinion have differed. When in 1924 the Irish Free State registered the 1921 agreement at Geneva, the British Government protested that the agreement was not an international one, but in the 1932 dispute over the payment of land purchase annuities by the Irish Free State, the British Government relied on the binding force of the agreement.[1] For its part, the Irish Free State recognized the agreement as binding between 1922 and 1932, when a change of government resulted in an alteration of the official view to one which alleged that the agreement had been signed under duress and therefore was not binding. Commentators have also adopted different views. Berriedale Keith held that the agreement recognized Ireland as an entity, while Mr. Noel-Baker thought that the form of the agreement was only a concession to Irish sentiment. In 1932 an eminent British lawyer took the view that the Crown could not make an agreement with itself but against this must be set the view of an Irish commentator in 1927 that the Crown was a multiple constitutional entity, and that the processes of approval and ratification gave the agreement full treaty status.[2] It is significant that the agreement is colloquially known in Ireland, both North and South, as "the Treaty," so this convenient designation will be used.

[1] *League of Nations Treaty Series,* XXVI, 10; XXVII, 449; XLIV, 263-269. (1932) Cmd. 4116.
[2] Arthur Berriedale Keith, *Journal of Comparative Legislation and International Law,* (3d Series) IV (1922), Part I, 104-108; Philip John Noel-Baker, *The Present Juridical Status of the British Dominions in International Law* (London, 1929), 319; Stafford Cripps, *House of Commons Debates* (5th series), 267, col. 695; Edward Joseph Phelan, "The Sovereignty of the Irish Free State," *Review of Nations,* I (March, 1927), 35.

The form of the Treaty was novel in 1922, though it resembles the agreement between the United Kingdom and Burma in 1947; but the Anglo-Burmese agreement was followed by a treaty and by the Burma Independence Act, 1947 (11 & 12 Geo. 6, c. 3), whereas the Anglo-Irish Treaty specifically conferred Dominion status on the new Irish Free State. The underlying assumption was that membership of the Commonwealth could be conferred in terms, rather than inferred from a constitutional relationship. The Treaty was a legislative recognition of the state of Commonwealth development as well as the legal foundation for the Irish Free State.

The first main feature of the Treaty appeared in the well-known Art. 1, by which Ireland was to have "the same constitutional status in the community of nations known as the British Empire" as the other Dominions—Canada, Australia, New Zealand, and South Africa. The Treaty did not seek to define the Commonwealth relationship in conferring Dominion status on the newly created Irish Free State; it merely referred to the facts of 1921. The Balfour definition, propounded in 1926, was to state that relationship as concisely as it has ever been stated, and later events were to alter the relationship, so that the pragmatism of 1921 gave rise to difficulties, but in this article of the Treaty lay the Irish Free State's legal claim to progress from the Dominion status accepted as a compromise towards the independence which was the ultimate aim.

The second main feature of the Treaty was its specific reference to the law, practice, and constitutional usage of Canada, which was to govern the relations between the Irish Free State on the one hand and the Crown and the Westminster parliament on the other. The inclusion of practice and usage in the constitutional apparatus of the new Irish Free State was to be expected, but the reference to them in a document later given statutory effect was a considerable innovation in British constitutional theory; the details as well as the outlines of the machinery were mentioned, and applied in new circumstances.

A third feature of the Treaty contained in Art. 4, was the much-discussed oath to be taken by members of the new legislature. The primary obligation was "true faith and allegiance to the constitution of the Irish Free State as by law established." It was only after this that faithfulness was sworn to the King, and then only "in virtue of the common citizenship of Ireland with Great Britain and her adherence to and membership of the group of nations forming the British Commonwealth of nations." Once again the terminology is significant, for the words "British Commonwealth" were placed on the statute-book at Westminster. In its content, the oath em-bodied the concepts of common citizenship and Commonwealth membership, which were very different from the ordinary idea of allegiance. As Dr. Leo Kohn remarked:

Paradoxical as it might seem, it was the expression of the Irish Free State's adherence to the British Commonwealth in the feudal rite of a oath of fidelity to a sovereign liege which symbolised the full measure of its free-dom in the new bond of association.[2a]

The Treaty was duly approved and incorporated in the 1922 Constitution of the Irish Free State, so that there came into ex-istence a fully fledged member of the Commonwealth which, un-like the older Dominions, had taken only a year to come to the birth. In considering its relative position it is necessary to remember that, as Professor K. C. Wheare has pointed out,[3] the inequalities of the Irish Free State's status in comparison with the United King-dom, although similar to those of the other Dominions, sprang from different sources according to the view taken of the source of the Constitution—an Act of the Westminster parliament, or the Treaty and the subsequent Constituent Assembly in Dublin: this difference of view was to lead to subsequent anomalies, but the practical effect was the same. Just as the United Kingdom's legisla-tive supremacy over Canada, to take the model used in the Treaty, was limited by convention, so s. 4 of the Irish Free State (Agree-ment) Act, 1922 (12 & 13 Geo. 5, c. 4) declared that Westminster's power was limited to "any case where, in accordance with constitu-tional practice, Parliament would make laws affecting self-govern-ing Dominions." (This was another instance of a legislative reference to constitutional convention.) Under Art. 3 of the Treaty and Art. 60 of the 1922 Constitution the Governor-General, as representative of the Crown, was to be appointed as in Canada, and by Art. 41

[2a] *The Constitution of the Irish Free State* (London, 1932), 56.
[3] *The Statute of Westminster and Dominion Status* (5th ed.; Oxford, 1953), 117-141.

of the Constitution he was given a power of reservation of bills, again exerciseable in accordance with Canadian practice. Also, the question of legislation with extraterritorial effect, which arose in Canada in *Croft v. Dunphy,* [1933] A. C. 156 (1932), was considered by the Irish courts in *R. (Alexander) v. Circuit Judge of Cork,* [1925] 2 I.R. 165, where the principle of *MacLeod v. Attorney General for New South Wales,* [1891] A.C. 455 was rejected in favor of wide powers. In judicial matters, a proviso to Art. 66 of the Constitution preserved the right of appeal to the Judicial Committee of the Privy Council by special leave, so that the judgments of the Irish Free State courts, like those of the Canadian courts, might not be final, another cause of later dispute. In sum, the choice of the oldest Dominion as the model for the youngest was the best that could have been made to insure the working of Dominion status, but it did not conceal the fact that Dominion status was, at best, a compromise for Ireland.

The Irish Free State resembled the other members of the Commonwealth in the respects which have just been mentioned, but in others she was in a distinctive position. First, as regards the area of her jurisdiction, it seems clear that this was intended to apply throughout the whole island, but was qualified by the position of Northern Ireland. Under Arts. 11 and 12 of the Treaty the Irish Free State's jurisdiction was not to be exerciseable in Northern Ireland for the "Ulster month," during which the Northern Ireland parliament could present an address opting out of the 1921 settlement. This was duly done and a Boundary Commission set up to determine "in accordance with the wishes of the inhabitants, so far as may be compatible with economic and geographic conditions the boundaries between Northern Ireland and the rest of Ireland. . . ." The subsequent fate of this Commission did not augur well for the settlement of disputes between Commonwealth members; in the result, no report was issued, but in 1925 the Treaty was amended by a tripartite agreement to which Northern Ireland was a party, to provide that Northern Ireland's jurisdiction should remain as fixed by the Government of Ireland Act, 1920. Acts of both the United Kingdom parliament (15 & 16 Geo. 5, c. 77) and the Irish Free State parliament (No. 40 of 1925) confirmed this agreement.

Another important respect in which the Irish Free State differed from the other Dominions was in the matter of defense. Under Art. 6 of the Treaty the Westminster government was to be responsible for the sea defense of the British Isles until other arrangements were made, while by Art. 7 the Irish Free State undertook to provide specified harbor facilities in peace time and, "in time of war or of strained relations with a foreign state," such harbor and other facilities as might be required for the purpose of sea defense. Thus a declaration of war from London would not only have involved the Irish Free State as a Dominion but would also have raised questions of modified neutrality or legal belligerence under the Treaty, despite the provision of Art. 49 of the 1922 Constitution under which the State could not be "committed to active participation in any war" without the assent of the Dublin parliament, the Oireachtas. The Irish Free State differed from Canada and South Africa in that her commitments were embodied in a fundamental constitutional document, while their obligations (in relation to such places as Halifax and Simonstown) were not so formal.

The Treaty also imposed certain internal limitations on the new Dominion. By Art. 8, Irish military establishments were to "bear the same proportion to those of Great Britain as the population of Ireland does to that of Great Britain," but this was given the flavor of international relations by a reference to "the observance of the principle of international limitation on armaments. . . ." As a consequence of its hiving-off from the United Kingdom, the Irish Free State had a liability for a portion of the National Debt (Art.5) and had to pay compensation to British officials (Art. 10). It was also subject to a prohibition on legislative discrimination on religious grounds (Art. 16). Thus, on the one hand the Treaty demonstrated that the concept of Dominion status had developed sufficiently to be applied directly to a fresh situation, but on the other hand that concept was subject to a certain amount of sea-change when it was transplanted to Ireland. The area of the new Dominion was reduced, its status in time of war rendered, to say the least, indeterminate, and it was subject to special internal limitations, in which it differed from the other Dominions. In a word, the Treaty bore the marks of compromise, for Dominion status was achieved, not as the result of development, but by a process of agreement and modification.

THE DEVELOPMENT OF DOMINION STATUS, 1922-1932

By her participation in the various Imperial conferences from the creation of the Irish Free State in 1922 to the passing of the Statute of Westminster in 1931, the new Dominion sought to achieve the development of Dominion status towards equality and eventual independence; development characterized the first phase of her relations with the Commonwealth. Generally, she sided with South Africa in seeking the maximum amount of power for the Dominions and, because of her link with the constitutional position of Canada, the Irish Free State was also concerned in the declaration of the position of Governor-Generals of the Dominions. But as well as assisting in the formal definition and declaration of Commonwealth relationships, the Irish Free State asserted in practice both her equal status and her right to take independent action.

The appointment of T. M. Healy, a prominent Nationalist Member of the Westminster House of Commons, as the first Governor-General of the Irish Free State set a precedent for the filling of such a position by a local appointee. In joining the League of Nations in 1923 the Irish Free State declared that she did so not as a member of the British Commonwealth but as a sovereign state, and her registration of the Treaty in 1924, and the supplemental agreement in 1926, raised the question of the relations of members of the Commonwealth *inter se*, a doctrine which has recently been analyzed out of existence by Professor R. Y. Jennings.[4] When in 1924 arrangements were made for the appointment of an Irish Free State Minister to Washington, there was no suggestion, as there had been when Canada made a similar proposal in 1920, that the new Minister should work with the United Kingdom Ambassador.[5] This independent appointment laid the foundation for the development of separate diplomatic corps for each of the members of the Commonwealth. The *inter se* doctrine arose again in 1929, when the Irish Free State differed from the other members of the Commonwealth in signing without reservation the optional clause of the Statute of the Permanent Court of International Justice.[6] Throughout this

[4] "The Commonwealth and International Law," *British Year Book of International Law*, XXX (1953), 320-351.
[5] (1924) Cmd. 2202; Green Haywood Hackworth, *Digest of International Law* (Washington, 1940), I, 65-66.
[6] (1929) Cmd. 3452.

time the Irish Free State had exercised her independent treaty-making power and, though the formal diplomatic unity of the Commonwealth had been preserved by the use of the Great Seal, in 1929 the Irish Free State in ratifying the Kellogg Pact was the first Commonwealth member to use a separate and self-contained instrument. Then in 1931 the Irish Free State acquired a seal of her own, and in this she was followed very shortly by South Africa, so that these two members of the Commonwealth were no longer dependent entirely on London for formal diplomatic purposes.[7]

The best way of describing the Irish Free State's position during the first decade of her existence is to emphasize that while she functioned as a Dominion in accordance with the terms of the Treaty she sought to exercise the powers so conferred upon her so as to make clear her claim to be an independent sovereign state. The Dominion nearest Westminster geographically helped to lead the constitutional movement away from Westminster predominance. But the binding force of the Treaty was always emphasized, and it was reasserted by President Cosgrave during the passage of the Statute of Westminster, 1931 (22 & 23 Geo. 5, c. 4) to refute a suggestion that the Irish Free State should be specifically prohibited from altering the Westminster legislation of 1920-1922 relating to Ireland.[8] Contract, not statute, was the basis of the Irish Free State's claim.

CONSTITUTIONAL DEVELOPMENTS IN THE IRISH FREE STATE, 1932-1937

The second phase of the Irish Free State's relations with the Commonwealth was one of transformation. There could have hardly been any greater contrast than that between Mr. Cosgrave's letter in 1931 and the claim made by Mr. de Valera in 1932 to abolish the oath set out in the Treaty. This was put on two grounds—that the oath was not mandatory in the Treaty and that there was an absolute right to modify the Constitution as the people desired, since this was a matter of internal sovereignty.[9] It will be noted that there was no allegation that the Treaty was not binding; this was regarded as irrelevant to the question of popular sovereignty. This claim also set the pattern for constitutional developments during the next five

[7] Robert Burgess Stewart, *Treaty Relations of the British Commonwealth of Nations* (New York, 1939), 191, 216.
[8] Arthur Berriedale Keith (ed.), *Speeches and Documents on the British Dominions 1918-1931* (London, 1932), 302.
[9] *Id.* at 460.

years. Instead of developing her status within the terms of the Treaty, the Irish Free State proceeded to make alterations in her Constitution which considerably changed her status.

The change in relations between Dublin and London was shown by the 1932 dispute about certain financial payments which the United Kingdom Government claimed were due to it but which the Irish Free State Government withheld. The claims were technical, turning on the interpretation of financial agreements made in 1923 and 1926, and were pre-eminently the type of problem which might have been settled by some form of Commonwealth tribunal. But although the Imperial Conference of 1930 had made recommendations about the composition of such a tribunal, the United Kingdom and Irish Free State Governments were unable to agree on the inclusion in such a tribunal of persons from countries outside the Commonwealth.[10] Not only was an opportunity of using some kind of arbitration procedure lost, but there also ensued an economic war, waged with tariff weapons, between the Irish Free State and the United Kingdom in which peace was not formally declared until 1938.

It is therefore in the amendments made by the Irish Free State in the 1922 Constitution that her next contribution to the development of Dominion status must be sought. It might seem strange that detailed matters of this kind should influence the general development of the Commonwealth, but such pragmatic processes are surely typical of the evolution of the Commonwealth relationship. Thus in 1933 there was passed the Constitution (Removal of Oath) Act (No. 6 of 1933), which not merely deleted the oath from Art. 17 of the 1922 Constitution but removed from the Constitution of the Irish Free State (Saorstát Eireann) Act, 1922 (No. 1 of 1922) the provision that the Treaty should override the Constitution in cases of conflict between the two documents. At one and the same time the sovereign independence of the Irish Free State was asserted and the Treaty relegated to a subordinate position where formerly it had been predominant. It might have been thought that the Irish judges would have upheld this action, while the English courts would have been inclined to hold against it. There is only one direct decision (an English one) on the point, but it is

[10] (1930) Cmd. 3717, 22-24; (1932) Cmd. 4116, 2-3.

clear that, paradoxically, exactly the opposite views were held. Since this issue was decided on an appeal to the Privy Council, this is an appropriate point to state the Irish Free State's position in relation to that tribunal.

The proviso to Art. 66 of the 1922 Constitution, preserving the right of the Privy Council to grant special leave for the hearing of appeals from the Irish Free State courts, was inserted at the request of the British Government, and it was aimed at providing protection for minority interests.[11] Lord Haldane's explanation in 1923, in *Hull v. McKenna*, [1926] I.R. 402, of the Judicial Committee's reluctance to entertain appeals from unitary Dominions, such as South Africa and the Irish Free State, included a reference to "the desire of the people." R. T. E. Latham observed that this would have prevented the hearing of any appeals from the Irish Free State, but in practice leave was granted in a number of cases, not all of which involved important constitutional questions on which the Privy Council's advice would have been appropriate.[12] But in *Wigg and Cochrane v. Attorney General for the Irish Free State*, [1927] A.C. 674 the Irish Free State refused to accept the Privy Council's decision as to the compensation to be paid to certain civil servants transferred to the new Dominion government in 1922, and the Oireachtas passed the Copyright (Preservation) Act, 1929 (No. 25 of 1929) to nullify the decision of the Privy Council in *Performing Right Society Ltd. v. Bray U. D. C.*, [1930] A. C. 377 on the right to collect royalties for copyright.

The Imperial Conference of 1926 recognized that "the wishes of the part of the Empire primarily affected" should determine the question of appeals, but in *Nadan v. R.*, [1926] A. C. 482 the Privy Council held that a Canadian attempt to abolish the appeal with special leave in criminal cases was invalid. This was the situation in 1933, when the Irish Free State passed the Constitution (Amendment No. 22) Act (No. 45 of 1933), which went further than the Canadian Criminal Code Amendment Act of that year (24 & 25 Geo. 5, c. 53) in that it purported to abolish all appeals from the Irish Free State to the Privy Council. This Act was considered by the Privy Council in the classic case of *Moore v. Attorney-General for*

---

[11] Darrell Figgis, *The Irish Constitution* (Dublin, 1922), 51-57.
[12] *The Law and the Commonwealth* (London, 1949), 553, n. 5.

the Irish Free State, [1935] A. C. 484 which, like the corresponding Canadian decision in *British Coal Corporation v. The King*, [1935] A. C. 500 established the right of Dominions to abolish the appeal.

The basis of the Privy Council's decision in *Moore's* case was that the Constitution of the Irish Free State derived from the Westminster parliament, that the Statute of Westminster, 1931 (22 & 23 Geo. 5, c. 4), gave the Dominions equal status with the United Kingdom, and that accordingly the Irish Free State was competent to abolish the right of appeal. As for the Treaty, the Judicial Committee said at p. 499:

The simplest way of stating the situation is to say that the Statute of Westminster gave to the Irish Free State a power under which they could abrogate the Treaty, and that, as a matter of law, they have availed themselves of that power.

This interpretation was in direct conflict with that of the Dublin Supreme Court in *The State (Ryan) v. Lennon*, [1935] I.R. 170. Though they differed on the effect of an amendment to the 1922 Constitution extending the time during which amendments could be made by way of ordinary legislation, all three judges were agreed that the Treaty was fundamental to the Constitution, and Fitzgibbon J. went so far as to say that any amendment purporting to sever the link between the Treaty and the Constitution would itself be illegal. On this reasoning, the view that the Irish Constitution had a solely Irish source imposed limitations, while the view that the Constitution had an English source gave complete freedom. Professor K. C. Wheare has pointed out that the link in the Treaty between the Irish Free State and Canada would, on the view of the Irish Courts, have limited the equal status of the Irish Free State,[13] but this particular view of Dominion status was not accepted by Mr. de Valera's government, which was determined to work towards its republican aim.

There were other occurrences in the Irish Free State at this time which underlined this aim. A dispute between the Government and the Governor-General resulted in his removal and replacement by a nominal figure, whose official status was much reduced. The Constitution (Amendment No. 20) Act, 1933 (No. 40 of 1933) removed

[13] *Op. cit. supra* note 3 at 113-120.

the Governor-General's function of recommending the appropriation of money, while in the same year the Constitution (Amendment No. 21) Act (No. 41 of 1933) deleted from the Constitution his power of reserving bills passed by the Oireachtas. In 1935 the Irish Nationality and Citizenship Act (No. 13 of 1935) expanded the provisions in Art. 3 of the 1922 Constitution by detailing the circumstances in which Irish citizenship could be acquired or lost, and purported to repeal all the British statutes and common law relating to nationality. This was not, however, recognized outside the Irish Free State as altering the status of British subjects, yet it did anticipate the scheme of the British Nationality Act, 1948 (11 & 12 Geo. 6, c. 56) by providing in detail for distinctive citizenship. The last group of constitutional amendments to be made before the 1922 Constitution was replaced in 1937 continued the separatist tradition which had been established in Dublin, and the process was hastened by the necessity of dealing with the abdication crisis in December, 1936. By the Constitution (Amendment No. 27) Act (No. 57 of 1936) references to the King and the representative of the Crown were deleted from the 1922 Constitution, and for diplomatic purposes and international agreements the Executive Council could use "any organ used as a constitutional organ for the like purposes by any of the nations referred to in Article 1 of this Constitution." Thus, as well as making internal changes, an alteration was made in the external exercise of executive authority. Simultaneously there was passed the Executive Authority (External Relations) Act, 1936 (No. 58 of 1936) which validated Edward VIII's Instrument of Abdication and provided that so long as the Irish Free State was associated with the members of the Commonwealth and "the King recognized by those nations as the symbol of their co-operation" acted for them in external affairs, he was to act in the same way for the Irish Free State on the advice of the Executive Council. The policy of "external association" consistently advocated by Mr. de Valera since 1922 had finally been given constitutional form.

In the space of four years Mr. de Valera's government had virtually transformed the Irish conception of Dominion status. Internally the Governor-General's functions and status had been reduced, and the office was finally eliminated from the Constitution. This differs from the course taken by South Africa in the Status of the Union Act, 1934 (No. 69), under which the Governor-General became the direct representative of the Crown. In judicial matters the Irish Free State had gone further than Canada in abolishing all appeals to the Privy Council. For external purposes the relationship between the Crown and the Irish Free State was changed to one of limited use of a symbolic figure. By eliminating the Treaty from the Constitution that document was formally given a self-contained foundation. In the view of the Irish government, the only links between Dublin and Westminster were tenuous ones, and these were entirely of Irish manufacture. In a decade and a half the chrysalis had grown to full maturity and was able to discard the cocoon which had originally encased it. Naturally the view taken of these events varies as the observer looks at them in Dublin, in London, or in other Commonwealth capitals, and the dichotomy of opinion to be found on all legal questions affecting Ireland prevents the reconciliation of views which differ fundamentally in their premises, but the action taken by the Irish Free State demonstrated the wide scope for development within the Commonwealth.

EIRE AND THE COMMONWEALTH, 1937-1949

The third phase of the relations between Eire and the Commonwealth was one of association. The passing of the 1937 Constitution stated the position which Eire considered she had reached. Ireland was a "sovereign, independent, democratic state" (Art. 5) and the national territory consisted of "the whole island of Ireland, its islands and the territorial seas" (Art. 2) but "pending the reintegration of the national territory," Dublin legislation was to have the like extent of application and extraterritorial effect as that of the Irish Free State (Art. 3). Art. 29, 4, (2) followed the External Relations Act of 1936 in providing that the government could use any organ, instrument, or method of procedure used for external relations "by the members of any group or league of nations with which the State is or becomes associated for the purpose of international co-operation in matters of common concern."

But this revolution in law (as Professor Wheare has described it)[14] was regarded by the United Kingdom and the other members of the Commonwealth " as not effecting a fundamental alteration in the position of the Irish Free State, in future to be described under the

[14] *Op. cit. supra* note 3 at 276.

new constitution as 'Eire' or 'Ireland,' as a member of the British Commonwealth of Nations." Canada, Australia, New Zealand, and South Africa concurred in this declaration, which was coupled with a statement that the United Kingdom government did not regard the 1937 Constitution as affecting "in any way the position of Northern Ireland as an integral part of the United Kingdom of Great Britain and Northern Ireland."[15] It is pleasant to record that this period, unlike the previous one, opened with an agreement between the Dublin and London governments rather than a dispute.

In so far as it affected the Constitution, the Treaty was, from the Irish standpoint, already a dead letter, but there remained in force provisions affecting Ireland's international status as well as her obligations to the United Kingdom government. The "economic war" was brought to an end by the Anglo-Irish agreements of 1938. Under the first of these, Articles 6 and 7 of the Treaty relating to coastal defense and the provision of harbor and other facilities were deleted and the "Treaty Ports" transferred to the Eire government. Not only was a perpetual source of friction between the two governments removed; Eire's control of her destiny in international affairs was now as complete as that of any sovereign state. The second of the 1938 agreements brought to an end the dispute on financial matters by providing for the payment by the Eire government of a sum of ten million pounds by way of final settlement. Both governments undertook to abolish the special duties imposed in 1932 on the importation of each other's goods. The way was now clear for the conclusion of the third agreement, which was a trade agreement between the two countries. (The 1948 Anglo-Irish trade agreements amended and expanded the provisions of the 1938 agreement in the postwar period when Eire was concerned with the furthering of her trade by means of agreements with European countries and the United States.)

The next significant matter was Ireland's neutrality in the Second World War. Whatever other effects that conflict may have had on the development of the Commonwealth, it disposed finally of the academic arguments about the impossibility of a Commonwealth member remaining neutral because of the unity of the Crown. In Eire's case, neutrality did not imply that her territory would be

[15] Nicholas Mansergh, *Documents and Speeches on British Commonwealth Affairs, 1931-1952* (2 vols.; London, 1953), I, 366-367.

used for hostile operations against the United Kingdom. Rather it was conceived as a declaration of the right of a small nation to dissociate itself from the conflicts of greater powers. Here again, one may notice the paradoxical situation that an Irish contribution, and a significant one, to the definition of Commonwealth relations was regarded in Irish eyes as primarily one of independent national action, or inaction.

Two wartime cases served to show the attitude adopted by the English courts to Eire's relations with the Commonwealth. *Hume Pipe, etc. Co. v. Moracrete Ltd.*, [1942] 1 K.B. 189 (1941) turned on a procedural point dealing with the service of a writ outside the jurisdiction of the English courts. It was held that since Eire was still a British Dominion the writ, and not merely notice of the writ, should be served, though at the same time it was recognized that Eire had ceased to be a part of the Ireland which was comprised in the former United Kingdom.

The basis of this reasoning was repeated in *Murray v. Parkes*, [1942] 2 K.B. 123 where a man born in Eire but resident in Britain since 1934 contended that he was not liable for national service since he was no longer a British subject. This argument was not based on nationality legislation but on broader constitutional grounds. It was argued that Eire had ceased to be part of the Dominions by virtue of the 1937 Constitution which had been recognized in the Anglo-Irish Agreements of 1938. Her power to sever this link stemmed from the Statute of Westminster as interpreted by the Privy Council in 1935 in *Moore's* case. The Court of Appeal rejected this argument by holding that no right to secede was implied in the Statute of Westminster, that there had been no claim to exercise that right, and that no secession had been recognized by the 1938 Agreements. Further, it held that the 1937 Constitution did not effect any change of nationality and that the appellant was still a British subject and therefore liable for military service. While the comments on secession were perhaps wider than was actually necessary for the decision of the case they served to indicate the natural tendencies of the English judicial view.

Eire's next contribution to Commonwealth affairs therefore lay not in the field of action but in the realm of theory; it consisted of yet another assertion of her unique position. Shortly after the end of the war in Europe a parliamentary question was put to Mr. de Valera. It was a simple one, whether Eire was a republic, and the reply was that she was. This was justified by reference to a number of dictionary definitions. Since the Crown no longer occupied a central place in the Irish Constitution, and was indeed used only for external purposes as an organ used by other members of the Commonwealth, it followed, in the Irish view, that the Constitution was a republican one. As Mr. de Valera put it:

We are an independent republic, associated as a matter of our external policy with the States of the British Commonwealth. To mark this association, we avail ourselves of the procedure of the External Relations Act . . . by which the King recognised by the States of the British Commonwealth therein named acts for us, under advice, in certain specified matters in the field of our external relations.[16]

He relied on the 1937 declaration of the United Kingdom government for the continued membership of Eire in the Commonwealth, but when the matter was raised again he was careful to point out that this, in the Irish view, did not imply any allegiance. In so far as any view implied the necessity of allegiance, Eire was to be regarded only as an associate.

These assessments of Eire's position differed radically from the orthodox view that the Crown provided a link between the Dominions. The concept of allegiance which had been the subject of so much dispute in the negotiations prior to the Treaty and in the post-1922 period might have proved a further stumbling block had any occasion arisen for the testing of the Irish and orthodox views. In the event, it was Eire's alteration of her position which led to a final determination of the question of her membership of the Commonwealth.

As in 1932 a change of government brought about a radical change of policy. The de Valera government during its period of office from 1932 to 1948 had not formally made a declaration of republican status, which was regarded as the goal to be achieved by the reintegration of the national territory; instead it had relied on the process of definition and interpretation which has just been described. The Fine Gael members of the government led by Mr. J. A. Costello were the spiritual successors of those who had accepted

[16] *Dáil Debates*, XCVII, col. 2573; Mansergh, *op. cit. supra* note 15 at II, 794-797.

the treaty and contributed to the development of Dominion status in the period 1922-1932: in some cases they were the actual persons concerned. As Professor Mansergh puts it, the realists of 1922 were also the realists of 1949. For them, as Mr. Costello declared to the Canadian Bar Association, "The harp without the Crown symbolized the ideal of Irish independence and nationhood. The harp beneath the Crown was the symbol of conquest."[17] Just as he had criticized the External Relations Act at the time of its passing, so when he came to power he acted on his view that the Crown was the symbol of free association between the members of the Commonwealth, whereas the External Relations Act spoke of the "symbol of co-operation." This might seem a very slender thread on which to hang a distinction between the position of Ireland and that of other members of the Commonwealth, but it was nevertheless a logical extension of the Irish view which preferred independence to Dominion status. Accordingly the External Relations Act was repealed, the description (but not the name) of the state was changed to "The Republic of Ireland," and executive functions dealing with external relations were vested in the President, on the advice of the government. The Republic of Ireland Act (No. 22 of 1948) was passed on December 21, 1948, and came into force on April 18, 1949, just thirty-three years after the first declaration of the Irish Republic in 1916.

Action was at last necessary from the other Commonwealth governments. In the United Kingdom this took the form of the Ireland Act, 1949 (12 & 13 Geo. 6, c. 41). Under this it was recognized that "the part of Ireland heretofore known as Eire" ceased to be part of His Majesty's Dominions from April 18, 1949. This part of Ireland was to be known for British purposes as the Republic of Ireland but was not to be regarded as a foreign country. The other provisions of the Act insured that British legislation would take effect accordingly, but an important declaration concerned Northern Ireland, which was to remain part of His Majesty's Dominions and of the United Kingdom until the parliament of Northern Ireland consented to a change. This drew from Dublin a repudiation of the claim of the British parliament to legislate for any part of Ireland, a protest against this particular piece of legislation, and a

[17] Mansergh, *op. cit. supra* note 15 at II, 799.

call for Irish unity. Against this, the United Kingdom government contended that when Eire left the Commonwealth it was a natural corollary to declare that Northern Ireland remained part of the Commonwealth.[18] The right of self-determination was accorded to Northern Ireland as well as to Eire.

Summing up the final phase of Eire's membership of the Commonwealth, the wide differences of view are immediately apparent. Neither the British government nor the English courts recognized that the 1937 Constitution made any difference in Eire's constitutional position; in their view she was still a member of the Commonwealth who, unlike other members, had chosen not to go to war. The de Valera government, on the other hand, held that the relationship between Dublin and London authorized by the 1937 Constitution was different from that between the United Kingdom and other Commonwealth countries, and the Costello government put the matter beyond all doubt. But having left the Commonwealth the Irish Republic does not stand towards the United Kingdom in the position of a foreign country. The special category of "citizens of the Republic of Ireland" recognized by British legislation is an indication of the new relationship; external association has disappeared and common citizenship has been replaced by recognition of status. In this, as in other matters, the Irish Republic stands alone.

The often-claimed right of secession had been exercised by Burma in 1947, in a manner reminiscent of the Anglo-Irish settlement, with agreement and Treaty, constituent assembly and Westminster legislation. But Eire's formal severance of her connection with the Commonwealth took the characteristic form of a constitutional amendment. It is somewhat ironical that shortly after the formal declaration of the Irish Republic India should have been permitted to remain within the Commonwealth although adopting a republican constitution. Pakistan also has taken similar action, so that the state which sought to reconcile republicanism and Commonwealth membership now possesses the first but not the second, while other countries enjoy both: but it is not necessary to remind American readers that the way of the pioneer is hard.

THE PERIOD AFTER 1949, AND THE POSITION OF NORTHERN IRELAND

In the period after 1949 the status of the Irish Republic as "not

[18] Mansergh, *op. cit. supra* note 15 at II, 821-836.

a foreign country" has been considered by the English courts in *Bicknell v. Brosnan*, [1953] 2 Q.B. 77 where a citizen of the Republic domiciled in England was alleged to be liable for national service because of his residence there. The Court of Appeal held that the combined effect of s. 3(2) of the British Nationality Act, 1948 (11 & 12 Geo. 6, c. 56) and s. 3(1) of the Ireland Act, 1949 included citizens of the Republic in the same category as British subjects. Accordingly, the appellant was held liable for national service. This special classification of Irish citizens is yet another recognition of a unique situation arising on one side of the Irish Sea because of events which have taken place on the other. It will be interesting whether any further new thing will yet come out of Ireland.

In all the transactions which have been described the part played by Northern Ireland was a negative one, since her existence naturally limited the South's area of effective jurisdiction; the tripartite agreement of 1925, in which Northern Ireland joined with the Irish Free State and the United Kingdom, determines the present position. But from time to time the question of Dominion status for Northern Ireland is raised unofficially. One comment on this possible development is provided by an academic lawyer in Belfast. Writing of "that position of independence coupled with allegiance to the Crown which is expressed by the phrase 'dominion status'," he said, "I cannot see why anyone should wish to exchange a position of eminence as a component part of a great power in order to rank as the smallest and least significant of an association of nations: to sink—in the words of Lord Craigavon—into the seventh or eighth class."[19] At present the possibility of a further Irish contribution to the subject of Dominion status appears to be remote. The South has moved from the compromise acceptance of Dominion status, through development of that status, to independence outside the Commonwealth; the North is not moving in the direction of independence and her position as part of the Queen's Dominions has been specifically recognized by the Westminster parliament.

II. Public International Law

The emergence of the Irish Free State as a person in international law is, naturally, closely bound up with the development of Do-

---

[19] Francis Headon Newark, "The Constitution of Northern Ireland: The First Twenty-Five Years," *Northern Ireland Legal Quarterly*, VIII (1948), 52, 62.

minion status. The new state understandably took every opportunity which it reasonably could of asserting its new status. At the Imperial Conference of 1923 the then Minister for External Affairs declared that in so far as the Irish Free State had had time to develop a foreign policy it concurred in the support given by the Dominions to the League of Nations. The League, and international organizations dealing with specific topics, provided opportunities for the assertion of the new status, and possible independent policies, of the Irish Free State. In 1923 the Oireachtas passed the League of Nations (Guarantee) Act (No. 41 of 1923) to conform with membership of the League, and in his address to the League on the admission of the Free State in that year President Cosgrave spoke of the new member participating as a sovereign state—a far cry and an explicit one from the normal Commonwealth position.

STATE SUCCESSION

The turbulent internal history which led to the setting up of the Irish Free State raised the question of state succession. It fell to the courts both in the Irish Free State and in the United States to survey the events of 1919-1922 with judicial retrospectivity, in an attempt to disentangle the extremely complicated question of the authority to legislate for Ireland. In 1926, in *Fogarty v. O'Donoghue*, [1926] I.R. 531, the Dublin High Court was asked to determine the ownership of certain trust funds which had been held on behalf of the second Dáil Eireann—the body which sought to legislate for Ireland before the setting up of the third Dáil, which regarded itself as a Constituent Assembly and adopted the 1922 Constitution. The trustees considered that they were bound to hold the money for the purposes which the second Dáil had sought, that is, the establishment of an independent republic. The Irish court, however, held that the Free State government set up under the 1922 Constitution had succeeded the second Dáil and directed that the funds should be paid over to the Minister for Finance. Since in this case the property was situate within the jurisdiction of the government which (on the Irish view) had succeeded the second Dáil, no question of international law arose, but the view taken of the facts is in direct conflict with that adopted by a New York court.

In *Irish Free State v. Guaranty Safe Deposit Co.*, 129 Misc. 551, 559-562, 222 N. Y. Supp. 182, 192-193 (Sup. Ct. 1927) a question arose of the title to funds raised by way of the Republican Loan, which had been collected in the United States in the early 1920's to assist in the struggle for Irish independence. When the Irish Free State government claimed these funds it was held that that government was the successor, not of the revolutionary Irish government but of the Westminster government. There was therefore no way of tracing the title to the funds collected on behalf of the republican government, and further the Irish Free State government had not undertaken any obligation in respect of the loan.[20] The only time it did so was in 1933 when it decided to make an *ex gratia* payment to bondholders. On this question of succession, an interesting parallel is provided by *Buckley v. Attorney-General and Power*, (1950) 84 I.L.T.R. 9. The question for decision in that case was the title to the funds of the Sinn Féin organization, which, as mentioned in the chapter on Constitutional History *(supra)*, had been active in the cause of Irish independence from 1905 and especially so during 1916-1922. In the course of a judgment which cast much light on the confused history of that period, Kingsmill Moore J. found that the organization which had functioned up to 1922, and to which the funds had been contributed, was a different organization from that which functioned after 1922.

DIPLOMATIC RECOGNITION AND REPRESENTATION

The confusion of the events in Ireland was not, however, an obstacle in the way of the recognition of the Irish Free State as an international person. Difficulties lay rather in the general position of the Dominions in the eyes of countries outside the Commonwealth which manifested a certain reluctance to recognize the Dominions as fully independent. As has already been mentioned, first the Irish Free State and then Canada appointed Ministers to Washington, thus asserting their right to independent external representation. In 1928 the United States reciprocated in the matter of representation by appointing ministers to Dublin and Ottawa so that the foundations of the Dominion diplomatic services were laid on a reciprocal basis. At the present time the Irish Republic has thirty-three representatives abroad, including eight ambassadors. Comparing these figures with

[20] Green Haywood Hackworth, *Digest of International Law* (Washington, 1943), V, 679-681; James Wilford Garner, "A Question of State Succession," *American Journal of International Law*, XXI (1927), 753-757.

those for Canada—the Canadian government has sixty-one representatives, of whom twenty-nine are ambassadors—it will be seen
that the representation of Ireland is fully proportionate, taking into
account the size of the Republic's jurisdiction.

Mention of Canada makes it appropriate to comment on the
method of accrediting Commonwealth representatives to Dublin. The
Canadian Ambassador in Dublin is accredited to the President of
Ireland, but the Australian government refused to follow suit on
the ground that this might be taken as implying the Canberra government's recognition of the Republic's claim to jurisdiction throughout the whole of Ireland. Since agreement could not be reached
on the Australian proposal that her ambassador should be accredited
to "The President of the Republic of Ireland," a proposal to appoint
an Australian Ambassador to Dublin was dropped, although an Irish
Ambassador is appointed to Canberra. In explaining the difficulties
which led to this situation, the Irish Minister for External Affairs
justified the acceptance of the United Kingdom Ambassador to Dublin (who was accredited to the President of the Republic of Ireland)
on the ground that it was necessary to maintain reciprocal diplomatic
relations with the United Kingdom both because of the close links
between the two countries and because of the outstanding cause of
contention—the existence of Northern Ireland within the United
Kingdom.[21] Thus the compromise of 1922 had echoes far removed
in both distance and time.

The Irish Free State equipped herself internally by the establishment of a Department of External Affairs in 1922. In this she
followed the lead of her republican predecessors, and set an example
to the other Dominions. The Australian, Canadian, and New Zealand Departments were established respectively in 1901, 1909, and
1919, but they were all to some extent subordinate in status or function. The Irish Free State was followed by South Africa in 1927, and
in the 1930's and 1940's the other Dominions followed suit.[22]

INTERNATIONAL ORGANIZATIONS

The establishment of an executive department and of diplomatic
representation were, of course, only the apparatus for asserting the

[21] *Dáil Debates*, CXLIV, cols. 38-40.
[22] Nicholas Mansergh, *Survey of British Commonwealth Affairs: Problems of
External Policy*, 1931-1939 (London, 1952), 71 n. 1.

existence of the Dominion in international affairs. The actual assertion of that existence showed itself in the participation in the work of such international bodies as the International Labor Organization. The ratification of the I. L. O. conventions was an especial part of the policy of the Irish Free State government in the early years of its existence and this trend has been continued.

The pages of the Dublin statute-book show how this policy has been implemented by legislation. On such matters as marine conventions, workmen's compensation, conditions of employment, and social security the I. L. O. conventions have been made part of the municipal law of the republic. An interesting aspect of this policy lies in the Irish ratifications of Conventions Nos. 87 and 98, relating to freedom of association and protection of the right to organize, and the application of the principles of the right to organize and to collective bargaining. Specific legislation on these points was unnecessary because of the fundamental rights guaranteed by the 1937 Constitution. Under Art. 40, 6, (1), (iii) liberty is guaranteed for the exercise, subject to public order and morality, of the right of citizens to form associations and unions which may, however, be controlled by laws enacted in the public interest; and collective bargaining is one of the means whereby the directive principles of social policy specified in Art. 45 of the Constitution may be carried out. On a more personal note, Mr. E. J. Phelan, the Irishman who drafted the 1919 constitution for the I.L.O. and the Philadelphia Declaration of 1944, which revived the organization, was also one of the first to assert the sovereignty of the Irish Free State on legal grounds.

At the present time the Republic participates in the work of a variety of international organizations, both governmental and nongovernmental. The former range from the International Civil Aviation Organization and the Universal Postal Union to such bodies as the International Bureau of Weights and Measures and the International Office of Epizootics. The subjects dealt with by the second type of organization to which the Republic subscribes vary from poultry science and seed testing to housing and town planning, geodesy, and geophysics. On this classification, the first category of organization comprises those in which immediate benefits derive from, or duties are imposed by, governmental membership; the second category comprises those organizations in which Irish experience on particular topics may be of assistance. In both cases the Republic plays her full part as an international person.

In the wider field of the organization of nations as such, Ireland's activities have been governed by the workings of international politics and practices which it is the function of international law to regulate. Mention has already been made of the Irish Free State's membership of the League of Nations and the part which that played in demonstrating different ideas about Dominion status. The Irish Free State sought election as an independent member of the council in 1926, but lacked the support of the United Kingdom and was not successful. She had, however, a seat on the council between 1930 and 1933. It is noteworthy that she was preceded by Canada and succeeded by Australia, from which it may be concluded that membership of the Commonwealth was regarded as a distinguishing feature by the other members of the League.[23] Mr. de Valera's Presidency of the League in 1932 and again in the crisis-ridden year of 1938 showed that the head of a small, recently created state might exercise considerable influence in international affairs. Further, as Professor Mansergh has pointed out, the policies adopted by Mr. de Valera of support for sanctions against Italy and refusal to intervene in the Spanish Civil War manifested a determination to overcome internal difficulties for the sake of fulfilling international obligations.[24]

On the other hand, it was reluctance to enter into international commitments which led to Eire's adoption of the policy of neutrality during the Second World War. Apart from the question of neutrality, the possibility of which had been established by the Anglo-Irish agreements of 1938, there remained outstanding Eire's claim to Northern Ireland, coupled with a realistic view which deprecated the participation of small nations in conflicts between major powers. Thus the constitutional settlement of 1920-1922 was used to buttress arguments against Eire's participation.

Between 1946 and 1955 the question of the Republic's joining the United Nations Organization was considered by the Security Council, but vetoed both separately and in conjunction with other applications. As a result, the direct participation in international discussions and

---

[23] Robert Burgess Stewart, *Treaty Relations of the British Commonwealth of Nations* (New York, 1939), 154.

[24] Mansergh, *op. cit. supra* note 22 at 324-327.

decisions which was possible before 1939 proved impossible in the first decade after the end of the Second World War. But if the main door to the U. N. building was closed to the Republic there were other doors through which she entered. Once again the policy of participating in specialized activities provided a valuable means of working in the international field. The Republic is a member of the Food and Agricultural Organization and of the World Health Organization. She participates in such U. N. work as the supervision and control of the distribution of narcotic and dangerous drugs and she has contributed to schemes for technical assistance and refugee relief, as well as to the U. N. children's fund. When in December, 1955, the main doorway opened to admit the Republic to the ranks of the United Nations, she entered not as a mere tyro but with considerable experience of the problems involved in international co-operation in the postwar period.

REGIONAL AGREEMENTS

In the narrower field of regional agreements between nations the Republic has also played her part, although once more the dispute about the position of Northern Ireland has determined the extent of the Republic's participation in such regional organizations. Thus, for example, the European Recovery Program and the foundation of the Organization for European Economic Co-operation (which was followed by the signing of the 1948 economic co-operation agreement with the United States) have brought the Irish Republic directly into the mainstream of European economic activity.

A second, and more direct, link between the Irish Republic and Europe has been provided by the Council of Europe, with its organization for co-operation on specific issues and its forum for the discussion of matters affecting Europe generally. When Minister for External Affairs, Mr. Seán McBride was a strong advocate of the maintenance of communication between the Committee of Ministers and the Assembly. It is significant that one of the reasons which he advanced for allowing ministers to express individual views in the Assembly was that this would permit the expression of opinion by a representative who might hold a minority view in international affairs.[25] As well as participating in the work of the Council, the Republic has ratified a number of the conventions agreed

[25] *Dáil Debates*, CXVII, col. 705.

upon by the Assembly. Of these, the most interesting is the Rome Convention of 1950, and the 1952 Protocol, for the protection of human rights. Not only have the Convention and the Protocol been ratified generally, but the Republic has made the declaration necessary for the purposes of Article 46, recognizing the compulsory jurisdiction of the projected European Court of Human Rights in the interpretation of the Convention. Further, it has, in accordance with Article 25, acknowledged the right of persons, nongovernmental organizations, or groups of individuals, to petition the European Commission of Human Rights against violations of the Convention by one of the signatories. The future relationship between this provision and the jurisdiction of the Irish courts might well prove instructive for other nations.

It will thus be seen that the achievement of Irish independence has not led to a policy of constitutional isolation; rather it has been the case that that independence is used to assist in the creation of organizations aimed at the strengthening of international co-operation. There is, however, one regional organization in which Ireland plays no part—the North Atlantic Treaty Organization. Her policy in this is determined by factors similar to those which produced the policy of neutrality during the Second World War. The claim to exercise jurisdiction over Northern Ireland conflicts with the Treaty's guarantee of the "territorial integrity, political independence or security" of signatories, particularly since the United States regarded the dispute about Northern Ireland as a matter for the Irish and United Kingdom governments.[26] Here again, the Irish policy of independent action is asserted and once more the events of 1920-1922 are perpetuated in their effect.

TREATY PRACTICE

Two further matters may be mentioned in connection with the Republic's place in international law—her treaty practice, and the view taken by her courts on the application of international law. Both of these stem from Art. 29 of the 1937 Constitution, which affirms "devotion to the ideal of peace and friendly co-operation amongst nations founded on international justice and morality" and "adherence to the principle of the pacific settlement of international disputes by

[26] *Texts Concerning Ireland's Position in Relation to the North Atlantic Treaty* (P. No. 9934, Stationery Office, Dublin, 1950).

international arbitration or judicial determination." To these ends the Republic "accepts the generally recognised principles of international law as its rule of conduct in its relations with other States." Clause 4 makes provision for the exercise of executive functions in connection with external relations, which has already been discussed. Under clause 5 international agreements (other than agreements of a technical and an administrative character) must be laid before the Dáil and must, if they involve public expenditure, be approved by that House in order to bind the Republic. By clause 6 no international agreement is to form a part of the domestic law of the state save as may be determined by the Oireachtas. Thus the lower House has the final say in determining whether the Republic is to be bound by financial obligations, while the legislature has control over its own domestic law. (It is noteworthy that India did not depart so far from the British precedent but merely included among the directives of social policy in her 1950 Constitution a reference in Art. 51 to the fostering of international peace and security. There is a similar reference in Art. 24 of the 1956 Pakistan Constitution.) The alteration of the municipal law to implement international agreements is common, and the Dublin statute-book contains many examples of this kind of alteration, ranging from the 1923 legislation to facilitate membership of the League of Nations to the Merchant Shipping (Safety Convention) Act, 1952 (No. 29 of 1952), giving effect to the 1948 London Convention on safety of life at sea. An example of general legislation to fulfil bilateral agreements is provided by the Consular Conventions Act, 1954 (No. 10 of 1954) under which the Republic was enabled to ratify the 1950 Consular Convention between Ireland and the United States, and the Supplementary Protocol of 1952.

The Irish Free State's contribution to the development of Dominion treaty practice—the framing of separate ratifications, and the use of an Irish seal—has already been mentioned. To show the way in which the Irish Republic's treaty-making power is exercised, the Treaty Series for 1953 may be taken as typical. Its seventeen documents included such multilateral agreements as the London Convention of 1946 on the meshes of fishing nets, the 1948 Convention on safety of life at sea, which has just been mentioned, and the 1953 Revision of the International Wheat Agreement. On the

European level, there was the ratification of the Rome Convention on Human Rights which has been referred to, conventions dealing with the standard of admission to universities and the valuation of goods for custom purposes, an agreement to set up a customs co-operation council, and protocols relating to the European Payments Union and the European Customs Union. It is indicative of the Republic's postwar development that the bilateral agreements included in the 1953 series were all trade agreements, either made or extended with such countries as Federal Germany, Ceylon, Finland, France, and Belgium. Just as the Republic's participation in international organizations shows her desire to implement the general aim of co-operation among nations, set out in Art. 29, 1 of the Constitution, so the exercise of her treaty-making powers manifests her intention to give practical effect to those powers to the greatest possible extent. The fact that she has left the Commonwealth does not alter her treaty relations with the member countries: and her participation in European affairs manifests her intention to share the modern life of Europe, with which continent she has many historic links.

THE ACCEPTANCE OF INTERNATIONAL LAW

The second point arising on Art. 29 of the 1937 Constitution relates to the acceptance "of the generally recognized principles of international law." Only a bare handful of cases turning on international law points have so far come before the Dublin courts, but the latest of these directly involved the interpretation of Art. 29. In *Norton v. General Accident, Fire and Life Assurance Co.,* (1939) 74 I.L.T.R. 123, the court had to consider the nature of diplomatic immunity. It held that this did not imply freedom from responsibility but merely immunity from jurisdiction and it followed the normal rule in holding that privilege lapses whenever the representative claiming it ceases to be accredited. A more substantial point was involved in *Zarine v. Owners of s.s. Ramava,* [1942] I. R. 148. In that case writs in rem were issued in respect of Estonian and Latvian ships berthed in Dublin which were on the high seas when these States became part of the U.S.S.R. in 1940. The U.S.S.R. moved to set aside these writs on the ground that that government now owned these ships. The High Court discussed the tendency towards the lifting of immunity from State-owned ships engaging in commerce, but the case turned on the fact that the Eire government did not recognize the U.S.S.R. as the government of either Estonia or Latvia, and both that Court and the Supreme Court held that this lack of recognition was sufficient to oust the claim of the U.S.S.R. Then in *Saorstát and Continental Steamship Co., Ltd. v. Morenas*, [1945] I.R. 291, a colonel in the Spanish Army was sued on a contract for the shipment of horses but moved to set aside the writ on the ground that the transaction was really an act of sovereignty on the part of the Spanish government. A certificate of the Spanish Minister to Ireland as to the defendant's official status and financial backing was not regarded as conclusive and the High Court gave the plaintiffs leave to enter judgment. On appeal to the Supreme Court it was held that, since the plaintiffs sought to recover only against the defendant, the government of Spain was not impleaded, but the defendant was given leave to defend the action in his personal capacity.

In all these cases the Irish courts followed previous decisions and did not seek to make any innovations in the application of the rules of international law, but in *The State (Duggan) v. Tapley*, [1952] I.R. 62 the Irish courts had to consider directly the reception of international law by Art. 29 of the Constitution. This case involved the interpretation of certain legislation authorizing the arrest in Ireland of persons who had committed offenses in Great Britain and from that point of view will be considered later in this chapter in relation to the conflict of laws. For the present purpose it may be noted that both the High Court and the Court of Appeal analyzed the provisions of Art. 29. Gavan Duffy P., in the lower court, held that the declaration of general principles in the three opening clauses was not inconsistent with the existence of legislation of the kind in question. Further, he held that Clause 5 relating to international agreements contemplated future events. The combined effect of these provisions was not, therefore, to cover the whole field of the Republic's international relations; there could still be passed agreements or legislation not covered by the Article. In the Supreme Court Maguire C. J. undertook a comprehensive study of the history of extradition, relying on the general acceptance of the negative doctrine that apart from special agreement no State is bound to grant extradition, holding that the *lex lata* did not exempt political offenders from extradition, and refuting arguments that either a treaty or some other form of reciprocal agreement was necessary for extradition. This survey ranged far in both space and time, and dealt with general principles rather than decided cases, differing in this from the general trend of British precedents.

SUMMARY, AND A NOTE ON THE POSITION OF NORTHERN IRELAND

Summarizing the development of Ireland's position in international law, we find the establishment of internal and external machinery for the conduct of foreign relations and co-operation in international affairs. The development of treaty-making powers in the Dominions was paralleled by the Irish Free State's participation in the work of the League of Nations and specialist international organizations. Until December, 1955, she was precluded from full participation in the work of the United Nations but did what she could in the work of specialized agencies. Further, her position as a European State enables her to play her full part in the movements for co-operation in Europe. Her treaty practice, the principles of international law accepted by the Constitution, and the application of international law in the Irish courts all combine to show how a small nation with an ancient history and a modern constitutional framework can assert to the fullest possible limit her position in international affairs. Both within and outside the Commonwealth an independent Irish stand was taken.

Before turning to the field of private international law the position of Northern Ireland merits consideration. It may seem anomalous to append this to a description of the application of public international law in the Republic, but the references which have been made to the Dublin claim to jurisdiction over Northern Ireland have shown that the existence of Northern Ireland as part of the United Kingdom has had a considerable effect on the policy adopted by the Dublin government. The Government of Ireland Act, 1920, the Treaty, and the 1925 Agreement fixing the area of Northern Ireland, and the declaration in the Ireland Act, 1949 (that Northern Ireland remains a part of His Majesty's Dominions and will not cease to be so without the consent of the Parliament of Northern Ireland) all combine to determine Northern Ireland's status as part of the United Kingdom. Against this must be set the Republic's claim to de jure jurisdiction over the whole of Ireland and its recognition of the present de facto scope of its legislation. Incidentally, if this long-standing dispute should ever reach the Hague, it is possible that eventually an authoritative decision may be given on the precise effect of the Treaty and its amendments.

This discrepancy between de jure and de facto jurisdiction has been reflected in Irish nationality law. In *In re Logue,* (1933) 67 I.L.T.R. 253 an Irish Free State court held that the area of jurisdiction of the Irish Free State (in Art. 3 of the 1922 Constitution, dealing with citizenship) meant the de jure jurisdiction, which extended throughout the whole island until Northern Ireland presented an address opting out. In Northern Ireland, on the other hand, it has been held in *R. (Stewart) v. Baldrick,* (1937) 71 I.L.T.R. 57 that the relevant area must be that of the de facto jurisdiction of the Irish Free State. Since, however, the Irish Free State claimed as its citizens those who were domiciled in the whole of Ireland on December 6, 1922, special provision was made in s. 3 of the Ireland Act, 1949 (12 & 13 Geo. 6, c. 41), to secure that such persons did not lose their status as British subjects. Here also the fact of Northern Ireland's existence had repercussions outside that area. Again, the Irish Nationality and Citizenship Act, 1956 (No. 26 of 1956), which replaced the Irish Nationality and Citizenship Act, 1935 (No. 13 of 1935), purported to apply to the whole island, and was the subject of a protest in the Northern Ireland parliament.[27]

Northern Ireland is only part of a person in the international law sense, and moreover her parliament is precluded, by s. 4 of the Government of Ireland Act, 1920, from legislating on such international law topics as the making of peace or war, treaties, relations with foreign states, extradition, fugitive offenders, or trade outside Northern Ireland. In the circumstances, there might seem little justification for referring to her at all in the context of international law, but there are two ways in which Northern Ireland may be affected by international law problems. The first of these concerns the signature by the United Kingdom of Great Britain and Northern Ireland of an agreement which requires the amendment of the municipal law. So far as any such amendment relates to Great Britain it can be undertaken by the Westminster parliament, but it is not impossible to foresee difficulties where the alteration re-

[27] *House of Commons Debates (Northern Ireland),* XL, No. 50.

quires an amendment of the law of Northern Ireland relating to one of the topics committed to the jurisdiction of that parliament. It is true that by s. 75 of the Government of Ireland Act, 1920, the Westminster parliament retains the right to override the local legislature, but against this must be set those constitutional practices which forbid interference with the exercise of delegated power. (In this respect the relations between London and Belfast resemble those between Canberra and the Australian states, as shown by *R.v. Burgess ex parte Henry*, (1936) 55 C.L.R. 608, rather than the relationship between Ottawa and the Canadian provinces, as exemplified by *Attorney-General for Canada v. Attorney-General for Ontario: re Weekly Rest in Industrial Undertakings Act*, [1937] A.C. 326.) This is the kind of problem which will normally be settled by agreement between the Belfast and London governments but it may have international repercussions. One such problem concerned the I.L.O. Convention No. 87 dealing with freedom of association and protection of the right to organize. The generality of this conflicted with the provisions of the Trade Disputes and Trade Unions Act (Northern Ireland), 1927 (17 & 18 Geo. 5, c. 20), restricting the right of civil servants to join trade unions. The case was not entirely covered by Art. 19(5) of the I.L.O. Convention since Northern Ireland is not in law part of a federation, nor was it covered by Art. 35(4) relating to self-governing, non-metropolitan territories, since Northern Ireland is in fact a self-governing part of the metropolitan territory of the United Kingdom. The difficulty disappeared on the adoption of another I.L.O. Convention, No. 98, with an exception for government servants, but it is an example of the way in which the devolution of power in a unitary state may cause international complications.

The second type of event in which Northern Ireland can make an appearance on the international scene is that in which she is enabled to do so by the United Kingdom parliament. So far, two main types of enablement have been given. Under the social welfare legislation passed under the postwar period the Westminster parliament has enabled the Northern Ireland parliament to enact corresponding legislation and this includes the power to make reciprocal arrangements for participation in social welfare services. In practice, these arrangements may be made generally for the United

Kingdom or even on occasion particularly on behalf of Northern Ireland. In the result, separate arrangements have been made with the Irish Republic, Australia, New Zealand, and some half-dozen European countries. A more particular use of this enabling device has authorized the enactment of parallel legislation with the Irish Republic on matters of common interest. Schemes for cross-border rail traffic, the development of drainage and hydroelectric works, and the preservation of a valuable salmon fishery have so far been active by means of parallel legislation in Belfast and Dublin. Thus, the constitutional difficulties stemming from the 1920-1922 period have been overcome and the device of parallel legislation used to bring about agreements similar to those reached by international bodies. Although not, at any rate from the Dublin standpoint, international, these agreements are as nearly international as it is possible in the circumstances for them to be, and they afford another example of the way in which Ireland makes a contribution to international affairs.

III. Conflict of Laws

At the beginning of 1920 there were three law-districts in the United Kingdom—England, Scotland, and Ireland; by the end of 1922 there were still three law-districts—England, Scotland and Northern Ireland—but the Irish Free State had been given a separate jurisdiction. The creation of two law-districts in Ireland where only one had existed before, and the carving of a new dominion out of the United Kingdom, gave rise to certain problems in private international law. Similar problems arose in India, but a quarter of a century before India achieved independence the courts in Belfast, Dublin, and London had to deal with this novel situation.

THE POSITION BEFORE 1920

Before the union between Ireland and Great Britain on January 1, 1801, Ireland had been treated as a foreign country for certain purposes by the English courts. It is true that, as explained in the chapter on Legal History (*supra*), in medieval times appeals lay from the Irish courts to the English King's Bench, and that from 1720 until 1782 the ultimate appellate tribunal for Ireland was the English House of Lords, not the Irish one. But this linking of judicial systems does not appear to have affected the rules governing original actions in the English courts. There are a number of English cases in the seventeenth and eighteenth centuries in which the English courts refused to take jurisdiction in cases relating to lands in Ireland,[28] although in *Kildare v. Eustace,* (Ch. 1686) 1 Vern. 419, 23 Eng. Rep. 559 the court declared that it was competent to deal with a trust of lands in Ireland, and said that the judges in England were the proper expositors of Irish law. Another example of the cleavage of jurisdiction caused by the Irish Sea is to be found in the construction of the statutes of limitation, where it was held that Ireland was "beyond the seas" in the legal as well as the literal sense. In *Lane v. Bennett,* (Ex. 1836) 1 M. & W. 70, 150 Eng. Rep. 350 it was held that the Act of Union had not affected this position.

The fact that the judicial systems of the three jurisdictions in the United Kingdom had a common apex in the House of Lords has led to certain protests, particularly on the part of Scots lawyers, against the tendency of English judges to assume that English law must necessarily be the best law, but it also meant that certain authoritative decisions were given on facts which had originated outside the home of the common law. Such leading cases as *Rex v. Millis,* (H. L. 1844) 10 Cl. & Fin. 534, 8 Eng. Rep. 344 (laying down the rule that a common law marriage must be celebrated by an episcopally ordained priest or deacon) and *Cooper v. Cooper,* (1888) 13 App. Cas. 88 (dealing with the capacity to make a marriage settlement) arose out of facts which took place in Ireland, and which came to the House of Lords after consideration by, respectively, the Irish and the Scottish courts. Yet here again the judicial link did not blur the boundaries of jurisdiction. This was clearly pointed out for Ireland in 1834, in the case of *Houlditch v. Donegal,* (H. L.) 2 Cl. & Fin. 470, 6 Eng. Rep. 1232 where the Irish Court of Chancery refused to take jurisdiction when a bill was filed there suing on a decree of the English Chancery. The House of Lords held that the English proceedings were in the nature of a foreign judgment and should be treated as such by the Irish courts. There could hardly be any clearer proof of the separateness of the jurisdictions, which was given legislative recognition by the Judgments Extension

---

[28] E.g., *Cartwright v. Pettus,* (Ch. 1676) 2 Chan. Cas. 214, 22 Eng. Rep. 916; *Barker v. Damer,* (K. B. 1691) Carthew. 182, 90 Eng. Rep. 710; *Fryar v. Vernon,* (Ch. 1724) Sel. Ca. T. King 5, 25 Eng. Rep. 191.

Act, 1868 (31 & 32 Vict. c. 54), providing for registration of the judgments of the superior courts, to take effect throughout the whole of the United Kingdom.

The Judgments Extension Act, 1868, provides a link with the views taken by the English courts as to events in Ireland in 1920-1922. Since new jurisdictions were being created in Ireland, s. 41(1) of the Government of Ireland Act, 1920 provided for the reciprocal enforcement of judgments of the Supreme Courts of Northern and Southern Ireland. However, since the 1920 Act never took effect in Southern Ireland, it was left to the courts to decide whether the Act of 1868 could work as between the United Kingdom on the one hand and the Irish Free State on the other.

The problem was considered by the English King's Bench in *Wakely v. Triumph Cycle Co.*, [1924] 1 K. B. 214 (1923) when it was held that the effect of the Westminster legislation was that the 1868 Act had ceased to have effect as regards the Free State even before the adoption of the 1922 Constitution. The Free State High Court, however, held in *Gieves v. O'Connor*, [1924] 2 I.R. 282, that the 1868 Act was still operative as regards the English and Scottish courts; so in 1925 the point was taken in the English Court of Appeal, which in *Banfield v. Chester*, 94 L.J.K.B. 805 confirmed the decision of the lower English court. In the result an English or Scottish judgment may be enforced directly in the Free State, but an action must be brought in the English or Scottish courts on an Irish judgment. A measure originally put forward in case of the litigant in the United Kingdom was adapted to operate in the smaller area of the United Kingdom as it is today, but ceased to operate reciprocally as regards the newly created Dominion. Moreover, the Foreign Judgments (Reciprocal Enforcement) Act, 1933, (23 & 24 Geo. 5, c. 13) was not extended to operate in respect of the Irish Free State.[29]

But the problems caused to the courts by the hiving-off of a part of the United Kingdom were not related solely to procedural

[29] *Cf.* Horace Emerson Read, *Recognition and Enforcement of Foreign Judgments in the Common Law Units of the British Commonwealth* (Harvard, 1938), 296; [John Foster Caldwell], "Reciprocal Enforcement of Judgments and Decrees," *Northern Ireland Legal Quarterly*, II (1938), 188; III (1939), 91, 135; IV (1940), 83.

matters. Good examples of the difficulties are provided by two cases in which the concept of domicil was considered. In *In re O'Keefe; Poingdestre v. Sherman*, [1940] 1 Ch. 124 (1939), the English Chancery Court had to consider the disposition of movables on the death intestate of a lady who had acquired a domicil of choice in Italy, but had not been naturalized there. Her father had been born, and was held to be domiciled, in county Clare, which in 1835 was part of the United Kingdom but by 1937 had become part of Eire. According to Italian rules the appropriate law for the disposition of movables was the "national law," but in this case the national law was not a unified system. In the result, Crossman J. held that the only part of the British Empire (*sic*) to which the intestate could be said to belong was the place where her father's domicil of origin lay, and accordingly directed that the law of Eire should apply. This decision has been subjected to the trenchant criticism of Professor Cheshire in the course of his attack on the "foreign court" theory. As he says:

> The succession to her property was governed by the laws of a country which she had never entered except during one short visit some sixty years before her death, which was not even a separate political unit until sixty-two years after her birth; of whose succession law she was no doubt profoundly and happily ignorant; and under the law of which it was impossible in the circumstances for her to claim citizenship.[30]

The result is indeed, as Professor Cheshire has said, out of touch with the realities of life, but it is difficult to see any alternative solution for the problem of the father's *lex domicilii*; the creation of the new law-district with a separate succession law (for Dublin has not yet followed London into the mysteries of the Birkenhead property legislation) was held to have some notional retrospective effect, though this was discovered only by a somewhat tortuous process.

The court used a similar "deeming" process to determine the proper law of a settlement *inter vivos* in *Iveagh v. Inland Revenue Commissioners*, [1954] Ch. 364. When the settlement was made in 1907, Ireland was part of a single fiscal unit, the United Kingdom, and there was no difference between the estate duty law of England and Ireland. When the tenant for life died in 1949, the Irish Re-

---

[30] *Private International Law* (4th ed.; Oxford, 1952), 79-80.

public was a separate fiscal unit, with her own system of estate duty law. By which law was estate duty to be charged? The court distinguished the case of *Duke of Marlborough v. Attorney-General (No. 1)*, [1945] Ch. 78 where the choice lay between two systems of law—those of England and New York—in force at the making of the settlement. It was held that the settlement was made by an Irish family, with an Irish domicil, though with many, perhaps overriding, interests in England, and that the proper law of the settlement being Irish, the law of the Irish Republic should be used for estate duty purposes. Here again a "deeming" process was used in the assumption that the law of the Republic should be given some retrospective effect. Just as in *O'Keefe's* case the court had to find the law which would have been applicable if Eire had been in existence in 1835, so in this case the court had to discover what law the parties to the settlement would have applied had Eire been a separate law district in 1907. As one commentator has pointed out, this "deeming" process has its complications,[31] but there seem to be few, if any, practical alternatives. The creation of the new law-district carries with it a certain element of notional retrospectivity, and indeed, this is only reasonable when it is remembered that the law-district did not spring from the air, but was rooted in the Irish soil, being itself a descendant of an older jurisdiction.

THE ATTITUDE OF THE IRISH COURTS

Before 1921 the conflicts problems which had come before the Irish courts appear to have been solved along traditional lines. But it is interesting to note in passing that there appears to be only one case, *Mayor of Limerick v. Crompton*, [1910] 2 I.R. 416, in which the Irish courts were asked to adjudicate on the proper law of a contract made between a party in Ireland and one in England. Presumably the close contacts and ease of communication between the two areas leant against the raising of points such as the proper forum for the arbitration of disputes. Or perhaps the party with the greater economic power insisted that contracts should be litigated in the law courts in the Strand rather than the Four Courts in Dublin. (This might provide an interesting field of research for some economic historian.) Be that as it may, the judges in both Belfast

---

[31] Valentine Latham, "Estate Duty and the Proper Law of a Trust," *International and Comparative Law Quarterly*, (Fourth Series) III (1954), 499-502.

and Dublin were, like their London counterparts, confronted with new problems by the drawing of a dividing line across the Irish law-district.

THE EXTENT OF JURISDICTION

Just as the area of the legislative jurisdictions of Northern Ireland and the Irish Free State gave rise to complications, so the question of the extent of judicial powers came before the newly constituted Northern Ireland courts shortly after they commenced to function. These cases resembled the ancient problem of the common law—the *locus commissi* of an act involving the shooting of an arrow from one county to another. This group of cases had another common feature, for they were all concerned with the interpretation of legislation providing compensation for personal injuries or damage to property suffered as a result of malicious action or riotous assemblies.

In *Fermanagh County Council v. Farrendon,* [1923] 2 I.R. 180 the Northern Ireland Court of Appeal held that a soldier injured in county Fermanagh (in Northern Ireland) could recover compensation from the council of that county when he was injured by a shot fired from county Donegal, in the Free State. Similarly when shots fired from county Donegal damaged property in county Fermanagh, the same Court held that compensation was recoverable, *Fermanagh County Council v. Donegal Presbytery Board of Education,* [1923] 2 I.R. 184. But a trans-border incident could not easily be brought within the scope of a code which had formerly applied throughout the whole country. The turbulent affairs of county Fermanagh were also the subject of a third case, *Plumb v. Fermanagh County Council; Orr v. County Councils of Fermanagh, Cavan, Monaghan and Tyrone,* [1923] 1 I.R. 54. In that case, a constable was wounded in county Fermanagh and dragged across the border into county Leitrim (in the Free State), where he died. The Northern Ireland Court of Appeal held that the former statutory power to make orders against "neighbouring counties" had become confined to counties in Northern Ireland, since the jurisdictions were mutually exclusive. But in the transitional process curious occurrences could take place, as in *R. v. McQuillan,* [1923] 2 I.R. 93 where a man was tried in Northern Ireland, after the Irish Free State had been constituted, for an offense committed outside Northern Ireland before that date.

The present-day problems to which the land frontier gives rise can be effectively overcome for certain specific purposes, as for instance in the parallel legislation in Belfast and Dublin relating to the Foyle fisheries. Under the Foyle Fisheries Act (Northern Ireland), 1952 (c.5), the Northern Ireland courts are enabled to try certain offenses committed in the Irish Republic by Northern Ireland residents, while under the corresponding Dublin Act (No. 5 of 1952) the Republic's courts may try similar cases involving Republican residents and originating in Northern Ireland. The exclusiveness of the two jurisdictions can thus be modified on a reciprocal basis.

DOMICIL

Just as problems relating to domicil arose in the English courts, so the Irish courts had to consider difficulties arising from the relationship between current situations and past events. Here mention may be made of a remarkable legislative method of dealing with the problem of domicil. An adaptation order (S.R. & O. 1922, No. 77) made under the Government of Ireland Act, 1920 provided that "For the purpose of determining the domicile of any person, Northern Ireland shall be deemed always to have been a separate part of the United Kingdom." Since the 1920 Act did not operate in Southern Ireland, this piece of subordinate legislation does not form part of its law, but it would be relevant to cases in the courts of Northern Ireland, England, or Scotland, though so far it has not been the subject of judicial consideration. Although it was not referred to in the *O'Keefe* and *Iveagh* cases it does support them to the extent that they applied the law of the Republic in the case of persons whose Irish domicil did not arise in the area which is now Northern Ireland; if Northern Ireland was to be regarded as always existing, by inference the rest of Ireland must have constituted a separate law-district.

Among the cases, perhaps the most novel arose on a petition for divorce presented in Northern Ireland in 1928. In *In re Egan*, [1928] N.I. 159 it transpired that the petitioner had been born in county Dublin and had lived in various parts of Ireland both North and South before becoming a civil servant in Ceylon in 1912, since when he had not resided permanently in Ireland although he intended to settle in the North. Where was he to be regarded as domiciled? The question had nearly arisen, but had not been decided, in *Platt v. Attorney-General for New South Wales*, (1878) 3 App. Cas. 336, dealing with the separation of Queensland from New South Wales. The Northern Ireland High Court had, therefore, to decide the problem without the assistance of authority, and it did so simply by holding that the petitioner could elect to be domiciled in North or South, that he had chosen the North, and that the court could, therefore, entertain the petition. In this case the facts were evenly distributed between North and South, so that the introduction of the element of intention was justifiable, but the virtual choice of a domicil of origin must be rare.

There were also cases, like the *O'Keefe* case, which necessitated a retrospective glance to a hypothetical past. Thus in *In re M*, [1937] N.I. 151, a legitimacy suit, the plaintiff relied on the subsequent marriage of her parents, and the material question was whether the father had been "domiciled in Northern Ireland" when he had lived all his life in county Antrim but had died in 1915, six years before that county became part of Northern Ireland. The court held that the phrase just quoted must be construed as "domiciled in that portion of Ireland which is now Northern Ireland." The principle applied in this case was exactly similar to that laid down under the Government of Ireland Act—the notional pre-existence of Northern Ireland as a separate law district. Moreover, an identical conclusion was reached, on similar facts, by an Eire court in *In re P.*, [1945] Ir. Jur. Rep. 17, so it is evident that Irish judges, both North and South, are willing to assume a hypothetical past existence for their respective jurisdictions. As Sir Arnold McNair (as he then was) pointed out in a somewhat similar case—he was dealing with the consequences of the cession of an area to another law district—this type of decision appears to be correct both on principle and on practical grounds.[32]

In sum, while the concept of domicil has not been weakened in Ireland, as has happened in Australia (*Walton v. Walton*, [1949] A.L.R. 148) and South Africa (*Ley v. Ley's Exrs.*, [1951] (3) S.A. 186 (A.D.)), it has been extended by the Irish courts, as it has by those in England, to deal with notional past situations.

[32] *The Legal Effects of War* (2d ed.; Cambridge, 1944), 390.

APPLICATION OF CONFLICT RULES

One of the most fruitful single sources of private international law cases in the Irish Republic has been the Irish Hospitals Sweepstake.[33]   (This was also the subject of an interesting case in the English courts, where in *R. v. Registrar of Joint Stock Companies, ex parte More*, [1931] 2 K. B. 197 a valiant but unsuccessful argument was put up in favor of the legality of the "Irish Sweep," on the ground that it was similar to certain eighteenth-century Irish state lotteries whose validity had been recognized.)   For instance in *Apicella v. Scala*, (1932) 66 I.L.T.R. 33 it was held that the purchase of sweepstake tickets and the sending of money and counterfoils was an offer, not an acceptance of an offer; the *lex loci contractus* was therefore the Irish Free State, where the transaction was legal. Again, in *McKie v. McKie*, [1933] I.R. 464 it was held, following *Castrique v. Imrie*, (1870) L.R. 4 (E. & I. App.) H.L. 414 that the decree of a California court in a divorce suit could not impose any restraint on sweepstake prize money still in Ireland, so that the effect of a "temporary restraining order" made in California was not recognized in Ireland.   Also, in *Dharamal v. Lord Holmpatrick*, [1935] I.R. 760 it was held that the prize money of an Indian infant should not be paid to her father (even though he was by Indian law her legal guardian) but should be administered by the court for the infant's benefit.   But a contrary view was taken five years later in *Orlando v. Earl of Fingal*, [1940] I.R. 281 where in similar circumstances payment out of court was ordered to the father of a fortunate New York infant.

In Northern Ireland matrimonial cases have caused the most frequent use of private international law concepts.   Thus the Northern Ireland courts refused to recognize a Florida decree of divorce which did not involve domicil (*In re E.E.L.*, [1938] N.I. 56), and more recently they have been concerned with the basis of jurisdiction in such matters as nullity suits.[34]   The Dublin courts cannot follow

[33] *Cf.* Frank Ernest Dowrick, "The Irish Sweep and Irish Law," *American Journal of Comparative Law*, II (1953), 505-515.

[34] For a commentary on a recent Northern Ireland decision, *Addison v. Addison*, [1955] N.I. 1, on jurisdiction in nullity cases, *cf.* P. R. H. Webb, "The Twilight of the Doctrine in *Inverclyde v. Inverclyde*," *International and Comparative Law Quarterly*, (Fourth Series) IV (1955), 557-563.   That Lord MacDermott (the Lord Chief Justice of Northern Ireland) was justified in refusing to follow *Inverclyde's* case was shown by the fact that that case was overruled by the English Court of Appeal in *Ramsay-Fairfax v. Ramsay-Fairfax*, [1956] P. 115.

their Belfast counterparts into the intricacies of divorce law, since Art. 41, 3, (2) of the 1937 Constitution forbids the enactment of laws providing for the dissolution of marriage. This does not, however, prevent the recognition of decrees granted elsewhere, as in *In re McComiskey; Gibson v. Patterson*, [1939] I.R. 573, where it was held that since no Irish law invalidated an English divorce decree, status should be determined in accordance with that decree and the law of the domicil.

ENFORCEMENT OF JUDGMENTS

On the procedural question of enforcement of judgments, it was perhaps natural that the courts of Northern Ireland should lean towards the interpretation placed by the judges in London on the effect of the creation of the Irish Free State. Thus in *Cailan v. McKenna*, [1929] N.I. 1 defendants who were resident in Northern Ireland applied to have the plaintiffs (who were resident in the Free State) give security for costs, on the ground that, if the defendants succeeded, they would not be able to extend the judgment to the Irish Free State. It was held that such security should be given, since the Judgments Extension Act, 1868, no longer extended there.

As has already been indicated, the Irish courts took the view that the 1868 Act still applied as between the Free State on the one hand and the English and Scottish courts on the other. Yet the English decision to the contrary, though it was not followed in the Free State, had its repercussions there. Though it was held in 1924, distinguishing the *Wakely* case ([1924] 1 K. B. 214), that the mere fact that a plaintiff was resident in England did not entitle an Irish defendant to ask for security for costs (*Gremson v. Lipman*, (1924) 58 I.L.T.R. 93), it was later held that the fact that an Irish judgment would have to be sued on in England as a foreign judgment was material in considering the giving of security for costs (*Perry v. Statham*, [1928] I.R. 580).

These Irish Free State cases related to disputes stretching across the Irish Sea, but a different attitude was shown towards cases originating across the land frontier in Northern Ireland. In *Edelstein v. Coleman*, (1938) 72 I.L.T.R. 142 an action was brought in Eire on a judgment obtained in Northern Ireland in respect of a contract made there for performance in England. The defendant was, however, domiciled and resident in, and a citizen of, Eire, and he did not appear in the Northern Ireland court, though he was served with a writ out of the jurisdiction of Northern Ireland. The Eire court applied the leading case of *Sirdar Gurdyal Singh v. The Rajah of Faridkote*, [1894] A.C. 670, in holding that a foreign judgment obtained in default of appearance was a nullity. For this purpose the recently created Northern Ireland jurisdiction was a foreign one, to which the Judgments Extension Act, 1868, was not applicable.

APPREHENSION OF ALLEGED CRIMINALS

A somewhat similar situation obtains in relation to the legislation dealing with the apprehension of alleged offenders. Since crossing the Irish Sea, or the border between Scotland and England, was a means of delaying, if not avoiding, arrest, the system of "backing of warrants" was instituted in the nineteenth century. Under this procedure, a warrant was issued for the arrest of the offender in the law-district in which the alleged offense was committed; this was then endorsed by a police officer or magistrate of the law-district to which the offender had fled; he could then be arrested in the latter district and returned to the former. The statutory authority for this in Ireland was s. 29 of the Petty Sessions (Ireland) Act, 1851 (14 & 15 Vict. c. 93), and after 1922 the courts had to decide how far this provision remained in force.

A curious anomaly, which still persists, emerged in the course of this judicial examination. Although the post-1922 adaptations of legislation permitted this system of "backing" warrants to operate as between England and Wales or Scotland on the one hand, and Northern Ireland or the Irish Free State on the other, there was no adaptation which permitted reciprocity of action between Northern Ireland and the South. This was first disclosed in the *O'Boyle and Rogers v. Attorney-General and O'Duffy*, [1929] I.R. 558. Two persons who had been sentenced and imprisoned in Northern Ireland escaped to the Irish Free State, and then sought an injunction preventing their arrest on the authority of a warrant issued by a Northern Ireland magistrate and endorsed in the Irish Free State. This injunction was granted, on the ground that there was no way in which the 1851 Act had been modified to operate as between the two areas. Yet the Act continued to function in respect of England and Scotland. In *The State (Dowling) v. Brennan and Kingston,* [1937] I.R. 483, (No. 2), [1937] I.R. 699, an Irishman was arrested on a Scottish warrant for failing to maintain his wife and family, who had gone to live in Glasgow. His first application for a habeas corpus was granted on a technical point—that the police officer who had endorsed the warrant in Dublin was not of the rank required by the legislation; but the basis of the decision (from which Gavan Duffy J. dissented) was that the Petty Sessions Act of 1851 remained in force by virtue of Art. 73 of the 1922 Constitution. When a fresh endorsement of the warrant was procured and another arrest made, the Supreme Court upheld the High Court's refusal of habeas corpus on the ground which has just been mentioned, although Gavan Duffy J. again protested that this was tantamount to enforcing two sets of criminal law in Ireland, that the offense came very near to being a civil one, and that the alleged offender had not in any event committed the offense within the jurisdiction of the Scottish courts.

Fifteen years later the same judge, having become President of the High Court, had to consider the point again, this time in relation to the 1937 Constitution. In *The State (Duggan) v. Tapley,* [1952] I.R. 62 the validity was challenged of an English warrant endorsed in Ireland, on the ground that extradition should be granted only in accordance with the principles of international law, and that legislation such as the Petty Sessions Act did not comply with those principles. Both the High Court and the Supreme Court held that the acceptance of the principles of international law did not prevent the operation of such legislation, which need not even be on a reciprocal basis. The basis of the decision in both courts was that Art. 50 of the 1937 Constitution had preserved the existing law just as the 1922 Constitution had done, and that the 1851 Act was part of that law.

Although the Dublin courts have held that reciprocity is not necessary, the English courts have held that the reciprocal arrangements for the backing of Irish warrants in England remain in force. In *R. v. Commissioner of Police, ex parte Nalder,* [1947] 2 A.E.R. 611 the English King's Bench Division held that the Fugitive Offenders Act, 1881 (44 & 45 Vict. c. 69) did not apply between England and the Republic, but that the backing of warrants under the summary jurisdiction legislation was still in force.

Mention of the Fugitive Offenders Act leads to a reference to the case of *The State (Kennedy) v. Little*, [1931] I.R. 39 where it was held that the 1881 Act remained in force as part of the law of the Irish Free State by virtue of Art. 73 of the 1922 Constitution, so that an Irish Free State national could be validly apprehended in Dublin for the alleged commission of false pretenses in Canada. In this case, the High Court was able to rely on an Australian precedent to the effect that the 1881 Act applied between the Australian States after federation as it had done before (*McKelvey v. Meagher*, (1906) 4 C.L.R. Part I, 265).

Thus criminals seeking refuge in Dublin from Great Britain and the Commonwealth may still be apprehended, but those from the North of Ireland are unapprehended. As Gavan Duffy P. put it in *Tapley's* case at p. 65, "I fear that offenders seeking to use that as a charter of immunity must put a severe strain on the law-abiding police authorities of the Border counties."

SUMMARY

Novel situations make fresh law, so there is only a slight basis for comparison of the Irish law with the Commonwealth position, but a few points may be noted.

The first is the way in which the courts in Belfast, Dublin, and London all created a notional domicil for some past period, without weakening the main concept. Perhaps the numerous Indian cases will produce some parallel judicial pronouncements. For instance, in *Allah Bandi v. Government of the Union of India*, A.I.R. 1954 All. 456 (D.B.) the area in which the husbands of two married women had been domiciled before the partition of India governed the case.

Secondly, the general application of private international law rules has been made in traditional ways, for subjects as widely varying as sweepstake tickets and matrimonial affairs.

Thirdly, the creation of the land frontier has led to certain difficulties relating to the respective jurisdictions, particularly in relation to such matters as the enforcement of judgments and the apprehension of offenders. This is a far cry from the full faith and credit provision in s. 118 of the Australian Constitution, or the Canadian provisions for the reciprocal enforcement of judgments, though federal jurisdictions are not on the same footing as the two Irish unitary ones.

Fourthly, in holding that the Petty Sessions Act, 1851 and the Fugitive Offenders Act, 1881 remained in force under the 1922 and 1937 Constitutions, the Dublin courts have taken a stand in which they have not been imitated by India. There the Supreme Court has held in *Madras v. C. G. Menon*, A.I.R. 1954 S.C. 517 that the 1881 Act was repugnant to the conception of a sovereign democratic republic, whereas the Dublin courts have reconciled the two.

In sum, in the development of Dominion status, the use of public international law, and the application of private international law rules, Ireland has had a considerable contribution to make, one which both paralleled and diverged from that of other Commonwealth countries.

4

Constitutional Developments
since 1920

IT MAY SEEM strange to deal with constitutional developments in
Ireland in the past thirty-five years, since there was also much unconstitutional development. The historian and the political scientist
must necessarily consider this background in some detail, and the
lawyer, in his search through the statutes and law reports, will find
much to remind him that life outside the law courts and the
legislative chamber was very far from settled. Yet the outlines
of constitutional development show how the processes of parliamentary democracy, though subjected at times to considerable strain,
were nevertheless adapted to meet the new circumstances of Irish
political life.

I. THE CONSTITUTION OF NORTHERN IRELAND

THE GOVERNMENT OF IRELAND ACT, 1920

The starting-point is the Government of Ireland Act, 1920 (10
& 11 Geo. 5, c. 67). This was the culmination of a series of events
referred to in the chapter on Constitutional History (*supra*)—the
suspension of the Home Rule Act in 1914, the rising in Dublin in
Easter, 1916, the all-party Irish Convention which reported in
1918, and the setting up in 1919 of the first Dáil Eireann by the
Sinn Féin members elected to the Westminster parliament at the
end of 1918. The Westminster parliament dealt with the situation
in Ireland in two ways. As a short-term measure the Restoration
of Order in Ireland Act, 1920 (10 & 11 Geo. 5, c. 31) was passed,
to deal with the guerilla warfare which was being waged; as a long-
term constitutional solution, there was enacted the Government of
Ireland Act, 1920. Unlike its predecessor of 1914, and unlike

Gladstone's and Asquith's Home Rule Bills, this was debated in the absence of the Irish Nationalists who had been eclipsed at the 1918 elections by the Sinn Féin party. Another difference was that the Ulster Unionists, who had resisted the previous measures, and sought exclusion from them, were prepared to accept the compromise of the 1920 Act—two parliaments in Ireland, where formerly there had been none. But Ulster, the historic northern province, was not to have jurisdiction over all that area, for three of her nine counties were to be subject to the new parliament of Southern Ireland. Instead, six of the Ulster counties were given the title of Northern Ireland, with a separate parliament subordinate to that at Westminster. The parliament of Southern Ireland never functioned effectively, so that the paradoxical situation was reached—and continues—that the Ulster Unionists, who never wanted Home Rule, are now working a modified Home Rule system. Indeed, a recent study of the development of Northern Ireland, historical and legal, political and economic, has been given the title of *Ulster under Home Rule*.[1]

The structure of the Government of Ireland Act, 1920, has been likened to that of a building with two wings linked by a central portion. One wing—Southern Ireland—collapsed almost as soon as it was built. The central portion was to be a Council of Ireland, described in the chapter on Constitutional History (*supra*); it was given functions throughout the whole of Ireland, but its main aim was to pave the way to the unification of the two separate parts of the island: "the date of Irish union" recurred throughout the Act of 1920, as originally enacted. But, although the right to elect members of the Council of Ireland was transferred to the Oireachtas of the Irish Free State by Art. 13 of the 1921 Anglo-Irish agreement, no elections took place, either in Belfast or Dublin. Eventually, under the tripartite 1925 Agreement, scheduled to the Ireland (Confirmation of Agreement) Act, 1925 (15 & 16 Geo. 5, c. 77; the Irish Free State Act was No. 40 of 1925), the Council of Ireland's powers in Northern Ireland were transferred to the government there, so that the Council of Ireland was abandoned without trial. The phrase "the date of Irish union" is no longer an effective part of the Act of 1920 as it applies in Northern Ireland.

[1] Thomas Wilson, ed., Oxford, 1955.

It is, therefore, with only one wing of the Irish building that constitutional lawyers in Northern Ireland are concerned, and the main objects of their interest are the structure of the Constitution and the relationship between the Northern Ireland and Westminster parliaments.

THE STRUCTURE OF NORTHERN IRELAND'S CONSTITUTION

The tripartite plan of legislature, executive, and judiciary is detailed in the 1920 Act. Like the majority of the Australian states, but unlike the Canadian provinces (except Quebec), Northern Ireland has a bicameral legislative system, attracting the powers, privileges, immunities, and disqualifications of the Westminster House of Commons (Act of 1920, s. 18(1) and (2)). The lower House, the House of Commons, consists of fifty-two directly elected members; the number of constituencies cannot be changed by the Northern Ireland parliament, although the system of election can be, and has been, changed (Act of 1920, s. 14). As for the upper House, the Senate, this was introduced into the 1920 Act only because the original unicameral system was altered for the proposed parliament of Southern Ireland, and similar provision was made for the North. All but two ex-officio members of the twenty-six members of the Senate are elected by the House of Commons for eight years, twelve retiring every four years (Act of 1920, s. 13 and Schedules 3 and 4). This system does not appear to have any exact parallel elsewhere in the Commonwealth, though the influence of the South African precedent may be seen.

As for the relations between the two Houses, Ministers may speak in either House, but vote only in that to which they belong (Act of 1920, s. 18(4)). The Senate cannot initiate financial legislation, or amend any Bill, in the words of s. 16 (3) of the Act of 1920, "so as to increase any proposed charges or burdens on the people." To resolve disputes between the two Houses, the device of a joint sitting may be used, in the same session for money bills, or in the succeeding session for other legislation (Act of 1920, s. 17). Since the Senate broadly reflects the state of the parties in the House of Commons, no such sittings have been held, but the similarity with the Australian and South African situations is obvious.

The precedents of the earlier Home Rule Bills were followed in providing Northern Ireland with an executive. Under s. 8 of the Act of 1920 executive power continues to be vested in the Crown, but is exercised by a Governor in relation to the administration of matters within the powers of the Northern Ireland parliament, a matter considered later in connection with the relations between Belfast and London.   The Letters Patent appointing the Governor provide for the issue of further instructions by the Crown, and in practice these regulate such matters as the giving of Royal Assent to Northern Ireland legislation, the reservation of bills, and the exercise of the prerogative of mercy.   There is a Privy Council with formal functions, but the power of advice rests with the Executive Committee of Northern Ireland, as the Cabinet of Northern Ireland is known; it is composed of the Ministers of Northern Ireland who must be or become members of the Senate or House of Commons. In comparing the position in Northern Ireland with that in other parts of the Commonwealth, it may be noted that the power of disallowance of acts, such as exists and is exercised in the Canadian provinces, does not exist.   Nor is reservation of bills obligatory in certain cases, as it is in the Australian states, and in the Indian states under Art. 31(3) of the 1950 Constitution.   In practice, there has been only one case of reservation in the thirty-five years of Northern Ireland's existence.   Again, just as constitutional practice regulates the position of the Governors of Australian states and the Lieutenant-Governors of the Canadian provinces, so the Governor of Northern Ireland stands in a similar position in the Northern Ireland Constitution.

The third element in the Constitution of Northern Ireland, the judiciary, has been described in the chapter on Legal History (*supra*), where mention was also made of the power of judicial review and of the method of reference of Northern Ireland legislation to the Judicial Committee of the Privy Council.

In its general structure the Northern Ireland Constitution resembles those of other parts of the Commonwealth, but a unique feature, which will be considered in some detail, is the relationship between the Northern Ireland and the Westminster parliaments.

THE RELATIONSHIP WITH THE WESTMINSTER PARLIAMENT

In deciding the powers to be devolved upon the new Irish legislature, the Westminster parliament used a number of general criteria.   The first of these was the principle of the supremacy of that parliament. This is enshrined in s. 75 of the 1920 Act, so that prima facie the Northern Ireland Constitution could be destroyed as easily as it was created—by a United Kingdom statute. There are, however, other considerations which modify the bare assertion of parliamentary sovereignty.

A second principle of the distribution of legislative power was that certain matters were to be excepted entirely from local jurisdiction. These were specified in s. 4 of the Act of 1920 and ranged from the Crown, peace and war, and defense matters, through foreign relations and trade outside the local jurisdiction, to weights and measures, trademarks, and copyright. These were the matters which, as in preceding Home Rule measures, were to be dealt with by the Westminster parliament for the whole of the United Kingdom.

Thirdly, certain matters were to be reserved to the Westminster parliament until "the date of Irish union." By s. 9 of the Act of 1920 these were to include such matters as the post office, and under s. 47 the Supreme Court was similarly reserved; these services were not to be transferred to Irish control until they could be administered on an all-Ireland basis. As events turned out, these "reserved" matters are now as much outside the jurisdiction of the parliament of Northern Ireland as those which the Westminster parliament intended to keep always within its power.

Similarly, the financial provisions of the Act of 1920, ss. 21 and 22, prohibit the Northern Ireland parliament from imposing an income tax or levying customs duties or variable excise duties: these and any taxes or duties substantially the same in character are fixed and collected by the Westminster parliament. Thus the Westminster parliament holds the strings of the larger purse, though it makes disbursements of the taxes it collects in Northern Ireland. The principle of parity of services in Great Britain and Northern Ireland involves not only similar rates of taxation, but payments to balance the costs in both areas; an agreement to this effect in relation to the social services was given statutory authority in 1949 by both the Westminster parliament (12 & 13 Geo. 6, c. 23) and the Northern Ireland parliament (1949 c. 3).[2]

[2] For discussions of Northern Ireland's finances see James Louis Montrose, "Legal Aspects of Taxation and Grant under the Northern Ireland System of Devolution" in Geoffrey Sawer, ed., *Federalism: An Australian Jubilee Study* (Melbourne,

A fifth principle was that the local legislature's powers to deal with the "transferred" matters should not be unrestricted. Thus it is made clear that the parliament of Northern Ireland cannot legislate in respect of matters outside its area nor can it override acts of the Westminster parliament passed after May 3, 1921, the day on which the Constitution of Northern Ireland came into being (Act of 1920, ss. 4 and 6). Also, this parliament is forbidden by s. 5 of the Act of 1920 to legislate on the basis of religious discrimination; it cannot endow any religion, nor can it (in words with more than an echo about them of the Fifth Amendment to the United States Constitution and the 1893 Home Rule Bill) "take any property without compensation." The width of this last prohibition has given rise to some litigation, and doubtless it will appear in the pages of future volumes of the *Northern Ireland Law Reports*. In comparison s. 51 (xxxi) of the Australian Constitution requires that the acquisition of property shall be on just terms, and Art. 31 of the 1950 Indian Constitution and Art. 15 of the 1956 Pakistan Constitution require the payment of compensation. But none of these provisions is exactly parallel to the restriction placed on the parliament of Northern Ireland by the Act of 1920.

Finally, by s. 19 of the Act of 1920, Northern Ireland retained the right to return thirteen members to the Westminster House of Commons, since there was not a complete devolution of power. The number of Northern Ireland M.P.'s was, however, reduced to twelve on the abolition of the university vote by the Representation of the People Act, 1948 (11 & 12 Geo. 6, c. 65).

The combined effect of these principles was to create a legislature with apparently no exact counterpart in the Commonwealth. The Northern Ireland parliament's powers are not specified, like those of the provincial legislatures of Canada or the provincial councils of South Africa; they are referred to generally as powers to legislate for the "peace, order and good government of Northern Ireland," and defined negatively, by specifying the matters on which only the Westminster parliament may legislate. This list of "excepted" and "reserved" matters is broadly similar to those in s. 91 of the

---

1952), 1; John Irvine Cook, "Financial Relations between the Exchequers of the United Kingdom and Northern Ireland" in Desmond Gorman Neill, ed., *Devolution of Government: The Experiment in Northern Ireland* (London, 1953), 18; and chapters in Thomas Wilson, ed., *Ulster Under Home Rule* (Oxford, 1955).

British North America Act, 1867 (30 & 31 Vict. c. 3) and in s. 51 of the Australian Constitution, though the latter list is more detailed than that in the Act of 1920. Once again certain distinctions place Northern Ireland in a different position from the Canadian provinces and the Australian states. Northern Ireland's powers are granted in respect of that area, just as the legislation of the provinces and the states is presumed to be confined to their respective jurisdictions; but both provinces and states have powers of amending their own constitutions, whereas Northern Ireland has no power to alter the Act of 1920. Northern Ireland resembles the Canadian provinces in that the residue of power lies with the central legislature, and she resembles the Australian states in that they are still bound by the Colonial Laws Validity Act, 1865 (28 & 29 Vict. c. 63) whereas Northern Ireland is prima facie bound by post-1920 Acts of the Westminster parliament, though she differs from those states in that the residue of power lies with them. In short, none of the federal schemes parallel the devolutionary position in Northern Ireland, though it is clear that the Commonwealth precedents have close resemblances to the Northern Ireland Constitution.

Under Art. 12 of the Anglo-Irish Agreement of 1921 Northern Ireland was to be given a month from the coming into operation of that article in which to decide whether to unite with the Irish Free State or to remain in the United Kingdom under the Act of 1920. The "Ulster Month," as it was called, began to run from December 5, 1922, and on December 8 the requisite address for opting out of the Irish Free State was presented by both Houses of the Northern Ireland parliament to the King. Northern Ireland therefore chose to continue her devolutionary existence though, as mentioned in the chapter on Ireland and the Commonwealth (*supra*), the area of Northern Ireland's jurisdiction was not fixed until 1925, by tripartite agreement and legislation in both Dublin and Westminster.

THE DEVELOPMENT OF THE NORTHERN IRELAND CONSTITUTION

The creation of Northern Ireland may not have been a conscious attempt to experiment in devolution, but the development of the Northern Ireland Constitution has provided an example of the working of a system of devolution. But before indicating the ways in which practice has altered the distribution of powers between Belfast and Westminster, two points may be mentioned for the purposes of comparison with the South of Ireland.

Under the Act of 1920, the system of proportional representation was to be used for elections to the Northern Ireland parliament. The first two such elections, in 1921 and 1925, were held on this system, but in passing the House of Commons (Method of Voting and Redistribution of Seats) Act (Northern Ireland), 1929 (19 Geo. 5, c. 5) the Northern Ireland parliament exercised its right to change the electoral system by introducing one of single-member constituencies, single votes, and simple majorities. In contrast, elections in the Irish Free State were, and those in the Irish Republic are, held on the proportional representation system. A second matter for comparison is the method used in the two areas for dealing with internal emergencies. In Northern Ireland the Civil Authorities (Special Powers) Act was passed in 1922 (12 & 13 Geo. 5, c. 5) providing for the making by the Minister of Home Affairs of regulations for the preservation of order; it was a lineal descendant of the Restoration of Order in Ireland Act, 1920. Offenses against the regulations were to be triable by courts of summary jurisdiction and extended powers of arrest were given; compensation was to be provided for damage caused. In *R. (O'Hanlon) v. Governor of Belfast Prison*, (1922) 56 I.L.T.R. 170 a challenge, by way of habeas corpus, to the validity of certain regulations was made shortly after the 1922 Act was passed, but the regulations were upheld as intra vires the statute. In a recent study Dr. J. Ll. J. Edwards has analyzed the use of the regulation-making power under the 1922 Act.[3] Other measures passed for the preservation of order in Northern Ireland were the Public Order Act (Northern Ireland), 1951 (c. 19) and the Flags and Emblems (Display) Act (Northern Ireland), 1954 (c. 10). In content, challenge, and decisions as to validity there is a close parallel with the Public Safety Acts passed in the Irish Free State, and the Offences against the State Act, 1939 (No. 13 of 1939) at present in force in the Irish Republic, to which later reference will be made. Also, it is interesting to note that the powers conferred by the Northern Ireland Act of 1922 proved useful on one occasion in facilitating the transfer of a person arrested in Northern Ireland across the border for trial in the Irish Republic for an offense com-

[3] "Special Powers in Northern Ireland," [1956] *Criminal Law Review*, 7-18.

mitted there; in *White v. Warnock*, (1947) 81 I.L.T.R. 35 a habeas corpus application was dismissed on the ground that the person concerned was no longer in custody or control in Northern Ireland.

The alteration of the election law and the preservation of law and order are matters with which the Northern Ireland parliament may properly deal, but amendments of the Government of Ireland Act, 1920 have to be undertaken by the Westminster parliament. These may take two forms; either they are made by acts passed specially for the purpose, or they arise incidentally in the course of Westminster legislation.

Amendments of the first kind have been made by five statutes, the Northern Ireland (Miscellaneous Provisions) Acts, 1928 (18 & 19 Geo. 5, c. 24), 1932 (22 & 23 Geo. 5, c. 11), and 1945 (8 & 9 Geo. 6, c. 12) and the Northern Ireland Acts, 1947 (10 & 11 Geo. 6, c. 37) and 1955 (3 & 4 Eliz. 2, c. 8). The first three of these are well-named "Miscellaneous Provisions" Acts and the last, though not so called, may be classified with these measures. In subject-matter they are extremely varied, but they have the common aim of enabling the Northern Ireland parliament to exercise its powers in relation to certain topics without the restrictions imposed by the Act of 1920. For example, Northern Ireland may now confer jurisdiction on its Supreme Court, prescribe standards for livestock and agricultural produce exported to other parts of the British Isles, repeal and re-enact United Kingdom statutes for the purpose of consolidating the statute law, lay down the procedure for trial of offenses whose substance it cannot alter, and amend the law relating to devolution of property on intestacy to correspond with the Birkenhead legislation passed at Westminster in 1922-1925. But the widest extension of powers was conferred by the Northern Ireland Act, 1947. As well as authorizing the passing of enactments similar to those governing the British National Health Service, and removing the restrictions on the taking of local government or public utility property (if accompanied by a transfer of functions in relation to that property), the 1947 Act gave power to legislate for water, electricity, and transport schemes extending "athwart the land frontier." As has been mentioned in Chapter III on International Law (*supra*), this power has been used to co-operate with the Irish Republic, by means of reciprocal legislation, on matters relating to drainage and hydroelectricity, fisheries, and common railway services. Set against the background of recent Irish history, this co-operation between a subordinate parliament within the United Kingdom, and an independent one outside the Commonwealth, marks a considerable advance.

The second aspect of amendments of the Northern Ireland Constitution is related to the everyday run of Westminster legislation. Just as Northern Ireland's powers have been extended by special legislation, so those powers have been preserved or extended by United Kingdom Acts dealing with particular topics. The process of extension of powers is a simple one, usually consisting of a provision that, notwithstanding the Act of 1920, the Northern Ireland parliament is to have power to make laws for purposes similar to those of the Westminster statute. These ad hoc enablements play a considerable part in the legislative activities of the Northern Ireland parliament, for they give power to carry out the policy of following "step-by-step" with Westminster. The best examples of these enablements are found in a series of Westminster acts passed in 1939 and 1940 to deal with the outbreak of war. Since the Northern Ireland parliament has no power to make laws in respect of "matters arising out of a state of war" it was necessary to enable them to legislate along the same lines as the Westminster acts.[4]

The process of preservation of Northern Ireland's powers is somewhat more complex. One method is to state clearly that so much of a Westminster act as relates to "matters with respect to which the Parliament of Northern Ireland has power to make laws" shall not extend to Northern Ireland; the differentiation is made as clear as possible. Another method of preserving local power is to provide that the Westminster act is to be deemed to be passed "before the appointed day" for the purposes of the Act of 1920. This means that the Northern Ireland parliament may alter such statutes, so that the repugnancy provision in s. 6 of the Act of 1920, similar to s. 2 of the Colonial Laws Validity Act, 1865 (28 & 29 Vict. c. 63), is virtually nullified. Other ways of preserving local powers are the delegation to the Northern Ireland parliament of the

[4] These enablements are listed in Sir Arthur Quekett, *The Constitution of Northern Ireland* (Belfast, 1946), III, 233.

right to determine if, and when, a Westminster statute shall apply there, and the specific designation of a Belfast or London Minister to administer a statute in Northern Ireland. An analysis of almost two hundred post-1920 Westminster statutes shows that, of these four methods, the first two are the most commonly used, in approximately equal numbers (seventy-two and sixty-six), while the second two are less frequently used, again in similar numbers (twenty-eight and twenty-five).

It will be seen that the day-to-day relations between the parliaments of the United Kingdom and of Northern Ireland are much more intimate than those in Canada and Australia; direct delegation of power from Westminster to Belfast is common and uncomplicated in comparison with the procedure devised for the transfer of powers from the Australian state capitals to Canberra, or the relations between Ottawa and the Canadian provincial capitals. Federation tends to rigidity, while devolution inclines to flexibility.

But the most important development in Northern Ireland's Constitution does not relate to the distribution of power, or the alteration of structure, or its operation *quoad* the Westminster parliament; rather it deals with the status of Northern Ireland itself. In the chapter on Ireland and the Commonwealth (*supra*) it was pointed out that, as a corollary of the recognition of the secession of the Irish Republic from the Commonwealth, the Westminster parliament provided in the Ireland Act, 1949 (12, 13, & 14 Geo. 6. c. 41) that Northern Ireland remains a part of His Majesty's Dominions and will not cease to be such without the consent of the Northern Ireland parliament. The extent to which the Westminster parliament has bound itself by this declaration may be a matter for argument, but at the very least the Mother of Parliaments recognized in this statute that the surviving twin of the Act of 1920 had developed into a mature adult.

JUDICIAL REVIEW OF NORTHERN IRELAND LEGISLATION

An innovation introduced by the Act of 1920 was that the courts had to consider the validity of legislation passed by a parliament in the United Kingdom. Up to 1921 the Privy Council had to determine the validity of Dominion and colonial legislation; from 1921 the validity of Northern Ireland legislation may be referred to

the Privy Council or it may arise for decision by the House of Lords
on appeal from the Northern Ireland courts. So far only a bare
dozen of such cases have appeared in the reports, but they are of
interest in a Commonwealth context in two ways, for they deal with
the distribution of legislative power and restrictions on the exercise
of such power, both matters frequently before the Privy Council.

Taking first the distribution of legislative power, it has been held
in *Hunter v. McKinley*, [1923] 2 I.R. 165 that the Northern Ireland parliament had no power to bar a police constable from voting
at an election for the United Kingdom parliament, and in *Morton
v. Air Ministry*, [1946] N.I. 136 it was decided that the words of
a Northern Ireland act relating to employment by public authorities
cannot be construed so as to apply to Crown servants employed by
the Air Ministry. These cases raise questions as to the "aspect" of
Northern Ireland legislation, the severability of valid and invalid
provisions, and the extent to which Northern Ireland legislation
may affect the powers vested in Westminster and Whitehall; all
of these are similar to matters with which Canada and Australia
are much concerned.

Also, Northern Ireland legislation regulating the sale of milk,
challenged by milk producers in the Irish Free State, has been upheld in *R. (Alexander) v. Minister of Agriculture for Northern Ireland* (1935, unreported) on the ground that it related solely to
Northern Ireland, and in *Gallagher v. Lynn*, [1937] A.C. 863 on
the ground that its primary purpose was the regulation of milk
supplies in Northern Ireland, not the prohibition of trade in milk
with areas outside Northern Ireland. The latter decision was one of
the House of Lords, and is important because Lord Atkin equated
Northern Ireland, in the matter of distribution of legislative power,
with the Canadian legislatures; *Gallagher v. Lynn* has passed into
the category of decisions used by the Privy Council in determining
the "pith and substance" of impugned legislation, being specifically
recognized as relevant in *Shannon v. Lower Mainland Dairy Prod-
ucts Board*, [1938] A.C. 708. Yet another case from Northern
Ireland, decided on a reference to the Privy Council under s. 51
of the Act of 1920, shows how that body determined the character
of a challenged tax, by the comparative analysis of the Act of 1920
and the legislation in question (*In re a Reference under the Govern-*

ment of Ireland Act, 1920 and s. 3 of the Finance Act (Northern Ireland) 1934, [1936] A.C. 352). All these decisions are well in the mainstream of Commonwealth precedent.

As for cases relating to constitutional prohibitions, the ban on religious discrimination has been invoked only once, and then unsuccessfully, in *Londonderry County Council v. McGlade*, [1929] N.I. 47. Significantly, the enactment impugned dealt with education, a subject which has given rise to Canadian litigation, such as *Roman Catholic Separate Schools Trustees v. R.*, [1928] A.C. 363. The cases on "taking property without compensation" have been relatively more numerous, and mainly concerned with the creation of a state-operated transport system. It was held in *O'Neill v. Northern Ireland Road Transport Board*, [1938] N.I. 104 that payment in stock is sufficient compensation for the transfer of a private operator's undertaking, and in *Ulster Transport Authority v. James Brown and Sons Ltd.*, [1953] N.I. 79 it was decided that restrictions on the operation of certain types of transport business amount to a taking of the property of such operators. This last case is particularly interesting, because it is paralleled by a decision of the Supreme Court of India, which in *Saghir Ahmed v. State of Uttar Pradesh*, A.I.R. 1954 S.C. 728 held that the creation of a transport monopoly in the State of Uttar Pradesh deprived private operators of property and was therefore contrary to Art. 31 of the 1950 Constitution.

In sum, while Northern Ireland legislation has been invalidated on only two occasions—in 1923 and 1953—the challenges which have been made have not merely emphasized the distinctiveness of the Northern Ireland Constitution; they have also shown their value in making comparisons with other parts of the Commonwealth, where similar problems are raised and comparable conclusions reached.

A SUMMARY OF NORTHERN IRELAND'S POSITION

This summary of the Constitution of Northern Ireland and its development has sought to show a novel situation—the creation of a subordinate legislature inside the United Kingdom—and its development with the aid of Commonwealth precedents, both statutory and judicial. Identical with no other Commonwealth constitution, but bearing traces of several, as well as of previous Home Rule

Bills, the Act of 1920 has survived both direct amendment and the preservation and extension of the local parliament's powers.   Enthusiasts for legislative devolution, such as those in Scotland, have often relied on the Act of 1920 as a precedent, though the Balfour Report on Scottish Affairs (1954, Cmd. 9212) suggested that similar provision for Scotland would "inevitably reduce the prestige and standing of Scotland and her representatives in Parliament at Westminster, and would thereby weaken her voice in British and world affairs."   On the other hand the Government of Wales Bill, a private member's measure rejected by the Westminster House of Commons in 1955, was largely modeled on the Act of 1920.

Outside the United Kingdom the Constitution of Northern Ireland provides interesting contrasts with those of the Canadian provinces and the Australian states; and recent proposals for the integration of Malta with the United Kingdom made specific reference to Northern Ireland's relations with Westminster (1955, Cmd. 9657).   Despite the fact that the Northern Ireland parliament is technically a subordinate one in an otherwise unitary state, the relations between Belfast and London have led to the federal precedents becoming relevant, and to judicial recognition of the quasi-federal relationship.   As Lord Thankerton remarked during the *Finance Act* case in 1936, "This Government of Northern Ireland has a sovereign Parliament except in so far as certain matters are reserved."   And an academic commentator has remarked some years ago that

> Within seven months of its coming into effect the Government of Ireland Act, 1920, was a legislative ruin, but sufficient remained of that ruin to provide a constitution for Northern Ireland which has endured for twenty-five years and which, with minor repairs and running adjustments, is capable of giving good service for a century or two to come.[5]

II. The Constitution of the Irish Free State

Although the Government of Ireland Act, 1920 formed, and continues to form, the basis of constitutional government in Northern Ireland, it had a very brief effective life in Southern Ireland.   The reason for this was that the First Dáil (which had been formed by the Sinn Féin party after the 1918 elections to the Westminster

---

[5] Francis Headon Newark, "The Constitution of Northern Ireland: The First Twenty-Five Years," *Northern Ireland Legal Quarterly*, VIII (1948), 52, 54.

parliament) resolved to treat the elections under the 1920 Act as elections to a second Dáil, which accordingly met on August 16, 1921. The official parliament of Southern Ireland met only on two occasions, and then only for the transaction of formal business. Naturally, it was not attended by the Sinn Féin members, and it was eventually dissolved on May 22, 1922, by a proclamation issued by the Lord Lieutenant under the Irish Free State (Agreement) Act, 1922 (12 & 13 Geo. 5, c. 4).

Meanwhile the Second Dáil had approved the Treaty, as had the "meeting summoned for the purpose of members elected to sit in the House of Commons for Southern Ireland." This meeting had also appointed the Provisional government authorized by Art. 17 of the Treaty, which continued to function as well as the Second Dáil. While the Dáil had resolved on May 22, 1922, to make provision for election to a Third Dáil, it was the Provisional government and the Lord Lieutenant who, five days later, set in motion the machinery for holding elections to the Provisional parliament which had been authorized by the Westminster Act. Thus there was a characteristic ambivalence in the status of the Provisional parliament. It derived from a United Kingdom enactment, but it also regarded itself as Dáil Eireann.

Immediately it was set up in January, 1922, the Provisional government took steps towards the drafting of a constitution by the appointment of a committee for the purpose. Perhaps some day the full story of what took place in the course of drafting, and in discussions with the British government, will be told. The draft which had been agreed on was published in June, just before the elections to the Provisional parliament. Subsequently the constitution committee compiled and published a collection of constitutions for the information of the Provisional parliament. These constitutions range from the post-1918 constitutions of Yugoslavia, Poland, Austria, Esthonia, Czechoslovakia, and Germany, back to that of the United States, so that the Irish document had two kinds of precedents— those of the older Dominions as well as those of European and American countries.

The dualism of the Provisional parliament-cum-Third Dáil appears in the document which finally emerged from it as the Constitution of the Irish Free State. "Dáil Eireann" the constituent act ran, "sitting as a Constituent Assembly in this Provisional Parliament, acknowledging that all lawful authority comes from God to the people and in the confidence that the National life and unity of Ireland shall thus be restored, hereby proclaims the establishment of the Irish Free State (otherwise called Saorstát Eireann) and in the exercise of undoubted right, decrees and enacts as follows." The first emphasis is laid on the Irish institution, the next on its constitution-making function, and the final reference to the recently constituted Provisional parliament. There is an echo here (though doubtless an unconscious one) of the medieval description of "the King in his Council in his Parliament," with the difference that there three institutions were mentioned, while in 1922 three different titles were given to the one body. Clearly there was room for divergent opinions on the origin of the Constitution.

For the purposes of comparison, however, the 1922 Constitution may be set against the constitutions of the older members of the Commonwealth—Canada and Australia, New Zealand and South Africa; such a contrast shows how great was the Irish divergence in 1922. Also, it was the later Irish Constitution of 1937 which was used as a model by the Asian democracies, so that comparisons with the more recent Commonwealth constitutions may be postponed for the moment. The external aspects of the 1922 Constitution were mentioned in the chapter on Ireland and the Commonwealth (*supra*); so the present description will be confined to the internal structure.

THE OPENING CLAUSES OF THE 1922 CONSTITUTION

Apart from the first article, conferring Dominion status on Ireland, under the title of the Irish Free State, the opening articles of the 1922 Constitution indicate clearly the nature of the new State. For instance, Art. 2 declared that "All powers of government and all authority legislative, executive, and judicial in Ireland, are derived from the people of Ireland," and were to be exercised through the constitutional organizations. This declaration of the origin of popular power is wider than that contained in the United States Constitution, and was therefore even further away from the constitutions of the older Dominions. Legislative sovereignty was subject to the provisions of the Treaty, and the shadow of the Westminster parliament loomed large in 1922, but the vesting of power in the

Irish people was complete, and it was acknowledged in the Westminster statute-book.

Another innovation was contained in Art. 3, conferring citizenship of the Irish Free State on certain persons, including those domiciled in "the area of the Irish Free State . . . at the time of coming into operation of this Constitution," a phrase pregnant with complexities. At that time, separate Commonwealth citizenship was to be found only in Canada, under 1910 legislation which had only limited effect; but in the Irish Free State citizenship was, under Art. 14 of the Constitution, the basis of electoral rights, a principle which did not apply in other parts of the Commonwealth until South Africa adopted it in 1931.[6]

The fourth article of the 1922 Constitution provided that Irish should be the national language of the Irish Free State, but that English should be equally recognized as an official language. In its wording it differed from s. 137 of the South Africa Act, 1909 (9 Edw. 7, c. 9) under which English and Dutch were both to be official languages, treated equally and given equal freedom rights and privileges. While official status and equality were conferred on the English language in the Irish Free State, the position of Irish as the national language was stressed.

Art. 5 also showed how the Irish Free State differed from the Dominions to whose company she was admitted. This article provided that the approval or advice of the Executive Council were necessary before any title of honor could be conferred on a Free State citizen in respect of services rendered in or in relation to the Irish Free State. This differs from Article 1, Section 9 of the United States Constitution in that the executive, rather than the legislature, is given control, but it is significant that the prima facie link is with a republican constitution rather than those of the Commonwealth countries, in which the Crown is the fountain of honor.

Thus the opening provisions of the 1922 Constitution give some pointers to its general tenor; this is brought out even more strongly in some of the succeeding sections.

FUNDAMENTAL RIGHTS

There is another strong link with the United States Constitution

[6] *Cf.* John Mervyn Jones, *British Nationality Law and Practice* (Oxford, 1947), 252-267.

in the next half dozen articles, setting out the rights enjoyed by persons in the Irish Free State. Art. 6 provided that "The liberty of the person is inviolable, and no person shall be deprived of his liberty except in accordance with law." It set out a method of challenging detention but included a saving clause (which had not been in the published draft constitution) for military acts in time of war and armed rebellion. The eighteenth-century struggle for the enactment of an Irish Habeas Corpus Act, which did not succeed until 1782, over a hundred years after it had been passed in England, was evidently not forgotten when the 1922 Constitution was being drafted. The other countries of the Commonwealth might rely on the ordinary law, but for the Irish Free State this right was declared to be a basic one, as was the inviolability of the citizen's dwelling, which under Art. 7 was not to be entered except in accordance with law.

Under Art. 8, freedom of conscience and religion were guaranteed, "subject to public order and morality," and there followed a number of prohibitions on religious discrimination, repeating Art. 16 of the Treaty and resembling s. 5 of the Government of Ireland Act, 1920. The nearest comparison was with s. 116 of the Australian Constitution, which likewise prohibited the establishing of any religion and the imposition of religious tests, though the Irish prohibition went further, extending to education. In this, s. 93 of the British North America Act, 1867 (30 & 31 Vict. c. 3) was comparable but more restricted. The Irish article also prohibited the diversion of religious property except for public utility purposes on payment of compensation, but nothing like the general restriction on the taking of property without compensation, which appeared in s. 5 of the Act of 1920, was included.

Art. 9 guaranteed the right to free expression of opinion, to assemble peaceably and without arms, and to form associations and unions. These rights were not to be exercised "for purposes opposed to public morality" and the second and third might be regulated by laws which contained no political, religious, or class distinction. Art. 10 gave a positive right to free elementary education.

This group of fundamental rights in the forefront of the Constitution were supplemented by others in later articles. In Art. 43 the legislature was prevented from enacting ex post facto legislation dealing with offenses, by Art. 70 trial "in due course of law" was guaranteed and the jurisdiction of military tribunals restricted, while Art. 72 provided that, except for minor offenses and offenses against military law, trial should be by jury. The latter article resembles s. 80 of the Australian Constitution, which is, however, rather closer to the Sixth Amendment to the United States Constitution than the Irish article, which appears to come from the opening words of the Fifth Amendment to the United States document.

In sum, the desire for a "Bill of Rights" inspired the draftsmen of the Irish Free State Constitution to follow the constitutional system across the Atlantic rather than that on the other side of the Irish Sea, from which the Irish system itself derived. In following the American precedent the Irish Free State went further in the express declaration of fundamental rights. With some minor exceptions the other Dominions relied on the ordinary law, while the Irish Free State preferred to incorporate these rights into her fundamental law.

THE LEGISLATURE

The Commonwealth pattern was more apparent in the composition of the legislative institutions of the Irish Free State. By Art. 12 the legislature, the Oireachtas, was to be composed of the King, a Chamber of Deputies which was given the familiar name of Dáil Eireann, and a Senate, Seanad Eireann. Apparently on a suggestion made by Berriedale Keith, the Oireachtas was given the sole power of making laws for the peace, order, and good government of the Irish Free State, thus importing a phrase traditional in the constitutional law of the Commonwealth.[7]

There were, however, some differences of detail between the way in which this bicameral Irish legislature was constituted and the setting-up of those of the older Dominions. For instance, the principle to be used in elections to the Dáil was to be that of proportional representation (Art. 26). The Senate was not to be nominated, as in Canada, but entirely elected, as in Australia, and was to be composed of sixty persons holding office for twelve years, fifteen retiring every three years. The candidates were to be proposed, on the ground of useful public service or special qualifications or attainments, as to two-thirds by the Dáil and as to the remaining

[7] Cf. Journal of Comparative Legislation and International Law (3d Series), V (1923), Part I, 121.

third by the Senate. From this panel, three times as large as the number of Senate vacancies, Senators were to be elected by citizens over the age of thirty (Arts. 14, 31-33). These provisions were fated to be the subject of considerable alteration.

Again, the privileges of members of, and reports of proceedings in, the Oireachtas were not linked with the corresponding privileges at Westminster, nor were they left to declaratory legislation, but were incorporated in the Constitution, as were general provisions about the conduct of business in each House (Arts. 18-23, 25). The Oireachtas did, however, resemble the Canadian, Australian, and South African parliaments in providing, in Art. 24, that there should be at least one session in each year. Likewise, the Dáil was placed in a position resembling that of the Canadian House of Commons, the Australian House of Representatives, and the South African House of Assembly in regard to money bills; but the Dáil's position was stronger in that if it rejected the Senate's recommendations, or if the Senate did not pass the money bill within twenty-one days of receiving it, the bill as passed by the Dáil was deemed to have been passed by both Houses of the Oireachtas. The Senate could delay ordinary bills (not financial or emergency measures) for a nine-month period, after which the Dáil's version could become law (Arts. 35 and 38). As for disagreements between the two Houses, the method of joint sitting was to be used only for debate, not for decision (Art. 38). In this the Oireachtas differed from the Australian and South African parliaments, where joint sittings may be decisive; the Canadian precedent of appointing additional senators was not followed.

In short, the Dominion pattern was altered to form a new pattern which, it was thought, would best fit the new circumstances. This was shown by the granting of franchise rights, the declaration of powers and privileges, and the predominant position given to the Dáil. The use of proportional representation and the composition of the Senate show how it was sought to combine popular representation with some safeguard for minority interests, though the latter would have liked a second chamber on the lines of that contemplated for Southern Ireland by the Government of Ireland Act, 1920, consisting of some ex-officio and some indirectly elected members. But it will appear that much time and thought have been spent on the composition of the Dublin Senate with diverse results illustrative of the complexity of the problem of constructing a satisfactory second chamber in a unitary state.

THE EXECUTIVE

Under Art. 51 executive authority was declared to vest in the King. This article made specific reference to the "law, practice and constitutional usage governing the exercise of the Executive Authority in the Dominion of Canada, by the Representative of the Crown." The specific reference to Canada was novel, but has recently been paralleled by the Ceylon Constitution which, by s. 4(2), applies the "constitutional conventions applicable to the exercise of similar powers, authorities and functions . . . by His Majesty."

The Governor-General was to be advised by an Executive Council of not less than five, nor more than seven Ministers. In the important matter of the dissolution of the Dáil the Governor-General was generally bound to act on the advice of the Executive Council. In the appointment of a person corresponding to the Prime Minister, the Governor-General was also restricted, for the President of the Executive Council had to be nominated by the Dáil. Also, the President nominated the other Ministers who were to comprise the Executive Council, but the Dáil had to assent to these nominations and if the Executive Council ceased to retain the support of the majority of the Dáil the Ministers had to resign, though by Art. 53 the Governor-General was not forced to act on the advice to dissolve the Oireachtas given by such a Council. Here again conventional practices were declared or modified, but an even better example of the declaration of a convention appeared in Art. 54 under which the Executive Council was to act collectively and be collectively responsible. By Art. 37 the Executive Council was specifically given the task of recommending the appropriation of money to the Governor-General.

Another innovation was the provision for appointment of Ministers not members of the Executive Council. By Arts. 55 and 56 they were to be recommended by an impartial Dáil Committee, nominated by the Dáil and appointed by the Governor-General, but responsible to and removable by the Dáil. The total number of Ministers—both the members of the Executive Council and the "extern Ministers" as they were called—was not to exceed twelve.

Thus both in relation to Cabinet and non-Cabinet Ministers the 1922 Constitution introduced innovations; for the former the general Canadian precedent was accompanied by a number of specific declarations, while the introduction of the latter marked an attempt to depart from traditional conceptions of cabinet government.

The fourth element in the 1922 Constitution was the judiciary, which has been described in the chapter on Legal History (*supra*).

REFERENDUM, INITIATIVE, AND AMENDMENT

The fifth main element in the 1922 Constitution had no counterpart in the constitutions of Canada, Australia, or South Africa.

By Art. 47 provision was made for the suspension for ninety days, on the written demand of two-fifths of the Dáil or a majority of the Senate, of a bill passed or deemed to have been passed by the Oireachtas. The purpose was to enable a proposal for a referendum to be made by three-fifths of the Senate or a twentieth of the registered voters. There were two exceptions to these provisions, both of them based on obvious necessity; the suspension of money bills was not permitted, nor could the referendum procedure be applied "to such Bills as shall be declared by both Houses to be necessary for the immediate preservation of the public peace, health or safety." With these exceptions, minority interests in the Dáil, or a majority in the upper house could, as some of their European counterparts were able to do, insure that a popular opinion was obtained on any measure, for the majority of the votes recorded on the referendum was to be conclusive of the decision of the people. This was a considerable inroad on the normal principles of parliamentary representation.

An even greater inroad on these principles was made by the succeeding article of the Constitution, Art. 48. This enabled the Oireachtas to make provision for the initiation by the people of laws or constitutional amendments: if the Oireachtas did not do so within two years, a petition by the voters could result either in legislation for initiation proposals or in a referendum. If initiation legislation was passed, proposals were to be made on a petition of fifty thousand registered voters, proposals rejected by the Oireachtas were to be submitted to a referendum, and proposals accepted were to be regarded as ordinary legislation. As Dr. Leo Kohn remarked of this elaborate procedure, "Despite the patent reluctance of the

Constituent Assembly to sanction the immediate introduction of the Initiative, the provisions adopted went further than those of almost any of its Continental models in enabling an extra-parliamentary system of legislation to be set up."[8]   Thus not only were the Dominion precedents exceeded, but even the Continental provisions were surpassed in this endeavor to insure the predominance of popular opinion.

In the use of the referendum for amendments of the Constitution the Irish Free State resembled Australia rather than Canada or South Africa.   In 1922 Canada had to look to Westminster for amendments of the 1867 Act, while South Africa, then as now, had to comply with the "entrenched sections" of the 1909 Act.   In Australia, by s. 128 of the Constitution, an absolute majority of each House was generally required, invariably followed by a referendum. By Art. 50 of the Irish Free State Constitution amendments "within the terms of the Scheduled Treaty" could be made by the Oireachtas in the ordinary way within a period of eight years, after which the suspensory and referendum provisions of Art. 47 were to apply, and the fate of an amendment would be determined by a majority of the registered voters or by two-thirds of the votes cast. Thus for a period the Irish Free State resembled South Africa in its power to make direct amendments, but later the Australian referendum system was to be used.   Once again the eclectic nature of the 1922 Constitution is apparent.

THE INAUGURATION OF THE 1922 CONSTITUTION

Art. 81 of the 1922 Constitution conferred on the Constituent Assembly, for a one-year period, the powers of the Dáil under the Constitution.   The first Senate was constituted by December 8, 1922, so that the legislative element of the Constitution was brought into being.   The first Governor-General to be appointed was the former Irish Nationalist member of the Westminster House of Commons, T. M. Healy.   Under Art. 75 the then existing courts were continued in existence, and so remained until the judicial system was recast by the Courts of Justice Act, 1924 (No. 10 of 1924).   With these three main bodies the Irish Free State was ready to function.

Both in the Dublin statute-book and in the reports of cases decided by the Dublin courts it is possible to trace something of the

[8] *The Constitution of the Irish Free State* (London, 1932), 241-242.

turbulent history of the Provisional government and parliament and of the inheritance into which the bodies set up under the 1922 Constitution entered. For instance, the powers of the Provisional parliament to take military measures to deal with the euphemistically termed "troubles" were challenged by way of habeas corpus but were upheld on the ground that a state of war existed, in which military measures were the only possible steps which could be taken. (*R. (Childers) v. Adjutant-General of the Forces of the Irish Provisional Government*, [1923] 1 I.R. 5; *R. (Johnstone) v. O'Sullivan*, [1923] 2 I.R. 13.) As mentioned in the chapter on Legal History (*supra*), legislation was necessary to provide for the winding-up of the Dáil courts. Again, in the Dáil Eireann Loans and Funds Act (No. 3 of 1924) provision was made in respect of the finances of the first and second Dáils. Another transitional matter, discussed in the chapters on International Law (*supra*) and on Administrative Law (*infra*), was the succession of the Irish Free State government to both the Provisional government and (in the view of the Irish courts) to the governments responsible to previous Dáils.

In all the circumstances, it is not surprising that the development of the 1922 Constitution should be uneven, for the new authorities could hardly expect constitutional development to proceed in an orderly way when so much unconstitutional development had taken place. For this reason the treatment of fundamental rights by the legislature and the courts is of special interest.

THE METHOD OF AMENDMENT

In considering the development of the 1922 Constitution the method of amendment is vital. If Art. 50 of the Constitution had remained unamended, the period for the making of amendments by way of ordinary legislation would have expired on December 5, 1930. However, Amendment No. 16 (made by Act No. 10 of 1929) extended this period for a further eight years, to 1938. This extension was challenged in the leading case on the 1922 Constitution, *The State (Ryan) v. Lennon*, [1935] I.R. 170, where both the High Court and the majority of the Supreme Court (Kennedy C. J. dissenting) held that such an amendment was intra vires the Oireachtas under Art. 50. One can only speculate on what would have happened if the original eight-year period had not been extended, for it is possible that the constitutional amendments of the 1930's would not have been accomplished so easily if the referendum procedure had been applied to them.

Another amendment of Art. 50 which was upheld in *Ryan's* case was made in 1928 by Amendment No. 10 (No. 8 of 1928). This removed constitutional amendments from the suspensory provisions of Art. 47, so that there was no possibility of a referendum being held. Constitutional amendments were not, however, the only enactments affected by Amendment No. 10, for both the referendum and the initiation procedure were deleted altogether, thus removing one of the distinguishing features of the 1922 Constitution—the element of direct popular control.

An attempt to use the suspensory and referendum procedure was made by the Dáil in 1927, but it was not followed by the necessary Senate resolution or voters' petition. In the following year a petition for the exercise of the initiative (with a view to abolishing the Oath in Art. 17) was signed but not formally presented. The Bill for Amendment No. 10 was then introduced, so that both the referendum for ordinary legislation and the provision for direct legislation disappeared from the Constitution before either had been used. In this respect the Irish Free State veered away from the Continental practice and moved back to the Commonwealth conception of representative government.[9]

The restoration of the referendum for constitutional amendments during the initial period was sought in 1934, when the abolition of the Senate was contemplated, but Amendment No. 25 never became law, being passed by the Senate but not considered by the Dáil. Another projected amendment of the 1922 Constitution which failed to become law, Amendment No. 19, introduced in 1933, was designed to reduce the Senate's delaying power from eighteen months to three; it was first postponed and later rejected by the Senate, but was never resolved by the Dáil to be enacted.[10]

FUNDAMENTAL RIGHTS

The aspect of the 1922 Constitution most frequently made the

[9] *Cf.* Donal O'Sullivan, *The Irish Free State and its Senate* (London, 1940), 219, 228-230.
[10] *Cf.* O'Sullivan, *op. cit. supra* note 9 at 410-411, 350-353.

subject of litigation was the declaration of fundamental rights. The exercise of these was declared to be qualified, but the various enactments passed by the Oireachtas for the preservation of public safety show the way in which a newly created constitution may be subjected to considerable strain because of the activities of those opposed to it, and the measures taken to deal with them. Naturally, these measures were challenged, usually by way of habeas corpus.

The very first Public Safety (Emergency Powers) Act, in 1923 (No. 28 of 1923), was challenged on the ground that it received the Royal Assent on the day on which it was passed, whereas an interval of seven days should have elapsed to allow for a possible suspension under Art. 47, since there was no declaration that the Bill was necessary for the preservation of the public peace, health, or safety. The challenge was upheld in *R. (O'Brien) v. Governor of Military Internment Camp and Minister for Defence*, [1924] I I.R. 32, and the defect speedily remedied by the passing of a second Act (No. 29 of 1923) containing the necessary declaration and scheduling the Act which had been impugned.

In 1924 the Public Safety (Powers of Arrest and Detention) Act (No. 1 of 1924) and the Public Safety (Punishment of Offenders) Temporary Act (No. 15 of 1924) re-enacted the provisions of the 1923 Act relating to powers of arrest and detention, and the punishment of offenses. The former could be exercised by a member of the Executive Council on such grounds as military necessity or public safety, or (for lesser periods) by the military or civil authorities on suspicion of the commission of certain scheduled offenses. Appeal Councils to advise on detention were constituted, and punishments specified for offenses ranging from armed revolt to arson. These Acts were to last only for a year, but the first was challenged in *R. (O'Connell) v. Military Governor of Hare Park Camp*, [1924] 2 I.R. 104. It was upheld on the ground that within its jurisdiction the Oireachtas was unrestricted and that there was nothing in the Constitution to prohibit an enactment authorizing the detention of untried persons, though Pim J. based his judgment on the ground that the Act was a temporary one, made in abnormal times.

Next in order of enactment was the Public Safety (Emergency Powers) Act, 1926 (No. 42 of 1926), which authorized the Executive

Council to proclaim an emergency, subject to revocation by a resolution of the Dáil or Senate within five days. Powers of arrest and detention were given for a number of offenses, from the overthrow of the government by violence to causing unlawful injury to land. In the following year the Public Safety Act (No. 31 of 1927), which was to last for five years, introduced a new provision. By s. 3 so much of the Act as contravened the Constitution was to be treated as an amendment of the Constitution—the converse of the usual severability clause. Another innovation was the power to declare certain associations unlawful and to penalize their members. By a proclamation (revocable by Dáil or Senate) special courts could be set up to try scheduled offenses. This Act was to last for five years but was repealed the following year; it was upheld in *Attorney-General v. McBride*, [1928] I. R. 451 on the ground that it was an amendment "by way of ordinary legislation" of Art. 6 of the Constitution, guaranteeing liberty of the person, though the method of amendment was criticized.

The direct method of amendment was used by Amendment No. 17, which inserted a lengthy Article 2A in the Constitution (No. 37 of 1931). This could be brought into force by a proclamation of the Executive Council, and while in force every section of the Constitution was to be read subject to it. It provided for a Constitution (Special Powers) Tribunal, composed of military members, with power to try persons for treasonable offenses, membership of unlawful associations, etc. and to impose the death penalty, if necessary. Special powers of arrest, detention, examination, and search were granted to the police, membership of unlawful associations was prohibited, and power was given to proclaim meetings. In short, this was a considerable encroachment, for the preservation of public safety, on fundamental rights. The very place in which it was inserted in the Constitution was indicative of the area of encroachment.

Once again it is *Ryan's* case which provides authority for the validity of the Amendment, though clearly the Supreme Court were not enamored of the provisions; in that case it was held that, since the Amendment was valid, prohibition would not issue to the Tribunal. But to insure that the Tribunal acted in accordance with the Article, both certiorari and habeas corpus orders were made against it. (*In re the application of O'Duffy*, [1934] I.R. 550; *The State*

(Hughes) v. Lennon, [1935] I.R. 128; *The State (Quinlan) v. Kavanagh,* [1935] I.R. 249.)

From this description of the various public safety measures it will be seen that various devices have been used in their enforcement—the necessity for a proclamation, the "unspecified amendment" clause, the direct and overriding amendment. In the result the fundamental rights of freedom of the person, inviolability of the dwelling, freedom to associate, and trial by jury were considerably restricted. But it will be remembered that these rights were not given in unqualified form in the Constitution; as O'Byrne J. put it in *O'Duffy's* case, there was no inconsistency between Art. 6 of the Constitution and the new Art. 2A (Amendment No. 17; No. 37 of 1931) save that the latter enlarged the methods whereby a person may be lawfully detained. While Art. 2A stood, the judges were prepared to use their powers to insure that its terms were strictly followed, so that the "due course of law" was followed even where that law contained special provisions not normally encompassed within that phrase. But in the last resort, if there was a conflict between the liberty of the person and a constitutional provision for the preservation of public safety, it was the latter which would prevail over the former.

THE SENATE AND ITS RELATIONS WITH THE DÁIL

The vicissitudes of *The Irish Free State and its Senate* have been described by its former clerk, Dr. Donal O'Sullivan, in a volume with that title; it is a detailed study of Irish life in the 1920's and 1930's, with special reference to the part played by the Irish Free State Senate. That body did not last as long as the 1922 Constitution, being abolished in 1936, but it was the cause of some important amendments in that document.

Thus Amendment No. 1, made in 1925 (No. 30 of 1925), was necessitated by the first triennial election to the Senate held in that year. Likewise the second triennial election, in 1928, produced a number of substantial alterations. By Amendment No. 6 (No. 13 of 1928) the system of direct election was abolished, and the members of the Dáil and Senate were constituted the electoral college; Amendment No. 7 (No. 30 of 1928) reduced the normal term of office to nine years, while Amendment No. 8 (No. 27 of 1928) reduced the age of eligibility for candidates to thirty years, and Amendment No. 9 left to ordinary legislation the formation of the panel of candidates (No. 28 of 1928). In the following year, 1929, Amendment No. 11 made provision for the filling of casual vacancies (No. 34 of 1929). This was to be the last of the amendments affecting the composition of the Senate until its abolition in 1936, which was brought about by tension between the two Houses as a result of the Senate's use of its suspensory power.

The Senate's suspensory power stemmed from Art. 38 of the Constitution, by which the Senate could delay for two hundred and seventy days an ordinary bill sent by the Dáil. In 1928 Amendment No. 13 (No. 14 of 1928) extended the suspensory period to eighteen months, after which the Dáil could present the bill again to the Senate, which had sixty days in which to deal with it; if agreement was not reached the Dáil could resolve that the bill become law. This amendment also abolished the possibility of joint sittings for debates on disputed measures. Among the enactments affected by the Senate's delaying power were the Constitution (Removal of Oath) Bill of 1932, a 1933 bill to reduce the period of the Senate's suspensory power to three months, and two measures in 1934—one to abolish university representation in the Dáil, the other to abolish the Senate itself. It is significant that while the suspensory power was used only three times before 1932, it was used eight times in the following four years.

As regards money bills, Amendment No. 12 in 1930 (No. 5 of 1930) made alterations in the procedure for determining, under Art. 35 of the Constitution, whether or not a bill was a money bill as respects which the Senate's powers were limited to recommendation and delay for a maximum of twenty-one days. Under Art. 35 as amended a quarter of the Senate members or two-fifths of the Dáil could require a reference to a Committee of Privileges, whose decision was final. This procedure was invoked only once, in 1935, when the Committee was constituted at the request of the Dáil, sat under the chairmanship of Kennedy C. J., and decided (on his casting vote) that the relevant enactment was a money bill.[11]

In the following year, on May 29, 1936, the Constitution (Amendment No. 24) Bill eventually became law (No. 18 of 1936),

[11] O'Sullivan, *op. cit. supra* note 9 at 522-524.

and the Senate of the Irish Free State was abolished by the simple device of altering Art. 12 of the Constitution to read ". . . [the Oireachtas] shall consist of the King and one House, the Chamber of Deputies. . . ." During the thirteen years of its existence the Senate initiated some twenty-five measures (ten of which became law), functioned as an active revising chamber, made a number of recommendations on money bills, and exercised its suspensory power on eleven occasions, eight of which resulted in bills becoming law without the Senate's concurrence.[12] While the alteration of the composition and powers of the Senate involved modifications of the framework of the 1922 Constitution, the abolition of the Senate was a somewhat drastic method of settling the difficulties arising from the use of the delaying powers. But the Irish experiment in unicameralism was shortlived and an upper house of the same name, but elected in a different way, was an integral part of the 1937 Constitution.

THE DÁIL AND THE EXECUTIVE COUNCIL

Apart from the question of its relations with the Senate, the main changes affecting the Dáil concerned its duration and the inclusion of university representatives. Amendment No. 4 (No. 5 of 1927) extended the four-year period of the Dáil's life to six "or such shorter period as may be fixed by legislation." Under the Electoral (Amendment) Act, 1927 (No. 21 of 1927) the maximum life of the Dáil was fixed at five years. As for the number of deputies, Art. 26 provided for this to be fixed by law, with a decennial revision to take effect on the subsequent dissolution. The Electoral Act, 1923 (No. 12 of 1923) accordingly fixed the number of members of the Dáil at one hundred and fifty-three. The Electoral (Revision of Constituencies) Act, 1935 (No. 5 of 1935) would have reduced this to one hundred and thirty-eight at the next dissolution. Coupled with this measure was the Constitution (Amendment No. 23) Bill, 1934, which was delayed by the Senate and did not become law until 1936 (No. 17 of 1936). This Amendment deleted Art. 27 of the Constitution, thus abolishing the right of the two universities existing in the Irish Free State in 1922— Dublin University and the National University of Ireland—to elect

---

[12] O'Sullivan, *op. cit. supra* note 9 at 605-628.

three members each to the Dáil. Once again the 1922 structure was drastically altered.

The Executive Council also underwent considerable alteration. In composition it was extended to a maximum of twelve members by Amendment No. 5 in 1927 (No. 13 of 1927) for the failure of the "extern Ministers" scheme was apparent. Two years later, by Amendment No. 15 (No. 9 of 1929) a new version of Art. 52 of the Constitution allowed one Minister of the Executive Council to be a member of the Senate; he could not, however, hold the offices of President, Vice-President, or Minister for Finance. As for functions, the Executive Council fell heir to the responsibilities of which the Governor-General was relieved in 1933, by Amendments No. 20 and 21 (No. 40 & 41 of 1933). An interesting feature of this legislation was that the chairman of the Dáil was designated as the person who should act on the advice of the Executive Council, as in the recommendation of financial legislation under Art. 37; and in the final batch of amendments made in 1936, it was the chairman of the Dáil who was given the task of summoning and dissolving the Oireachtas under Art. 24 and of signing legislation under Art. 41 and 42. In view of these provisions, Amendment No. 2, passed in 1927 (No. 6 of 1927), is relevant, for it provided for the automatic re-election of the retiring chairman of the Dáil, but the difficulty was that he would not be chairman until chosen by the members, who in their turn could not elect a chairman until summoned by a chairman. The demise of the 1922 Constitution prevented any difficulty arising, but the point is indicative of the speed with which the 1922 Constitution was altered in 1936, both in its internal structure and in its external activities.

A SUMMARY OF THE DEVELOPMENT OF THE 1922 CONSTITUTION

By the end of 1936 the Constitution of the Irish Free State was indeed "a thing of shreds and patches." One might have expected a Westminster statute, such as the Government of Ireland Act, 1920, to be subject to frequent modifications and alterations, but in its operation in Northern Ireland the main structure of that Act has remained unchanged, though the details have been modified in Northern Ireland's favor. In contrast, the basic elements of the Irish Free State's Constitution were radically altered. Provision was made in the Constitution itself for those circumstances of internal emergency which necessitated the making of inroads on fundamental rights, the relationships between the two Houses of the Oireachtas were modified, and then a unicameral system was instituted; the functions of the head of the new Dominion were first reduced and then abolished. Of the main elements of the Constitution, only the judiciary survived unscathed, and while the status of the courts was enhanced by the abolition of the appeal to the Privy Council, the application of their powers was limited by the detailed provisions of Art. 2A of the Constitution, inserted by Amendment No. 17 (No. 37 of 1931). Such novelties as the popular initiation of legislation and the appointment of "extern Ministers" disappeared, but the extension of the period for amending the Constitution shows that the preliminary stages of parliamentary amendment had not been passed, for evidently it was thought to be too soon to entrust the fate of amendments directly to public opinion. But clearly some changes were necessary when the Irish Free State accomplished in some sixteen years something which the United States has not yet achieved during the century and three-quarters of its existence—the passing of over two dozen amendments to the Constitution.

III. The 1937 Constitution of the Irish Republic

In 1937 the various Dominion constitutions had reached crucial stages in their respective developments. This was particularly noticeable in Canada, where the effect of the Privy Council's judgments restricting the rights of the Dominion parliament aroused critical comments. She was still twelve years away from the power of amendment conferred by the British North America (No. 2) Act, 1949 (12, 13 & 14 Geo. 6, c. 81). Australia was, then as now, beset by the problem of interstate trade, on which the Privy Council had in the previous year pronounced judgment in the case of *James v. Commonwealth of Australia*, [1936] A.C. 578. In addition, her attempts at altering the Constitution by referenda had succeeded in only four cases in the thirty-seven years of her existence. In South Africa in 1937 the case of *Ndlwana v. Hofmeyr*, [1937] A.D. 229 had decided that the effect of the Statute of Westminster was to override the "entrenched" sections of the South Africa Act, 1909. A further thirteen years were to elapse before the recent constitutional crisis laid bare the real nature of South African sovereignty and the manner in which South Africa's powers could be validly exercised. In New Zealand, a decade was to elapse before the passing of the New Zealand Constitution (Amendment) Act, 1947 (11 & 12 Geo. 6, c. 4) but there the Constitution functioned without any inherent difficulty which might at any time arise in the path of legislative development.

By contrast, in 1937 the Irish Free State, after no less than twenty-five amending statutes of constitutional importance, could argue that the power of constitutional amendment which she claimed had been recognized by the British courts. It is true that the decision in *Moore v. Attorney General for the Irish Free State*, [1935] A.C. 484 had been based on the view that the 1922 Constitution originated in an act of the Westminster parliament, which could be amended by the Dublin legislature after the passing of the Statute of Westminster. Yet the existence of the Privy Council decision gave added weight to the Irish Free State's view of her powers, although the reasoning behind the decision would not have found favor in the Dublin courts. Paradoxically those courts had themselves, in *The State (Ryan) v. Lennon*, [1935] I.R. 170 held that the terms of the Anglo-Irish Agreement of 1921 restricted the power to amend the 1922 Constitution. In these circumstances it is not surprising that the doctrine of the popular will was prayed in aid to authorize the making of a new constitution, and that the draft of the new fundamental document was not subjected to judicial scrutiny which might prove unfavorable. The draft constitution was approved by the Oireachtas (which at that time consisted only of the lower house, Dáil Eireann) and was, under the Plebiscite (Draft Constitution) Act, 1937 (No. 16 of 1937), submitted to a referendum at the same time as a general election was held in July 1937. It came into force on December 29, 1937, and under Art. 48 the 1922 Constitution was repealed as from that date.

While it bore certain resemblances to its 1922 predecessor, the 1937 Constitution is a fundamental document which stands by itself, and is interpreted in accordance with its own terms; the domination of the Treaty no longer exists. Again, while the 1937 Constitution resembles those of the older Dominions in some of its details, its general structure is very different from those based on acts of the Westminster parliament and the conventions of the British Constitution. But the most interesting comparisons which may be drawn are not with the constitutions of the older Dominions but with those of the newer members of the Commonwealth, where some of the Irish provisions appear with only verbal changes. It is against this background of change that the various provisions of the 1937 Constitution must be considered; not only was it a turning point in the constitutional development of the Irish Free State, it was also a new departure in constitutional trends within the Commonwealth.

THE PREAMBLE AND PRELIMINARY PROVISIONS

The distinguishing features of the Constitution are epitomized in the preamble and the opening articles. Just as the 1922 Constitution had stressed the divine and popular source of power, so the preamble to the 1937 document commenced "In the Name of the Most Holy Trinity, from Whom is all authority and to Whom, as our final end, all actions both of men and States must be referred." As an Irish commentator has pointed out, the Catholic Confederation which met in Kilkenny in 1642 had commenced its Articles of Confederation in similar fashion, so that the people of the Irish Free State in 1937 were following a native precedent almost three centuries old.[13] In the preamble there are, in addition, phrases which reflect both the stormy history of recent developments in Ireland and the general aims both implicit and expressed in this fundamental law. Phrases like the "heroic and unremitting struggle to regain the rightful independence of our Nation," "the common good," "the dignity and freedom of the individual," "the unity of our country" are, in their Irish context, redolent with memories of the past and pregnant with hopes for the future.

Likewise, the first article makes a claim which, in 1937, no other Dominion had incorporated in its fundamental law: this was an affirmation of the inalienable, indefeasible, and sovereign right of the Irish nation "to choose its own form of Government, to determine its relations with other nations, and to develop its life, political, economic and cultural, in accordance with its own genius and traditions." Several centuries of Irish history lie behind this affirmation

[13] Vincent Grogan, "The Constitution and Natural Law," *Christus Rex*, VIII (1954), 201, 207.

of right.   In the two succeeding articles, the events of more recent times are reflected, for while Art. 2 asserts that "the national territory consists of the whole island of Ireland, its islands and territorial seas," Art. 3 recognizes that "pending the re-integration of the national territory" and without prejudice to the right to exercise jurisdiction over the whole of the national territory, laws are to have the same area, extent, and extraterritorial application as those of the Irish Free State.   While de jure jurisdiction is claimed over the whole island, de facto jurisdiction does not extend to Northern Ireland and recognition of this state of affairs is embodied in the Constitution.

Having dealt generally with the nation, the Constitution next proceeds to deal with the position of the state.   It is named Eire or, in the English language, Ireland (Art. 4), a nomenclature which still gives rise to difficulty; it is declared to be sovereign, independent, and democratic (Art. 5).   It has two official languages (Irish being the first and English the second (Art. 8)); its citizenship is to be determined "in accordance with law" (Art. 9), and the natural resources within the jurisdiction are vested in the State (Art. 10). It was not until 1949, with the coming into force of the Republic of Ireland Act, 1948 (No. 22 of 1948) that the state was given the official description (but not, be it noted, the name) of the Republic of Ireland.

These preliminary articles relating to nation and state exhibit some characteristics of the Irish Constitution.   The reference to the divine origin of power is one, for it opens the door to the interpretation of the Constitution in accordance with natural law, such as Kennedy C. J. had suggested in *Ryan's* case was possible in construing the 1922 Constitution.   Next, the right to self-determination is specifically claimed and in Art. 6 it is declared (in terms similar to Art. 2 of the 1922 Constitution) that

All powers of government, legislative, executive and judicial, derive, under God, from the people, whose right it is to designate the rulers of the State and, in final appeal, to decide all questions of national policy, according to the requirements of the common good.

These powers are exercisable only by or on the authority of the organs of State established by the Constitution, so that popular power is not unrestricted but is channeled into constitutional forms.

While the provisions relating to the area of jurisdiction are peculiar to Ireland and the distinction between the Irish nation and the state more than a theoretical one, the claim to self-determination and the description of Ireland as a sovereign, independent, democratic state had echoes in the other parts of the Commonwealth. The loudest of these was in India, where the 1950 Constitution in the preamble declared India to be a sovereign democratic republic. But what was at most implicit in the Dominions constitutions in 1937 was made express in Eire.   Likewise the Indian Constitution declares its popular origin, but whereas the Indian people's will was expressed through the Constituent Assembly, the Irish referendum gave direct authority for the acceptance of the Constitution.   The authority for the adoption of the 1956 Pakistan Constitution was also a Constituent Asembly, and the state was declared to be "a democratic state based on Islamic principles of social justice."

Two other characteristic features of the Irish Constitution appear in phrases occurring in these opening articles.   One of these is the reference in Art. 6, 1 to the decision of national policy "according to requirements of the common good."   The common good is one of the principles on which the Constitution is based, and the protection given to fundamental rights is an application of the principle. The second phrase refers in Art. 9, 1, (2) to the future determination "in accordance with law" of Irish nationality and citizenship.

Many of the provisions of the Constitution contemplate their implementation by the ordinary legislative process, thus insuring flexibility of detail.   It is against this background of general principles that any analysis of the Constitution must be made.

THE PRESIDENT

There could hardly have been a greater example of divergence from the traditional conception of the Dominion constitution than the institution of the presidency of Eire.   Under the 1922 Constitution the position of the representative of the Crown had been greatly reduced in status and functions, and finally eliminated.   Under the 1937 Constitution the head of the state is the President.   By Art. 12 any Irish citizen of thirty-five years or over may, on the nomination of twenty members of the Oireachtas or by four county borough or county councils, be elected, by direct vote on the proportional representation system, President for a period of seven years. The President is eligible only once for re-election, a provision which preceded by some fourteen years the Twenty-second Amendment to the United States Constitution. No provision is made for a Vice-President, but where the President's incapacity is established (by the Supreme Court) or on his death, resignation, removal, or failure to act, a Commission may act under Art. 14. To assist the President there was constituted a Council of State consisting of certain Ministers and ex-Ministers, judges and ex-judges, and a maximum of seven members appointed by the President. The President is not responsible to the Oireachtas or any court, but he may be impeached before the Oireachtas (Arts. 12, 10 and 13, 8).

The direct election of the Irish President distinguishes this officer from appointed Governor-Generalships; and both the President of India, under Arts. 54 and 55 of the 1950 Constitution, and the President of Pakistan, under Art. 32 and the First Schedule of the 1956 Constitution, are selected indirectly by members of electoral colleges.

As head of state, the President is charged with the exercise of civil, military, and diplomatic functions (Arts. 12, 1; 13, 4 and 5). Generally, however, these functions must be exercised on the advice of the Government (Art. 13, 9); the President's absolute discretion is confined to such matters as the refusal of a dissolution to a Taoiseach (Prime Minister) with minority support (Art. 13, 2, (2)) and the appointment of additional members of the Council of State (Art. 31, 3). He must consult the Council of State before convening a meeting of either or both Houses of the Oireachtas (Art. 13, 2, (3)) or addressing the Oireachtas or the nation on matters of national or public importance, and these messages must be approved by the Government (Art. 13, 7). The Council of State must also be consulted on the settting up of a Committee of Privileges to determine whether legislation is a money bill (Art. 22, 2), and on the referring of bills to the Supreme Court (Art. 26, 1) or to the people (Art. 27, 4). Again in such matters as the appointment of the Taoiseach the President must act on the nomination of the Dáil (Art. 13, 1, (1)), while in the dissolution of the Dáil, the appointment and resignation of members of the Government, and the appointment of the Attorney-General he acts on the advice of the Taoiseach (Arts. 13, 2, (1); 13, 1, (2) & (3); 30, 2).

In comparison, the powers of the Indian and Pakistan Presidents are much wider than those of the Irish President. Under Art. 75 of the 1950 Constitution the Indian President has complete discretion in the choice of Prime Minister; Art. 37 of the 1956 Constitution provides that the Pakistan President has discretion to appoint a Prime Minister "most likely to command the confidence of the majority of the members of the National Assembly," to hold office during the President's pleasure. The President of India is advised by a Council of Ministers (1950 Constitution, Art. 74) and that of Pakistan by a Cabinet of Ministers (1956 Constitution, Art. 37 (1)), and Arts. 85 and 50 of the respective Constitutions give these Presidents power to summon, dissolve, and prorogue the respective legislatures. A point of importance is that both Art. 53 of the Indian Constitution and Art. 39 of the Pakistan Constitution vest executive authority in the respective Presidents, while the Irish President has no such power. In both India and Pakistan there is scope for the development of convention, while in the Irish Republic the President's powers are restricted and explicit. In 1937 only South Africa, in s. 4 of the Status of the Union Act, 1934 (No. 69), had sought to make the acceptance of advice obligatory, except in relation to appointment or dismissal of Ministers or of dissolution. While constitutional conventions remain unwritten in the Canadian and Australian Constitutions, the United Kingdom conventions have been expressly applied in Ceylon, by S. 2 of the Ceylon (Independence) Order in Council, 1947. Once again it appears that Ireland has provided a distinctive institution, by limiting the activities of the President of the Republic.

THE LEGISLATURE

If the President under the 1937 Constitution differed greatly from the Governor-General under the 1922 Constitution, there were distinct resemblances between the legislatures created by the two documents, though the second bore traces of the constitutional developments in the intervening years.

The new Oireachtas consists of the President, Dáil, and Seanad, with sole and exclusive power of making laws for the state, and power to create subordinate legislatures and functional or vocational councils (Art. 15, 1-3). As in 1922, the franchise right is set out, and the powers and privileges of the Oireachtas detailed; the ban on ex post facto offenses and the declaration of the exclusive power of raising military forces are repeated (Arts. 16; 15, 7-15; 15, 5; 15, 6). In the new Constitution the right to decide on participation in war is vested in the Dáil (Art. 28, 3).

The Dáil is elected by proportional representation, it has control over the choice of Taoiseach and Government, it must consider the Government's financial provisions, and money bills must be initiated there (Arts. 16, 2, 5; 13, 1; 17; 21 & 22). In these respects it resembles its 1922 predecessor. Another point of resemblance is that, while by Art. 16, 5 the maximum life of the Dáil is fixed at seven years, its actual life is five years, under the Electoral (Amendment) Act, 1927 (No. 21 of 1927). The Dáil consists of a hundred and forty-seven members, so that it is the same size as the 1922 House, less the six university members who now sit in the Senate.

In contrast, the Senate constituted in 1937 differed from its 1922 counterpart. The most important change is that, instead of holding office for a fixed period, Senators have to be re-elected at a general election held not more than ninety days after each dissolution of the Dáil. By Art. 18 the number remains at sixty, but the six university representatives now sit in the Senate, not the Dáil, and eleven members are nominated by the Taoiseach after the Dáil reassembles. The remaining forty-three Senators are chosen by election from five electoral panels representing Culture and Education, Agriculture and Fisheries, Labor, Industry and Commerce, and Public Administration. Under the Seanad Electoral (Panel Members) Acts, 1947 (No. 42 of 1947) and 1954 (No. 1 of 1954) the candidates are nominated for these panels by registered nominating bodies and by members of the Oireachtas, and the electorate consists of members of the Oireachtas and the local government bodies. Despite the elaborate apparatus contrived for these elections, the results have demonstrated the difficulties in the way of constructing a second chamber which will operate satisfactorily in a unitary state.[14]

[14] The composition of the Senate is discussed in Arthur Watson Bromage and Mary C. Bromage, "The Vocational Senate in Ireland," *American Political Science Review*, XXXIV (1940), 519-538. For a more recent commentary see Frederick

The usual period for the Senate's consideration of bills is ninety days, but for money bills it is twenty-one days and for emergency purposes it may be abridged by a certificate of the Taoiseach, a resolution of the Dáil, and the concurrence of the President (Arts. 23, 21, and 24). The subordinate position of the Senate is clear, for the Dáil's version of disputed legislation prevails, if that House so resolves within a hundred and eighty days after the end of the Senate's period for consideration. Thus two particular problems of the bicameral system—the elective body's control of financial legislation, and the solution of disputes between the two houses—have both been solved in the Irish Constitution by the imposition of time limits after which the measure as passed by the Dáil becomes law. There are no requirements as to passage in successive sessions, or dissolution, or joint sittings such as occur in different forms in Commonwealth constitutions; the directly elected body has the final say.

After the brief experiment in unicameralism which has been described earlier in this chapter, the 1937 Constitution restored the bicameral system. It was some thirteen years later that New Zealand abolished her upper house by the Legislative Council Abolition Act, 1950 (No. 3 of 1950), and the Pakistan parliament consists of the President and a single chamber, the National Assembly, under Art. 43 of the 1956 Constitution; but both India and Ceylon have bicameral legislatures, which remain in the majority of Commonwealth constitutions, although the composition of the second chamber is not the same in any two countries. The Irish experiments in the composition of second chambers have not been undoubted successes; but the answer may well be that it is beyond the wit of man to devise an entirely satisfactory second chamber and that this may well be easier in federal states, which provide at least a foundation for a representative upper house.

THE EXECUTIVE

With the abolition of the office of Governor-General in 1936, executive power in the Irish Free State passed to the Government. In the 1937 Constitution this power is vested in the people but exercisable by the Government, which must have seven members and may have as many as fifteen, though only two may be mem-

---

Basil Chubb, "Vocational Representation and the Irish Senate," *Political Studies*, II (1954), 97-111.

bers of the Senate (Art. 28, 1 & 2).   Under Art. 28, 8, Ministers may speak in either House, as was then possible in South Africa, and is now permitted also in India.   Like the Executive Council under the 1922 Constitution, the Government is collectively responsible to the Dáil and has the duty of making provision for finance (Art. 28, 4).

The position of the Taoiseach is shown by his right to advise that the Dáil be dissolved, which was formerly done by the Executive Council; he must resign if he cannot obtain a majority in the Dáil; he has power to require the termination of appointment of a member of the Government, and his resignation automatically entails that of the Government (Arts. 13, 2; 28, 9-11).   An interesting innovation was that the deputy premier was given, by Art. 28, 6, the title of Tánaiste, the name of the prospective successor to the head of the old Irish family group.

Thus in 1937 the Irish Government differed from others in the Commonwealth in that it was declared to be a collective body, responsible to the lower house.   The principles of personal responsibility for advising a dissolution, and of Ministers holding office during the Taoiseach's pleasure were introduced, though the continued requirement of the support of the majority in the Dáil naturally provides a check on the exercise of those powers.   It is noteworthy that the express vesting of power in the Head of the Government, subject to the support of the elective house, is not general in the Commonwealth.   In the older constitutions the Westminster convention persists that the Prime Minister is only *primus inter pares*.   In Ceylon, the United Kingdom conventions have been specifically applied but the principle of collective responsibility is stated in s. 46 of the 1946 Constitution.   The principle has also been stated in Art. 75 (3) of the Indian Constitution and in Art. 37 (5) of the Pakistan Constitution but the Irish provisions for the nomination of the Premier and Government, and the rule as to automatic resignation, have not been followed.   The Irish Constitution sets out the relevant rules in concise form, and so far these have proved workable.

The judicial element in the 1937 Constitution has been described in the chapter on Legal History (*supra*); so the next question for consideration is that of the "Bill of Rights" provisions.

FUNDAMENTAL RIGHTS

The 1922 Constitution had specified certain individual rights which had, until then, remained unformulated in the law of the Commonwealth, and recognized only by judicial decision. In 1937, this process of definition was taken a stage further by providing that the state guaranteed, in its laws, to respect these rights, to protect them from attack, and, in the words of Art. 40, 3, (2), "in the case of injustice done, [to] vindicate the life, person, good name, and property rights of every citizen."

The right to be tried "in due course of law" was repeated and, as in 1922, the right to trial by jury in criminal cases conferred by Art. 38 was qualified in relation to minor offenses triable by courts of summary jurisdiction, and to offenses triable by special courts or military tribunals.

In other specifications of fundamental rights there are similar qualifications to enable the state's duties to be performed. For instance, the general statement in Art. 40, 1 that "All citizens shall, as human persons, be held equal before the law" was followed immediately by an interpretation provision, that "This shall not be held to mean that the State shall not in its enactments have due regard to differences of capacity, physical and moral, and of social function." The conception of equality was further underlined by prohibitions on the conferring of titles of nobility by the state, and on a citizen's acceptance, without the prior approval of the Government, of titles of nobility or honor (Art. 40, 2). The right of individual liberty was restated in the form "No citizen shall be deprived of his personal liberty save in accordance with law" and the habeas corpus procedure was repeated, with the addition of special provisions to operate where it is alleged that detention is in accordance with an invalid law, or where a death sentence has been pronounced. As in 1922 this clause is not to restrict the activities of the defense forces during war or armed rebellion (Art. 40, 4).

The rights of free expression of opinion, of peaceable assembly, and of forming associations and unions were repeated, but the qualifications were made more explicit. The state is to endeavor to insure that the organs of public opinion should not use their rightful liberty of expression (including criticism of Government policy) "to undermine public order or morality on the authority of the State," and blasphemy, sedition, and indecency are punishable "in accordance with law"; laws may prevent or control meetings which might cause a breach of the peace or a danger or nuisance to the public; and the right to form associations and unions may be regulated and controlled "in the public interest," but political, religious, or class discrimination is prohibited (Art. 40, 6).   Most of these personal rights are restatements, expanded and with detailed reservations, of those in the 1922 Constitution, but the next two Articles made much greater advances on the 1922 position.

Under Art. 41 the state recognized the family "as the natural primary and fundamental unit group of Society, and as a moral institution possessing inalienable and imprescriptible rights, antecedent and superior to all positive law," to be protected "as the necessary basis of social order and as indispensable to the welfare of the Nation and the State."   Similarly, it was recognized that "by her life within the home, woman gives to the State a support without which the common good cannot be achieved" and the state accordingly endeavors "to ensure that mothers shall not be obliged by economic necessity to engage in labour to the neglect of their duties in the home."   There is also a pledge to guard and protect the institution of marriage, a prohibition on the enactment of laws providing for the dissolution of marriage, and a ban on the remarriage within the state of persons whose marriages have been dissolved abroad.   This article embodies a particular philosophy in the broad framework of constitutional development, and has two aspects—the general duty placed on the state, and the particular application of that philosophy in cases coming before the courts.   As will be seen, the potentialities of this process of interpretation are greater than its achievements so far.

Art. 42 acknowledged the family as the primary and natural educator of the child, and guaranteed the right and duty of parents to educate their children.   While the state cannot oblige parents to violate their consciences by sending their children to schools provided or designated by the state, as "guardian of the common good" it has the duty of seeing that children "receive a certain minimum education, moral, intellectual and social," of providing free primary education and other educational facilities, and, in cases where parents neglect their duty towards their children, "to supply the place of the parents." Here the duty of the individual is balanced against the power of the state, the latter being confined to the general protection of individual rights, which it must support, may regulate to a limited extent, and can appropriate to itself only in narrowly defined circumstances.

There is a similar balance between individual rights and state duties in Art. 43, dealing with private property, which again had no counterpart in the 1922 Constitution. This article acknowledges that "man, in virtue of his rational being, has the natural right, antecedent to positive law, to the private ownership of external goods" and the state is prohibited from passing any law "attempting to abolish the right of private ownership or the general right to transfer, bequeath and inherit private property." This is qualified by a statement that the exercise of these rights "ought, in civil society, to be regulated by the principles of social justice," and the state is given power to delimit by law the exercise of these rights "with a view to reconciling their exercise with the exigencies of the common good." There could hardly be a clearer statement of the Irish view of relationship between the rights of citizens and the state's general function—the former an inherent possession, the latter a duty to harmonize the exercise of individual rights.

Art. 44 dealt separately with the matter of religion, of such great moment in Ireland. The article recognizes "the special position of the Holy Catholic Apostolic and Roman Church as the guardian of the faith professed by the great majority of the citizens" and it also recognizes the religious denominations—some specified, the others unspecified—in existence in 1937. The resemblance between the recognition of the special position of the Roman Catholic Church and the 1801 concordat between Napoleon and Pius VII is evidently coincidental.[15] After this general declaration came a series of specific provisions. Freedom of conscience, and of the profession and practice of religion, are guaranteed "subject to public order and morality." There are prohibitions on the endowment of religion, on religious discrimination (especially in education) and the taking of religious property "save for necessary works of public utility and on payment of compensation," and every religious denomination has the right to manage its own affairs.

[15] A suggestion that the 1937 provision was taken from the 1801 Concordat has been denied by Mr. de Valera. *Irish Times*, October 14, 1955.

In sum, the recognition of the family, the express provisions relating to education, the possibility of restraining private property in the public interest, and the recognition of religious denominations are innovations showing clearly the philosophy on which the Constitution is based, though the extent to which philosophical ideals will be reconciled with judicial reasoning is still indeterminate.

For purposes of comparison, the Indian and Pakistan Constitutions are relevant, for Ceylon has chosen to rely on the common law, but has incorporated in s. 29 (2) of the 1946 Constitution a prohibition on laws involving religious discrimination on the lines of s. 5 of the Government of Ireland Act, 1920. In the 1950 Constitution India has included among the list of fundamental rights a ban on discrimination on the ground of caste (Art. 15 (1)), the abolition of untouchability (Art. 17), and a prohibition on traffic in human beings (Art. 23). Other provisions which emphasized the difference between Indian and Irish conditions are those which allowed freedom of movement throughout India and residence and settlement there (Art. 19 (1) (d) and (e)) and gave protection for minority interests (Arts. 29 and 30). On the other hand, the Irish Constitution might well have contained provisions such as the Indian declaration of equality of opportunity for state employment (Art. 16) and of the right to practice a profession or carry on a trade or business (Art. 19 (1) (g)). Again, Art. 31 of the 1950 Constitution, relating to the taking of property and the payment of compensation, is much more elaborate than the Irish recognition of the right of private property. Also, Art. 32 of the Indian Constitution confers specific remedies for the enforcement of fundamental rights, which the Irish Constitution does only for the liberty of the person.[16]

Similarly, Part II of the 1956 Pakistan Constitution provides a number of contrasts with the Irish Constitution of 1937. In the matter of personal liberty, Art. 7 of the Pakistan Constitution (like Art. 22 of the Indian Constitution) provides for an advisory board in cases of preventive detention, for which there is no corresponding Irish provision. Pakistan, like India, has constitutional guarantees of freedom of movement (Art. 11), of nondiscrimination in state employment (Art. 17), and of protection for linguistic and cultural

[16] For the judicial views of Part III of the Indian constitution, see Alan Gledhill, *Fundamental Rights in India* (London, 1955).

minorities (Art. 19), as well as a prohibition on slavery (Art. 16); the Irish Constitution did not contain anything on these points. Other matters of contrast are the qualified Pakistan prohibition on the taking of property without compensation (Art. 15), and the provision in Art. 22 for the issue of writs for the enforcement of fundamental rights. Again, both the Indian Constitution, by Arts. 25 and 26, and that of Pakistan, by Art. 18, guarantee religious freedom but do not refer to specific religious denominations, as the Irish Constitution does.

In sum, even brief comparisons of this kind show how the Irish model may be adopted and adapted; and it can fairly be claimed that the Irish Declaration of Fundamental Rights in 1937, like that of the United States a century and a half earlier, provided a precedent for subsequent constitutional development in other parts of the world.

THE DIRECTIVE PRINCIPLES OF SOCIAL POLICY

In another respect the 1937 Constitution provided a constitutional model for India and Pakistan. Art. 45 contained a set of "Directive Principles of Social Policy" which were included "for the general guidance of the Oireachtas" and are not cognizable by the courts. Indeed, judges might have difficulty in determining whether the state was securing "a social order in which justice and charity shall inform all the institutions of the national life" (Art. 45, 1). (In *Pigs Marketing Board v. Donnelly (Dublin) Ltd.*, [1939] I.R. 413 Hanna J. commented that the term "social justice" (in Art. 43) was too nebulous for a court of law, and if that spirit were to prevail in dealing with the social directives their judicial effect would be slight.)

Once again it is the common good which must be served, by securing that citizens have the means of making reasonable provision for their domestic needs, by insuring that ownership and control of material resources are evenly distributed and that essential commodities are not concentrated in the control of a few, and by establishing as many families as possible in economic security on the land. In addition, the state is to favor and supplement private enterprise (which must, however, be conducted efficiently), to safeguard "the economic interests of the weaker sections of the community," and

to prevent exploitation of workers.   Just as the articles dealing with
fundamental rights show the balance which must be held between
the individual and the state, so the "directive principles" of Art.
45 indicate the way in which the Oireachtas should frame its
legislation to ensure social justice, both by individual effort and by
state activity.   But once a law emerges from the Oireachtas, the
only standards applicable to it in judicial review are those in other
articles of the Constitution, since Art. 45 provides only standards
of policy, not ultimate criteria of legal validity.

It is interesting to note the alterations made in the corresponding
sections of the Indian Constitution, where different problems necessitated different policy directives.   Such matters as the organization
of village *panchayats*, the provision of a uniform civil code throughout India, and the special protection to be given to the Scheduled
Castes arise from specifically Indian conditions (Arts. 40, 44, and 46).
But the right to equal pay, to public assistance, and to maternity
relief given by Arts. 39(a), 41, and 42 are matters which in the Irish
Republic are left to be dealt with by the Oireachtas in the ordinary
course of legislation, as are the raising of the standard of living, the
organization of agriculture, and the protection of public monuments,
all of which are included in the Indian aims (Arts. 47 to 49).   Two
other Indian aims, the separation of the judiciary from the executive
(Art. 50) and the promotion of international peace and the fostering
of respect for international law (Art. 51) are, in the Irish Constitution, not merely directives but effective articles of the Constitution
(Arts. 35, 2, and 29).

Another comparison may be made with Part III of the Pakistan
Constitution, which is distinctive in that it included among its
aims the promotion of Moslem unity and Islamic principles (Arts.
24 and 25).   Here also the aims of international peace (Art. 24)
and the separation of judiciary from executive (Art. 30) are directives in Pakistan but embodied in the Irish Constitution.   Other
distinctive provisions in this part of the Pakistan Constitution relate
to the discouraging of prejudice (Art. 26) and the protection of
minorities (Art. 27).   Again, the "principles of social uplift" in Art.
28 and the provisions of Art. 29 for "the promotion of social and
economic well-being of the people" differ widely from the general
Irish provisions, but the ultimate aims are similar.

Thus in both India and Pakistan the Irish foundation has been used but the architecture of the structures is distinctive; the plan of the Irish architect was modified to suit other conditions.

AMENDING THE CONSTITUTION

The method adopted in 1937 for the amendment of the Constitution was similar to that chosen in 1922. There was a three-year period during which amendments could be introduced by ordinary legislation, after which any amendment had to be agreed to both by the Oireachtas and the people, on a referendum. Bills for the amendment of the Constitution must be so titled, and before signing, the President must satisfy himself that the provisions of the Constitution have been duly followed (Art. 46).

Only two amending acts were in fact passed. The First Amendment of the Constitution Act, 1939 (p. xi) altered the emergency provisions in Art. 28, 3, (3) to include the period of "an armed conflict in which the State is not a participant," while the Second Amendment of the Constitution Act, 1941 (p. viii), added periods after war, armed conflict, or armed rebellion had terminated but as respects which the Oireachtas had not declared the emergency to have ceased to exist. The 1941 Act also made a variety of minor alterations in other provisions of the Constitution. The referendum has not been used, either for an amendment of the Constitution or the consideration of a bill of national importance, deemed to have been passed by the Oireachtas under Art. 23 and referred to the people by the President under Art. 27. Art. 47 provides that a simple majority of those voting on the referendum will suffice to approve a proposal to amend the Constitution, but that to veto a measure of any other kind referred to the people this majority must include at least a third of the voters on the register. The Oireachtas has set up the machinery for the referendum (No. 8 of 1942 and No. 30 of 1946), but so far it remains unused.

In comparison with the new Asian constitutions the Constitution of the Irish Republic has greater rigidity, since popular approval must be obtained for amendments. In India the power of amendment conferred by Art. 368 requires a special majority—two-thirds of each House of the Union Parliament who are present and vote, and who must comprise a majority of the total membership of each

House.   For certain matters (including the amendment of the amending procedure itself) ratification by at least half of the legislatures of the Part A and Part B states is required, while in other cases the Constitution confers power directly on the Union Parliament in the ordinary course of legislation (*e.g.*, the creation or reconstitution of states, Art. 4 (2)).   Similarly the Pakistan Constitution provides in Art. 216 that a majority of the National Assembly, and a two-thirds majority of the members present and voting, are needed for constitutional amendments, which are to be made by ordinary legislation.   The approval of either or both of the Provincial Assemblies is necessary for alterations affecting the Provinces and relating to specified topics, but the bulk of the schedule in the 1956 Constitution may be altered by ordinary legislation passed by a simple majority.   In Ceylon a special majority of two-thirds of the House of Representatives is required (s. 29 (4)).

Thus only in the Irish Republic and in Australia does the referendum survive.   Having long been denied a voice in the legislative process, the Irish people now retain ultimate power.

SUMMARY

From the comparisons made between the present Irish Constitution and the Constitutions of India, Pakistan, and Ceylon, it will be seen how far advanced Eire was in 1937, when conceptions of the Commonwealth were such that the "revolution in law" effected in Dublin was not regarded as altering her position in the Commonwealth.   But whether her link with the Commonwealth was one of membership or association, the structure of Eire's Constitution marked a considerable step forward in Commonwealth constitution-making.

It was republican in all but name, with no link with the Crown in its provisions, and only a tenuous link, for limited purposes, enacted and repealable by ordinary legislation.   If in the division and distribution of powers it resembled other Commonwealth constitutions, in such matters as the declaration of fundamental rights the 1937 Constitution went far beyond the Dublin precedent of 1922.   And with the "directive principles of social policy" the Eire Constitution introduced a new conception into Commonwealth constitutional law, outside the ambit of judicial review.   The older countries of the East wishing to arrange their constitutional affairs on modern lines have in the Irish Constitution a precedent of an old country emerging into new life, and fashioning new constitutional machinery along fresh lines.

THE COURTS AND THE 1937 CONSTITUTION

In their consideration of the 1937 Constitution the Dublin courts have had to consider the nature and attributes of the state as well as the validity of legislation. On the juristic problem of the nature of the state, judicial authority is so far slight. In *Comyn v. Attorney-General*, [1950] I.R. 142 the question for decision was whether the state should pay compensation as if it were a government department. In holding that the state was a distinct juristic entity, Kingsmill Moore J. summarized the state's functions under the 1937 Constitution, and concluded that that document retained nothing of the British theory of the Crown as a corporation sole, whose executive functions are carried out on its behalf by various instrumentalities. The Constitution did not define the nature of the new entity which had been substituted; that has to be gleaned from the contents of the Constitution. The learned judge confined himself to deciding that the state could hold property and in this he was upheld by the Supreme Court. In the field of constitutional theory the Irish Republic and the newer members of the Commonwealth have much in common, but a great deal remains unexplored.

THE PRESIDENT'S POWER OF REFERENCE

The ordinary method of testing Irish legislation is in litigation before courts, but the Constitution itself provides a special method. The President, after consultation with the Council of State, may under Art. 26 refer bills (other than money bills, constitutional amendments, and emergency measures) to the Supreme Court for a decision as to repugnancy of a bill, on any ground, to the Constitution.

This power of reference may be compared to that under s. 51 of the Government of Ireland Act, 1920 of referring Northern Ireland legislation to the Privy Council. It is not as wide as the power to give advisory opinions on constitutional matters possessed by the Canadian Supreme Court (*Attorney-General of Ontario v. Attorney-General of Canada*, [1912] A.C. 571). The Supreme

Court of India has also a wide power, under Art. 143 of the 1950 Constitution, to give advisory opinions on law and fact, and Art. 162 of the 1956 Constitution gives the Pakistan Supreme Court similar power.   In these cases a presidential reference is required, not a dispute, as is necessary in Australia (*Re Judiciary and Navigation Acts*, (1921) 29 C.L.R. 257).

So far the President's power of reference has been used on only two occasions; on one of these the legislation was upheld, on the other it was adjudged repugnant to the Constitution.   In *In re Art. 26 of the Constitution and the Offences Against the State (Amendment) Bill 1940*, [1940] I.R. 470, the legislation challenged permitted the arrest and detention of persons considered by a Minister to be acting "prejudicially to the preservation of public peace and order or to the security of the State."   This was held not to confer on the Minister power to administer justice, contrary to Art. 34; it was further regarded as preventive rather than punitive and did not contravene Art. 38 under which no person was to be tried on a criminal charge "save in due course of law"; nor did it infringe Art. 40, 3, guaranteeing "as far as practicable" citizens' personal rights; further, it did not contravene the provisions of Art. 40, 4, providing that "no person shall be deprived of his personal liberty save in accordance with law."   In sum, the general provisions of the Constitution did not prevent the taking of measures considered necessary by the executive for the preservation of the state.

The second reference was *In re Art. 26 of the Constitution and the School Attendance Bill 1942*, [1943] I.R. 334.   S. 4 of the bill gave the Minister for Education power to determine whether a child was receiving suitable education.   The Supreme Court held that under Art. 42, 3, (2) all the state could do was to require a minimum standard of education.   Under the bill the Minister might prescribe a higher standard than the minimum, varying from child to child, and relating to the manner as well as the standard of education.   The section was therefore repugnant to the Constitution, and the President was advised accordingly.   In these two cases the emphasis was on personal liberties, and a similar tendency appears in the cases arising in ordinary litigation.

THE SCOPE OF JUDICIAL REVIEW

The extent to which the Dublin courts will go to emphasize the distinction between legislative and executive matters was indicated by Gavan Duffy J. in *In re Loftus Bryan's Estate*, [1942] I.R. 185 when he refused to follow a section of the Land Law (Ireland) Act, 1887 (50 & 51 Vict. c. 33) purporting to give the Irish Land Commission freedom from court orders. Judicial matters were the sole concern of the courts under Art. 34. This did not, however, prevent the Supreme Court from drawing the distinction between judicial and administrative procedures. In *Fisher v. Irish Land Commission*, [1948] I.R. 3 the Supreme Court held that the Commission, in inquiring into cases of resumption of land under s. 39 of the Land Act, 1939 (No. 26 of 1939), was acting as an administrative authority not a judicial one, though they were bound to act judicially.

A landmark in judicial review was *Buckley and Others (Sinn Féin) v. Attorney-General*, [1950] I.R. 67. In that case funds had been lodged in court in 1924 by the former Sinn Féin organization. In 1942 representatives of the organization brought an action asking for payment of these funds. While the action was pending the Sinn Féin Funds Act, 1947 (No. 13 of 1947) was passed, vesting these funds in trustees for certain purposes, and ordering the staying of all further proceedings in the action. In the High Court, Gavan Duffy P. refused to abdicate jurisdiction in a case in which the court was duly seized, and on appeal the Supreme Court held that the 1947 Act was ultra vires because it was repugnant to the rights of private property in Art. 43 of the Constitution, because it was an unwarrantable interference by the Oireachtas with the judicial functions of the courts, and because the courts could review the action of the legislature under Art. 43, 2, (2) of the Constitution, in reconciling the exercise of the rights of private property with "the exigencies of the common good." The separation of legislature and judiciary is clearly shown by this case, as are the extent to which the courts will exercise judicial review and the protection which the courts will afford to private property despite an attempt to regulate the exercise of such rights.

EMERGENCY POWERS

Another type of case in which the Dublin courts have had to exercise judicial review is that where individual rights were involved. Thus Art. 28, 3, (3) contains a wide provision for dealing with war or armed rebellion; the Constitution cannot be invoked to "invalidate any law enacted by the Oireachtas which is expressed to be for the purpose of securing the public safety and the preservation of the State" in such cases, and anything purporting to be done under such legislation cannot be challenged. As already mentioned, this Article was amended so that the legislature was able to make provision for what was officially named "the emergency," but better known as the Second World War.

In exercise of this power, Emergency Powers Acts were passed in 1939 (No. 28 of 1939) and 1940 (No. 16 of 1940) and under the Emergency Powers Orders which they authorized military courts were established to try certain specified offenses, including murder, for which the penalty was death by shooting. Two challenges were made to the jurisdiction of these courts. In *In re McGrath and Harte; and in re the Constitution*, [1941] I.R. 68, it was held, inter alia, that the reference to the emergency in the long titles of these acts sufficed to bring them within Art. 28 of the Constitution, so that the other articles of the Constitution could not be invoked to invalidate them. In the second case, *The State (Walsh) v. Lennon*, [1942] I.R. 112 it was held that habeas corpus would lie to determine the validity of detention authorized by emergency powers, but that the powers conferred by emergency legislation enacted in accordance with the Constitution could not be impugned. Thus, the courts will scrutinize the resultant legislation to ensure that the constitutional provisions are followed, but further than that they cannot go. The compliance with constitutional provision bars judicial investigation as firmly as it was barred when in *Liversidge v. Anderson*, [1942] A.C. 206 (1941) it was held that the grounds for a Minister's statement under emergency powers could not be investigated.

In one way or another, emergency powers feature in all Commonwealth constitutions. In Canada such an event as war justifies federal interference with provincial matters (*Re Reference as to Validity of the Wartime Leasehold Regulations*, [1950] S.C.R. 124), while in Australia the federal defense power in s. 51(vi) of the Constitution has been widely interpreted, and extended to the apprehension of war (*Marcus Clark & Co. Ltd. v. Commonwealth*, (1952) 87 C.L.R. 177). In India the powers of the Union Government over the states are, under Part XVIII of the 1950 Constitution, greatly extended during the existence of a presidential proclamation of emergency and certain fundamental rights may be suspended. Similar powers are contained in Part XI of the 1956 Constitution of Pakistan. In unitary states such as New Zealand, South Africa, and Ceylon the problem is rather one of the flexible exercise of power. In the Irish Republic the position is that, in certain circumstances, and subject to procedures specified in the Constitution itself, the Constitution may be overridden by emergency legislation.

FUNDAMENTAL RIGHTS

In the ordinary course of events the courts have had to consider questions involving such fundamental rights as those of liberty and association, as well as the special provisions in the 1937 Constitution relating to the family and education.

The case of *In re Philip Clarke*, [1950] I.R. 235 is an example of the way in which the habeas corpus procedure was invoked to test an alleged deprivation of personal liberty. The question in that case was the validity of the Mental Treatment Act, 1945 (No. 19 of 1945), which gave a member of the Gárda Siochána the right to detain a person believed to be of unsound mind, either for his personal safety or for the safety of the public. Both the High Court and the Supreme Court held that the 1945 Act did not infringe the Constitution; it is, indeed, the kind of legal provision which the Constitution contemplates.

The right of the citizens to form associations and unions was tested in *National Union of Railwaymen and Others v. Sullivan*, [1947] I.R. 77. The legislation involved was Part III of the Trade Union Act, 1941 (No. 22 of 1941) which gave a Trade Union Tribunal power to grant to a union the exclusive right to organize workmen of a particular class. An effort by the Irish Transport and General Workers' Union to put this legislation into operation in relation to certain workmen was challenged. In the High Court Gavan Duffy J. argued that the 1941 Act merely regulated the exercise of the right to form associations and unions, but the Supreme

Court held that the legislation was invalid as infringing the right to associate. Another aspect of the right to association was examined by a Circuit Court in *Buckley v. Rooney*, [1950] Ir. Jur. Rep. 5. In that case it was held that an agreement between an employer and a trade union that only members of the union should be employed for certain work did not infringe Art. 40. Accordingly, an employee whose contract was properly terminated because he was not a member of the union could not obtain damages against an official of the union who procured the dismissal. The exercise of the recognized right to form associations and unions did not render unlawful the diminution of private rights in a lawful way.

The provisions of Arts. 41 and 42, relating to the family and to education, have been invoked in a number of cases of an unfortunate type, relating to the custody of children where a marriage is broken up, as may happen where the parents are of different religions. A group of four cases will indicate the present state of the law of the Irish Republic on this point.

In *In re Kindersley*, [1944] I.R. 111 a father sought the custody of his son who was residing in Eire with his mother (contrary to an order of the Court of Appeal in England, where he was a ward of court). The High Court and the Supreme Court held (in accordance with the view of the law then recognized) that the father was entitled to custody, the latter court holding that the welfare of the child was the paramount consideration. Here the Constitution was not adjudged to have made any alteration in the law.

This view was reinforced by *In re Frost, Infants*, [1947] I.R. 3 when it was held that the Constitution did not displace the father's rights to have his children educated as he wished, subject to the children's welfare. An antenuptial agreement did not abrogate the father's rights. But a different view of the effect of the Constitution was taken by Gavan Duffy P. in *In re Tilson*, [1951] I.R. 1, where a father educated his children contrary to an antenuptial agreement. The learned judge held that that agreement was binding as a solemn undertaking, and that the welfare of the children demanded that they should be educated by the mother in accordance with the agreement. In the Supreme Court the ground for decision was that under Art. 42 the duty of education was vested in both parents, and was not revocable by one party alone. Black J., dissenting, relied on the common law rule followed in *In re Frost*, but that case was distinguished by the majority on the ground that there the antenuptial agreement had been varied by a postnuptial agreement to separate.

Again, in *In re O'Brien*, [1954] I.R. 1, it was held that Arts. 41 and 42 must apply in cases of dispute between a parent and a non-parent, but that in cases in which the family has broken up the Articles are not applicable. Thus the father's common law right is preserved by, and in accordance with, Arts. 41 and 42 as against a non-parent, while it may be restricted by an antenuptial agreement. The interpretation of the general words of the Constitution does not justify any more definite conclusion, and indeed these are pre-eminently cases of the sort where facts have a great bearing on the choice of legal principles to be applied. (It may be noted in passing that in the law of Northern Ireland the father's superior rights at common law have not been completely abrogated by the paramountcy of the child's welfare (*In re B. an Infant*, [1946] N.I. 1).

Another aspect of Art. 42 appeared in *Minister of Education and Attorney General v. Doyle* (1955, unreported). In that case the provision challenged was s. 10 of the Children Act 1941 (No. 12 of 1941) which authorized a District Justice to send a child to an industrial school in specific circumstances. The Supreme Court took the view that a parent who consented to such a course was entitled to withdraw that consent, and that the section impugned was therefore invalid since it was contrary to Art. 42, guaranteeing the parental function in educating children. In principle, this decision is similar to the *School Attendance Bill* case, for both decisions were in favor of parental rights as against state control.

The protection of property conferred by Art. 43 was considered in a number of cases. In *Pigs Marketing Board v. Donnelly (Dublin) Ltd.*, [1939] I.R. 413, Hanna J. held that all legislation interfering with contractual or proprietary rights does not per se infringe the provision of Art. 43. He also held that matters of detail requiring expert knowledge might be delegated by the legislature without surrendering its exclusive jurisdiction under Art. 15, 2, (1), which was not infringed by the creation of a price-fixing board.

Again, in *Foley v. The Irish Land Commission and the Attorney-General*, [1952] I.R. 118 the tenant of a land purchase holding had not resided in a house built for him some eight years previously, so the Land Commission directed him under s. 2 of the Land Act, 1946 (No. 12 of 1946) so to reside, and commenced proceedings against him when he did not comply with the direction. The Supreme Court held that the requirement as to residence did not abolish a right of personal property, but was a delimitation of these rights, within the meaning of Art. 43, 2, (2). The court also held that if the Land Commission's power was one of a judicial nature, it was not repugnant to Art. 37, but it found that the Land Commission had failed to act judicially.

Summing up this outline of the principal cases on the 1937 Constitution, one may discern certain essential points. The first is the definite assertion of the power of judicial review, even in the teeth of specific legislative action. Next, the wide scope of government activity under the Constitution is demonstrated, not only by the fact that only three statutory provisions have so far been found repugnant to it, but also in the way in which emergency legislation and the setting-up of special courts have been held to be in conformity with the Constitution. The third point is that personal rights guaranteed by the Constitution may be restricted by such provision as may be made "in accordance with law." Finally, as the custody of children cases show, common law rules may be modified or altered in emphasis by the Constitution.

A comparison between the interpretations placed on similar provisions by the Irish courts on the one hand, and the Indian and Pakistan courts on the other, would be extremely valuable. Meantime, two quotations will illustrate the different views which may be taken of influences other than merely legal ones on constitutional interpretation. Looking back, an American commentator has concluded that

. . . it is clear that the impact of modern Catholic political, social and economic ideas on legal development in present-day Ireland has been rather less significant or substantial than the adoption of the radically new Constitution of 1937 might have seemed at the time to foreshadow.[17]

In contrast, an Irish commentator has concluded an analysis of the principles of interpretation with a look to the future:

[17] Edward McWhinney, "The Courts and the Constitution in Catholic Ireland," *Tulane Law Review*, XXIX (1954), 69, 86.

Our Courts and lawyers are not, however, left to the hazards of the unaided application of pure reason. They have judicial knowledge of the universal declarations of human rights. Further, the Constitution recognises the truth of the Christian religion. Divine Revelation in the Old and New Testaments and the exposition of the Doctors of the Church are their binding precedents. The pronouncements of modern Christian Leaders on the application of Divine Teaching to appease human problems are available for their guidance. Finally, in seeking for enlightenment, it is not too much to ask the individual, whatever his personal religious persuasion, to have particular regard to the Social Encyclicals, in view both of their intrinsic merit and of the special position of the Holy Catholic Apostolic and Roman Church as the guardian of the faith professed by the majority of the citizens.[18]

Clearly future decisions of the Dublin courts are likely to be of importance in comparative constitutional law.

SUMMARY

This chapter on Irish constitutional development in the past three and a half decades has sought to demonstrate three matters relevant to Commonwealth affairs.

The first is the distinctive position of Northern Ireland, whose quasi-federal relationship with the United Kingdom, derived from special historical circumstances, may yet prove important if any form of devolutionary government should be conferred on Scotland, or if Malta should be integrated in the United Kingdom. Secondly, the 1922 Constitution of the Irish Free State showed how Dominion and European models could be used in the framing of a new Dominion constitution, and the development of that Constitution showed how such a framework was altered in a comparatively short period of years so that it was transformed into a virtually republican structure. Thirdly, the 1937 Irish Constitution showed how a new legal framework could be adopted by a Commonwealth member, and how that model could be adapted to different circumstances such as those of India and Pakistan.

In these three ways Ireland, both North and South, has made a contribution of some importance to constitutional developments in the Commonwealth.

---

[18] Vincent Grogan, "The Constitution and Natural Law," *Christus Rex*, VIII (1954), 201, 218.

5

Administrative Law

THE CHAPTERS on Legal History and Constitutional History (*supra*) traced something of the development of the common law and of parliamentary government in Ireland, at times paralleling and at other times diverging from the situation on the other side of the Irish Sea. Similar trends can be seen in the development of administrative law, particularly in that part of it relating to delegated legislation. For instance, in his *Notes on the Delegation by Parliament of Legislative Powers*[1] Sir William Graham-Harrison gave as an early example of delegated legislation a statute of 1337 (11 Edw. 3, c. 1) which prohibited the export of wool but gave the king and council the right to lift the ban; this statute included Ireland in its scope. The parliamentary activities of Henry VIII, which were regarded by the Donoughmore-Scott Committee on Ministers' Powers[2] as delegating wide authority to legislate, were not repeated in the Irish parliament, but an interesting example of this process appeared on the Irish statute-book in the seventeenth century. This was the 1665 Act of Explanation (17 & 18 Car. 2, c. 2) passed to remedy the defects of the 1662 Act of Settlement (14 & 15 Car. 2, c. 2). Under the 1665 statute the Lord Lieutenant and council were empowered during a period of seven years to "make and establish rules, orders and directions for the better regulating of all cities, walled towns, and corporations in Ireland, and the electing of magistrates and officers therein."

Again, as Professor John Willis has shown in the appendix to his work on *The Parliamentary Powers of English Government Departments*,[3] in the nineteenth and early twentieth centuries there are

[1] Privately printed, London, 1931. [2] (1932) Cmd. 4060.
[3] Cambridge, Mass., 1933.

numerous examples of Westminster statutes passed to deal with Ireland and providing that rules were to have effect as if they were enacted in the parent act, that confirmation of instruments was to be conclusive evidence that they were validly made, that outlines of legislation were to be filled in by orders, that schemes were to be made or confirmed, and that acts were to be modified. In short, the variety of Irish affairs was dealt with by the methods used for similar purposes in other parts of the United Kingdom. In the increased output of Westminster legislation Ireland had its full share; so it was inevitable that the delegation of legislative power should also include Irish authorities.

With the outbreak of the First World War and the passing of the consolidated Defence of the Realm Act, 1914 (5 & 6 Geo. 5, c. 8), there was a considerable increase in the bulk of subordinate legislation, and at the end of the wartime period Ireland was responsible for two kinds of such legislation. The Restoration of Order in Ireland Act, 1920 (10 & 11 Geo. 5, c. 31), authorized the making of regulations covering a very wide field, while the Government of Ireland Act, 1920 (10 & 11 Geo. 5, c. 67) involved the making of a considerable number of Transfer Orders, to insure that the new administration in Northern Ireland would be clothed with the necessary powers, and Adaptation Orders, to alter the terms of legislation to make it fit the changed circumstances. As the pages of Sir Arthur Quekett's volumes on *The Constitution of Northern Ireland*[4] show, the constitutional skeleton of the 1920 Act had to be clothed with muscles and sinews, veins and flesh, to give it administrative life. Even today the distribution of functions between various departments of the Government of Northern Ireland is governed, in the main, by a series of notifications issued by the Lord Lieutenant in 1921. In the Irish Free State the setting up of the new state was achieved by the issuing of a number of notices and proclamations by the provisional government to insure that the new constitutional machinery was brought into operation.

Since the administrative systems of both Northern Ireland and the Irish Republic spring from a common source, it is not surprising that the use of administrative powers in both Belfast and Dublin should be similar, although the respective constitutions are different

[4] Belfast, 1928-1946.

in form. Here two observations are relevant. First, neither Northern Ireland nor the Irish Republic, in common with the United Kingdom and other Commonwealth countries, has enacted any equivalent of the United States Administrative Procedure Act, 1946 (60 Stat. 237, 5 U.S.C. §§ 1001-1011); the various processes of government have been left to develop individually, without any over-all legislative regulation. Secondly, there has been no investigation, in either Belfast or Dublin, of the scope of administrative law, similar to that carried out by the Donoughmore-Scott Committee on Ministers' Powers, or of the working of administrative tribunals and inquiries, such as is now being undertaken by the Committee under the chairmanship of Sir Oliver Franks. Thus Irish administrative law is ripe for a much more detailed comparative investigation than is possible in this chapter.

THE SCOPE AND FORMS OF DELEGATED LEGISLATION

Since 1921 both the Belfast and Dublin parliaments have frequently delegated parts of their legislative power, subject to various kinds of parliamentary control. (The Dublin parliament has not exercised its power under Art. 15, 2, (2) of the 1937 Constitution to create subordinate legislatures.) To illustrate the nature and extent of this delegation some of the subordinate instruments issued in the two areas in the year 1952 will be summarized, as a random sample of the present-day working of this branch of administrative law.

In 1952 the annual volume of Northern Ireland Statutory Rules and Orders showed that two hundred and thirty-four instruments were issued and that of these twenty were local and eighteen temporary. In the same year, according to the volumes of Statutory Instruments published in Dublin, three hundred and eighty-nine orders were issued, and while these were not classified in the same way as those issued in Northern Ireland, about fifty of these might be regarded as of local application. A significant feature of these volumes is the similarity of their subject-matter. Thus, for example, where the Ministry of Labour and National Insurance made reciprocal arrangements, under the National Insurance and Industrial Injuries schemes in force in Northern Ireland, with France and the Benelux countries, in the Irish Republic the Minister for Social Welfare made similar reciprocal arrangements with Great Britain and the Isle of Man. Then both the Northern Ireland Ministry of Agriculture and the Minister for Agriculture in the Irish Republic had occasion to make orders to deal with outbreaks of foot and mouth disease; the common origin of the agricultural legislation in force in the two areas is indicated by the fact that the main statute relied on by both authorities was the Diseases of Animals Act, 1894 (57 & 58 Vict. c. 57). The taking of censuses of production in both areas was regulated by orders made for this purpose, the Ministry of Commerce for Northern Ireland doing so under the Statistics of Trade Act (Northern Ireland), 1949 (c. 7), while the Minister for Industry and Commerce in the Irish Republic did so under the Statistics Acts, 1926 and 1946 (No. 12 of 1926 and No. 34 of 1946). This Belfast Ministry and Dublin Minister had another problem in common, for both made orders authorizing the abandonment of small railway lines in their respective areas. Similar methods of dealing with housing problems were shown by the regulations made by the Northern Ireland Ministry of Health and Local Government and the Minister for Local Government in the Irish Republic, under which applicants for housing grants were informed of the conditions with which they would have to comply to become entitled to assistance of this kind. Again, in 1952 the Ministry of Home Affairs for Northern Ireland made provision for the expenses incurred by election officials, and for the pay and pensions of the Royal Ulster Constabulary. In Dublin the Minister for Finance made changes in the payments to election officials in the Irish Republic, and the Minister for Justice made alterations in the pay and pensions of the Gárda Siochána.

Of course, the similarity of subject matter of these subordinate instruments does not necessarily imply identical conditions in the North and South of Ireland. For instance, the schemes operating in Northern Ireland under the Health Services Act (Northern Ireland), 1948 (c. 3), under which a number of regulations were issued in 1952, differed considerably in scope from the schemes contemplated by the Irish Republic's Health Act, 1947 (No. 28 of 1947), which was to be extensively amended by the Health Act, 1953 (No. 26 of 1953). Again, the National Insurance (Industrial Injuries) Act (Northern Ireland), 1946 (c. 21) and the National Insurance Act

(Northern Ireland), 1946 (c. 23) do not operate in the same way in Northern Ireland as the Social Welfare Act, 1952 (No. 11 of 1952) does in the Irish Republic. Apart from detailed operation, there are also differences in the devices used to deal with particular problems. Thus, for example, under the Wages Councils Act (Northern Ireland), 1945 (c. 21), councils set up for different industries make proposals as to the wages to be paid to workers in those industries; these proposals are incorporated in orders made by the Ministry of Labour and National Insurance. In the Irish Republic, on the other hand, similar proposals made by committees for different industries are submitted to the Labour Court, set up under the Industrial Relations Act, 1946 (No. 26 of 1946).

Another important difference, stemming from the constitutional position of Northern Ireland, is that the delegated legislation in force there may be authorized either by the Westminster parliament or the Northern Ireland parliament. Thus, for example, in 1952 of the two thousand three hundred and nineteen Statutory Instruments emanating from Whitehall ten of these related specifically to Northern Ireland while many others were applicable by reason of the fact that they applied to the whole of the United Kingdom. This accounts for the fact that the volume of Northern Ireland Statutory Rules and Orders does not contain any equivalent of the Dublin Statutory Instruments made to deal with such matters as the control of imports and the fixing of maximum prices, which occupied a considerable portion of the 1952 volumes. Also, in 1952 the Rules Committee of the Northern Ireland Supreme Court, acting under powers conferred by the Supreme Court of Judicature Act (Ireland), 1877 (40 & 41 Vict. c. 57), made a number of alterations in the Rules of the Supreme Court, but since this is not a matter with respect to which the Northern Ireland parliament has power to make laws, these were not published as Northern Ireland Statutory Rules and Orders. On the other hand, the High Court Rules made in Dublin by the Superior Courts Rules Committee, under the Courts of Justice Acts, 1924 to 1949, were among those included in the volumes of Statutory Instruments for that year. Although, because of the different constitutional conditions in the two areas, one set of rules was published while the other was not, the principle behind the delegation of legislative power—that the details of court procedure should not be

set out in statutes but should be determined by a representative committee—was the same in both cases; and the composition of the committee, representing the Bench and both branches of the legal profession, was similar in both Belfast and Dublin.

In all common law jurisdictions in recent times emergencies have
been a source of much delegated legislation. In the chapter on Constitutional Developments since 1920 (*supra*) reference was made to
the emergency provisions in Commonwealth constitutions, from which
flowed legislation and delegated legislation to deal with such emergencies as the Second World War and its aftermath. In Northern Ireland the Emergency Powers (Defence) Act, 1939 (2 & 3 Geo. 6,
c. 62) applied as it did in the rest of the United Kingdom, so that
authority was given for the operation there of the Defence (General)
Regulations made under the 1939 Act. To insure effective local administration the powers conferred by these regulations on departments of the United Kingdom government were often subdelegated
to Northern Ireland government departments, and Sir Arthur
Quekett pointed out that this process of administrative devolution
might well result in the production of documents which were the
"great-grandchildren," or even the "great-great-grandchildren" of
the "parent" Act passed in 1939. Again, at an early stage the
Northern Ireland courts had to consider the effect of an order made
under Defence Regulations on a Northern Ireland Act, and they held
that the Northern Ireland provision must be read subject to the Defence Regulation (*Swain v. The Producers Bacon Co. (Collin Glen)
Ltd.* (1939, unreported)). However, the emergency provisions did
not impose any undue strain on the constitutional relations between
Belfast and London, because of the extent of administrative collabora-
tion. In 1952 six Northern Ireland instruments were made under authority delegated from Whitehall as a result of continued emergency
legislation. In the Irish Republic there was no corresponding necessity for such a chain of delegations; the Emergency Powers Act, 1939
(No. 28 of 1939) corresponded to the Westminster act of that year.
Like the Defence Regulations, the Emergency Powers were continued
after the ending of the emergency, and in 1952 a great deal of the
economic regulation of the life of the country took place by means
of instruments made under orders continued in this fashion.

Another example of emergency legislation which, like so many enactments of this kind, has remained on the statute-book, was the Emergency Imposition of Duties Act, 1932 (No. 16 of 1932). This Act, which was passed at the beginning of the "economic war" with the United Kingdom, gave the Executive Council power to impose and vary customs, excise and stamp duties, by means of an order which was to have statutory effect when it was made but had to be confirmed by act of the Oireachtas within eight months. This Act was much wider in scope than the Westminster Import Duties Act, 1932 (22 & 23 Geo. 5, c. 8), but differed from it in that confirming legislation was required. Extensive use of the Dublin Act was made during 1952, when some twenty-seven orders were made, the necessary statutory authority being given by the Imposition of Duties (Confirmation of Orders) Act, 1952 (No. 10 of 1952), and the Imposition of Duties (Confirmation of Orders)(No. 2) Act, 1952 (No. 21 of 1952). Another example of a wide delegation of power to regulate economic affairs was the Control of Imports Act, 1934 (No. 12 of 1934) which gave the Executive Council power to make quota orders prohibiting the importation of goods except in specified quantities. Such orders must be approved within six months by each House of the Oireachtas. In 1952, fifty-one quota orders were made under the authority of this legislation.

Having seen something of the way in which delegated legislation has been used both in Northern Ireland and the Irish Republic in the course of ordinary administration, and also to deal with emergency situations, one should note the diversity of forms used for this purpose. This variety is most noticeable in the Statutory Rules of Northern Ireland, where the rule-making authorities vary from the Governor and Privy Council of Northern Ireland to an individual Minister. As a result, the subordinate instruments range from Orders in Council through rules and regulations made by government departments (with or without the concurrence of another department or Minister) to warrants and directions given by Ministers. In the Irish Republic, on the other hand, delegated legislation may be issued by the Government, by an individual Minister (with or without the concurrence of another Minister), or by a separate body such as the Labour Court or the Agricultural Wages Board. The result is that most of the legislation is described simply as "Orders," though the term "Regulations" is also used, while "Rules of Court" are in a special category. Nevertheless, despite this variety of form, diversity of scope, and difference in application, it will be seen that the use made in both Belfast and Dublin of delegated legislation is in the main similar in both areas. Like their Commonwealth counterparts, both governments, faced with the complexity of modern administration, have made considerable use of the flexible forms of delegated legislation.

PARLIAMENTARY CONTROL AND PUBLICATION

The references to the Dublin legislation relating to imposition of duties and control of imports have demonstrated two methods by which a legislature can exercise control over the powers which it delegates to subordinate law-making bodies; a confirmatory act may be required, or the assent of the legislature may be obtained by means of a resolution of either or both houses. However, in both Belfast and Dublin the most widely used provision for the exercise of parliamentary control is that of the "negative resolution," by which members of the legislature are given the opportunity of annulling the statutory instrument, but without prejudice to anything already done under the instrument at the time of the annulment. In three of the twenty-six Northern Ireland statutes passed during 1952 (to continue with this random example) there was a delegation of legislative power and in all three cases the "negative resolution" procedure was authorized. Similarly, of the thirty Dublin acts passed during the same year seven used this method of control, and the Social Welfare Act (No. 11 of 1952) combined this method with that of approval of draft regulations laid before the Oireachtas. There is, however, a substantial difference in the statutory periods during which members of the different legislatures can propose annulling resolutions. Members of either house of the Oireachtas have twenty-one days on which the relevant house sits in which to take this action. In Northern Ireland the period was fixed by the Rules Publication Act, 1925 (15 & 16 Geo. 5, c. 6) at five sitting days, but was not to be shorter than ten actual days; by the Statutory Rules (Period of Laying) Act (Northern Ireland), 1950 (c. 12) these periods were increased to ten and twenty days respectively. In his *Notes on the Delegation by Parliament of Legislative Powers* (*supra* note 1) Sir William Graham-Harrison suggested that the 1925 Northern Ireland precedent would not be valid at Westminster, because the period was rather short and because "sitting days" did not provide a satisfactory criterion for the Westminster parliament. It is noteworthy that the Statutory Instruments Act, 1946 (9 & 10 Geo. 6, c. 36) specifies forty actual days (other than days on which the Westminster parliament is prorogued or dissolved) as the period during which peers and M.P.'s may pray for the annulment of the subordinate legislation produced by Whitehall departments.

Recently more direct methods have been used to scrutinize the flow of delegated legislation. In 1944 the Westminster House of Commons set up a Select Committee on Statutory Instruments, to draw the attention of the House to such matters as the imposition of charges on the revenue, the exclusion of the jurisdiction of the courts, unusual or unexpected uses of the delegated power, unauthorized retrospective effects, or unjustifiable delay in publication or in laying before parliament. Two years later a Joint Select Committee of the Senate and House of Commons of Northern Ireland was set up to scrutinize Statutory Rules, Orders, and Regulations. The terms of reference of the Belfast Committee were similar to those of its Westminster counterpart. Then in 1954 the Dublin Senate set up a Select Committee on Statutory Instruments, whose terms of reference were identical with those of the Northern Ireland Committee. A convenient way of comparing the activities of these three bodies is to examine their working during the first four months of 1955, at the end of which the Dublin committee made its first report.

During the relevant period the Westminster committee considered one hundred and eighty-five instruments, asked for memoranda on four of these and, after some correspondence with the responsible department, reported one of the instruments to the House on the ground that it was an unusual exercise of the powers conferred by the parent statute. The committee of Dublin Senators considered one hundred and two documents during its first period of activity, had correspondence with government departments about sixteen of these, and called one witness. In their first report they called the attention of the Senate to these sixteen documents on such grounds as the unexpected use of powers, delay in laying before the Oireachtas, and the form and purport of orders. In the course of these investigations doubt was thrown on the validity of one order and in another it was agreed that the order was void since it had not been laid in draft for the requisite period. The committee did not, however, confine itself to criticism of these instruments, for it also made a number of general recommendations about the form of future orders. The activities of the Joint Select Committee in Belfast during the same period display a different emphasis. Thirty-six instruments were considered, departmental memoranda relating to these were submitted, witnesses were called to explain the meaning of almost all these documents, and the committee discussed both the effect and the policy of many regulations. In the result, five instruments were mentioned to the Northern Ireland parliament as imposing a charge on public funds. From this comparison it appears that the Belfast committee has gone much further than its Dublin and Westminster counterparts in requiring explanations and examining the policy of delegated legislation. Where the Dublin and Westminster bodies are concerned with form, the main preoccupation of the Belfast committee is content.[5]

In addition to providing methods for the scrutiny of delegated legislation, the three parliaments have legislated to deal with the important matter of publishing copies of subordinate instruments. At Westminster, the Statutory Instruments Act, 1946 replaced the Rules Publication Act, 1893 (56 & 57 Vict. c. 66), but the latter enactment continued in force in so far as it concerned certain matters, such as the Rules of the Northern Ireland Supreme Court, with which the parliament of Northern Ireland has no powers to deal. As respects matters within the powers of the Northern Ireland parliament, the publication of subordinate instruments is governed by the Rules Publication Act, 1925. This Act specified the Northern Ireland rule-making authorities and defined a statutory rule as:

Every exercise by a rule-making authority of a statutory power which is of a legislative character (whether described as a rule, regulation or order or by any other name).

Provision was made for the numbering, printing, and publishing of Statutory Rules and Orders, with exceptions for orders whose pub-

---

[5] For a comparison of the activities of scrutiny committees in different parts of the Commonwealth see Sir Cecil Thomas Carr, "Parliamentary Control of Delegated Legislation," *Public Law,* I (1956), 200, 211-215.

lication is deemed by the rule-making authority to be unnecessary. Annual volumes of all instruments (other than temporary local or unpublished orders) are issued, classifying the orders according to subject matter and giving lists of those omitted. The distinction between public general and local statutes is followed in differentiating between the various types of Statutory Rules and Orders, and questions arising under the Act are determined by the Northern Ireland Ministry of Finance, with the concurrence of the Lord Chief Justice and the Speakers of the two Houses of the Northern Ireland Parliament.

In the Irish Republic there was no similar legislation until the passing of the Statutory Instruments Act, 1947 (No. 44 of 1947). Until then an aura of doubt had prevailed concerning the application of the Rules Publication Act, 1893. In *The State (Quinlan) v. Kavanagh and Others*, [1935] I.R. 249 Kennedy C. J. had assumed at p. 264 that the Act applied, but in *In re McGrath and Harte*, [1941] I. R. 68 his successor, Sullivan C. J., had pointed out at p. 78 that the Act had not been adapted for application in the Republic. The 1947 Act settled the matter by repealing and replacing the British enactment. The term "statutory instrument" was defined to include "an order, regulation, rule, scheme or bye-law made in exercise of a power conferred by statute," so that the Dublin Act avoids the question whether or not an instrument is "of a legislative character." As well as providing for the numbering, citation, and printing of Statutory Instruments, the Act authorized the deposit of copies in a number of specified libraries. The Dublin Attorney-General exercises the powers which in Belfast are entrusted to a committee. He has to certify whether persons or bodies are exercising any function of government or discharging duties in relation to public administration; whether an instrument "affects the public generally or any particular class or classes of the public"; or whether Statutory Instruments should be exempted because of local, personal, or limited application or temporary operation. There is no statutory authority for the preparation of annual volumes, but in practice a series commenced publication in 1948. Unlike the Belfast volumes and the annual volumes of Whitehall Statutory Instruments, those published in Dublin are arranged in chronological order and are not classified.

In these different ways the parliaments at Belfast, Dublin, and Westminster have made statutory provision to inform the public of the legislation made by subordinate authorities. The next matter for consideration is the complementary branch of administrative law, that relating to administrative decisions and tribunals.

ADMINISTRATIVE DECISIONS AND TRIBUNALS

In both Belfast and Dublin, as in Whitehall and elsewhere, the administrative decisions of government departments and subordinate tribunals play an important part in the working of the constitutional systems. An Irish investigation on the lines of Sir Carleton Allen's recent work on *Administrative Jurisdiction*[6] would be most welcome, but in the absence of this a few examples must suffice to illustrate the way in which administrative tribunals operate in both Irish jurisdictions. In the Irish Republic these tribunals derive their ultimate authority from Art. 37 of the 1937 Constitution, providing for the limited exercise of judicial functions otherwise than by courts and judges, while in Northern Ireland administrative authority is exercised under the ordinary law. Despite the constitutional differences there are certain similarities in the way in which administrative jurisdiction is exercised in both Belfast and Dublin.

An obvious source of such similarity is the statute law which formerly applied throughout the whole of Ireland. For example, the Housing of the Working Classes Act, 1890 (53 & 54 Vict. c. 70) when it was originally enacted applied to England and Wales, Scotland, and Ireland. One of its features was the holding of local inquiries where there were objections to the confirmation of orders made by local authorities; it was on a provision of this kind that the classic English case of *Errington v. Minister of Health*, [1935] 1 K.B. 249 (1934) was decided. Another feature of the Victorian legislation was the requirement of arbitration for disputes about the amount of compensation for land. It is, therefore, not surprising to discover that in the housing legislation in force in both Northern Ireland and the Irish Republic these two principles continue to be used. In neither jurisdiction is there separate legislation on the lines of the Westminster Acquisition of Land (Authorisation Procedure) Act, 1946 (9 & 10 Geo. 6, c. 49), providing a uniform procedure for the

[6] London, 1956; reprinted from *Public Law*, I (1956), 13.

acquisition of land by local authorities otherwise than for housing purposes, nor has the Lands Tribunal Act, 1949 (12, 13 & 14 Geo. 6, c. 42) been followed, so that no single body is entrusted with the decision of compensation disputes. But the vesting order procedure used in Belfast, and the method of making compulsory acquisition orders authorized by Dublin legislation, together with the continued use of the Acquisition of Land (Assessment of Compensation) Act, 1919 (9 & 10 Geo. 5, c. 57), combined to insure the continued application in both areas of the general principles of previous legislation.

Another example of the similar ways in which administrative topics are treated by the Belfast and Dublin legislatures is provided by the law relating to town and country planning. Under the Planning Acts (Northern Ireland), 1931 (21 & 22 Geo. 5, c. 12) and 1944 (c. 3), the Ministry of Health and Local Government has the task of considering planning schemes made by local authorities, of holding local inquiries into objections to schemes, and of approving or disapproving such schemes. In the Irish Republic under the Town and Regional Planning Acts, 1934 (No. 22 of 1934), and 1939 (No. 11 of 1939), the Minister for Local Government has a similar task. There are two additions in the Dublin legislation—the Oireachtas may annul a planning scheme which has been approved, and a statutory right of appeal to the High Court is given to a person whose property has been affected by a scheme. As for appellate jurisdictions exercised by the Belfast Ministry and the Dublin Minister, both have the duty of determining appeals by persons aggrieved by the refusal of a local authority to permit the development of land. Thus Northern Ireland and the Irish Republic have devised similar administrative procedures for the solution of this type of problem, and they have also in common the fact that as yet neither has passed any enactment corresponding to Westminster's Town and Country Planning Act, 1947 (10 & 11 Geo. 6, c. 51).

The two previous examples have shown a similarity in original and appellate ministerial jurisdictions. Another type of modern administrative system is that used to decide the rights of persons under social welfare schemes. Under a Social Services Agreement made between the Northern Ireland Ministry of Finance and the United Kingdom Treasury in 1949 it was agreed that the social welfare and health services schemes in Northern Ireland should be in general parity and conformity with those in force in the rest of the United Kingdom. In these circumstances it is not surprising that the details of the National Insurance Acts (Northern Ireland), 1946 (cc. 21 and 23), and of the amending legislation, should be almost identical with the acts passed at Westminster, and the same is true of the schemes themselves. As in Great Britain, two methods are used for the determination of claims and questions arising in relation to social benefits. Questions as to whether a person has satisfied the necessary conditions are determined by the Ministry of Labour and National Insurance, which may refer points of law arising out of such questions to the Supreme Court; in addition, a person aggrieved by a decision of the Ministry on a question of law may appeal to the Supreme Court. Other questions are determined in the first instance by an insurance officer, from whom an appeal may be taken to a local tribunal; questions of fact are decided by an officer, or a tribunal may refer them to local referees for a report. From the tribunals an appeal lies to an umpire, who has the status of a County Court judge and acts as final appellate authority for these statutes and other social welfare legislation. In outline, the system of appeals in the Irish Republic under the Social Welfare Act, 1952 (No. 11 of 1952), is similar. Disputed questions go first of all to a deciding officer, who may decide the matter himself or may, like an insurance officer in Northern Ireland, refer the question to a higher authority. Under the 1952 Act this authority is an appeals officer, who may be assisted by an assessor. There is no appeal from such a decision on matters relating to claims or disqualification but on other matters, such as the question of insurable employment and the status of a person as a contributor to the scheme, the Minister for Social Welfare may, if requested by the chief appeals officer, refer the matter for decision by the High Court. Alternatively, a dissatisfied person may appeal on a question of law to the High Court. As in Northern Ireland, decisions may be reviewed in the light of changed circumstances. The details of the Irish Republic's social welfare scheme are not the same as those of the Northern Ireland national insurance scheme, but the problem of adjudicating on the rights of persons involved in the schemes is dealt with in like manner in both areas.

Yet another type of administrative body is the independent tribunal which deals with the activities of public corporations (which

are mentioned briefly in the succeeding section). Convenient examples are provided by the tribunals established under the Transport
Act (Northern Ireland), 1948 (c. 16) and the Irish Republic's Transport Act, 1950 (No. 12 of 1950). The Northern Ireland Transport
Tribunal is deemed to be a court of record and it has a wide range of
functions. Thus it determines maximum charges which may be
made by the transport undertakings, the main one being the Ulster
Transport Authority; it fixes the conditions for services and facilities
provided by those undertakings, and it hears and determines applications for the total discontinuance of railway services. An appeal
lies on a point of law to the Supreme Court, and the relative importance of this tribunal may be gauged from the fact that a Lord
Justice of Appeal was appointed as its first chairman. The functions
of the corresponding Transport Tribunal in the Irish Republic are
more limited, but its equivalent status may be gathered from the fact
that witnesses appearing before it are entitled to the same immunities
and privileges as a witness appearing before the High Court. The
Tribunal's main task is to consider applications from Coras Iompair
Eireann, the state transport undertaking, for relief from the duty
to provide railway services or from the liability to keep canals open
for navigation. In addition, the Tribunal has a duty to advise the
Minister for Industry and Commerce on matters which he may refer
to it. The two tribunals differ in the effect of certain of their decisions. If the Ulster Transport Authority obtains an order from
the Northern Ireland Transport Tribunal permitting it to discontinue
railway services on a particular line, that line cannot be abandoned
until an order to that effect is made by the Ministry of Commerce
for Northern Ireland. On the other hand, an exemption order made
by the Dublin tribunal allowing Coras Iompair Eireann to discontinue railway services entitles that body if it so wishes to make an
abandonment order without any further procedure. Despite these
differences in function, the corresponding jurisdictions of the two
transport tribunals facilitated the co-operation on railway services between Northern Ireland and the Irish Republic which was mentioned
in Chapter III on International Law (*supra*).

Yet another type of administrative tribunal is concerned with the
organization of professional bodies. A convenient Irish example is
provided by the arrangements in the two areas for the exercise of

disciplinary control over members of the solicitors' profession. In Northern Ireland the statutory authority for this lies in the Solicitors Act, 1938 (2 Geo. 6, c. 14), under which the Lord Chief Justice appoints a disciplinary committee from members of the Incorporated Law Society of Northern Ireland. This committee conducts investigations into allegations relating to the professional conduct of solicitors, and their report is presented to the Lord Chief Justice, who may strike an offending solicitor off the rolls or suspend or censure him. In the Irish Republic the corresponding procedure is set out in the Solicitors Act, 1954 (No. 36 of 1954), under which the disciplinary committee is appointed by the Incorporated Law Society of Ireland from its members. This committee has jurisdiction, after investigation, to make the necessary disciplinary orders, but an appeal lies to the Chief Justice. In *O'Farrell and Gorman v. Incorporated Law Society of Ireland* (1956, unreported) the validity of these provisions was challenged as an unconstitutional delegation of judicial power, but the challenge was not sustained. Once again a common statutory origin explains the similarities in these procedures, for the profession in the whole of Ireland was formerly regulated by the Solicitors (Ireland) Act, 1898 (61 & 62 Vict. c. 17).

These are only examples of the way in which the power to adjudicate is distributed in Northern Ireland and the Irish Republic; as already indicated, there is room for a comparative study of this topic. But the similarities which have been mentioned do not obtain in every part of this branch of administrative law. For example, neither the United Kingdom as a whole nor Northern Ireland has anything comparable to the Irish Republic's Censorship of Publications Acts, 1929 (No. 21 of 1929), and 1946 (No. 1 of 1946). Under these Acts a Censorship of Publications Board is given power to ban the importation and sale of books judged to be indecent or obscene, or advocating contraception or abortion. From the decisions of the board, an appeal lies to the Censorship of Publications Appeals Board, whose chairman must be a judge, or a barrister or solicitor of seven years' standing. Mr. Norman St. John-Stevas has examined the operation of this system in his recent work on *Obscenity and the Law*[7] but for the present purpose it will suffice to note that in the Irish Republic a special system of administrative adjudication has been

[7] London, 1956.

devised to cope with a situation which in the United Kingdom is dealt with by the ordinary courts. Again, the Adoption Act, 1952 (No. 25 of 1952) set up a special board of six members, with a judge or other legally qualified person as chairman, to hear applications for, and to make, adoption orders. In Northern Ireland and Great Britain this is a matter for the lower courts rather than a special tribunal.

Other opportunities for comparison and contrast are to be found in the procedures for the regulation of economic affairs. Mention has been made already of the powers of the Irish Republic's Labour Court in fixing wages and conditions of work. Another of its functions is the investigation of trade disputes, either on its own initiative (if there is a likelihood of a stoppage of work or no other negotiating machinery is available), or at the request of the parties to the dispute.[8] The activities of the court have played an important part in the industrial life of the Irish Republic in the past ten years, and a student of labor relations would find it of interest to compare these activities with the negotiating machinery and ad hoc tribunals used in Northern Ireland and Great Britain, as well as with the varieties of industrial conciliation and arbitration legislation used in the Australian Commonwealth and states, and with the work of the New Zealand Court of Arbitration. Again, the activities of the Commission established under the Monopolies and Restrictive Practices (Inquiry and Control) Act, 1948 (11 & 12 Geo. 6, c. 66), and the court constituted under the Restrictive Trade Practices Act, 1956 (4 & 5 Eliz. 2, c. 68), might well be compared with the working of the Irish Republic's Restrictive Trade Practices Act, 1953 (No. 14 of 1953). This set up a Fair Trade Commission, with power to make fair trading rules and to inquire into the observance of these rules. Reports of the Commission require legislative action (as did those of the British Monopolies Commission) so that this aspect of economic control has not passed out of the hands of the Oireachtas as has happened at Westminster, where independent adjudication is now used. Another useful comparison could be made between the Irish legislation and, say, that of New Zealand relating to monopolies and that of Canada relating to restrictive practices.

[8] *Cf.* Ronald James Patrick Mortished, "The Industrial Relations Act, 1946," *Public Administration in Ireland* (Dublin, 1949), II, 75.

This brief summary has sought to show something of the scope of administrative adjudication in both Northern Ireland and the Irish Republic in relation to such matters as the acquisition of property, town and country planning, social welfare, and the activities of transport undertakings and the members of a branch of the legal profession. In these fields there are similarities between the systems used in the two areas, but the Irish Republic has also made certain innovations. A study of these systems and innovations, in comparison with the administrative procedures used in other common law jurisdictions, would be of interest alike to lawyers, political scientists, and economists.

A NOTE ON PUBLIC CORPORATIONS

A brief reference to the subject of public corporations must suffice to end this précis of administrative procedures in the two parts of Ireland, before the attitude of the courts and the legal position of the two governments are considered. In Northern Ireland the main use of the statutory corporation before the Second World War was to insure the economic development of the area. Thus the Electricity (Supply) Act (Northern Ireland), 1931 (21 & 22 Geo. 5, c. 9), constituted an Electricity Board whose activities have spread throughout Northern Ireland so that now there are only three suppliers of electricity—the Board and the Belfast and Londonderry Corporations. In 1935 the Road and Railway Transport Act (Northern Ireland) (25 & 26 Geo. 5, c. 15) authorized the constitution of the Northern Ireland Road Transport Board, which was given the responsibility of operating almost all road services for passengers and the carriage of freight "for hire or reward." By the Transport Act (Northern Ireland), 1948 (c. 16) this Board was reconstituted as the Ulster Transport Authority and its powers were increased to include the operation of railway services. In the postwar period the statutory corporation has been utilized for the provision of social services. For example, the Northern Ireland Tuberculosis Authority was set up under the Public Health (Tuberculosis) Act (Northern Ireland), 1946 (c. 6) to combat this disease. The Health Services Act (Northern Ireland), 1948 (c. 3) differed from the corresponding measures passed by the Westminster parliament for England and Wales and Scotland in that the Northern Ireland legislation set up independent boards to operate the various health schemes. Thus the Northern Ireland General Health Services Board and the Northern Ireland Hospitals Authority are charged with the duty of providing health services, while the function of the Ministry of Health and Local Government is to co-ordinate these services. Another important development was the setting up under the Housing Act (Northern Ireland), 1945 (c. 2) of a Housing Trust. This independent body was given the task of assisting local authorities to meet the postwar housing shortage, and it has been responsible for changing much of the face of the countryside during the past decade.

In the Irish Free State the necessity for setting up statutory corporations was recognized early in the existence of the new Dominion. The Electricity Supply Board was set up by the Electricity (Supply) Act, 1927 (No. 27 of 1927), and in 1933 began the process of regulation of railways which led in 1944 to the passing of the Transport Act (No. 21 of 1944) and the formation of Coras Iompair Eireann, which operates road and rail services. A variation of the normal type of statutory corporation was provided by the creation, under statutory authority, of government-financed joint stock companies. In this way the Agricultural Credit Corporation was set up under the Agricultural Credit Act, 1927 (No. 24 of 1927), and the Industrial Credit Corporation was constituted by statute in 1933 (No. 25 of 1933). The Air Navigation Transport Act, 1936 (No. 40 of 1936) authorized the formation of Aer Rianta to hold the shares in a similar company, Aer Lingus, which is responsible for the operation of air services from the Irish Republic to Great Britain and Europe. In 1934 there was constituted another publicly financed company, the Turf Development Board Limited, which under the Turf Development Act, 1946 (No. 10 of 1946) became a statutory corporation with the name of Bord na Mona. Under the Public Hospitals Act, 1933 (No. 18 of 1933) a complex structure composed of a private company, representative committees, and appointed boards is used to organize that well-known feature of Irish life, the Irish Hospitals Sweepstakes. Another important Irish matter is the subject of development and regulation by the Racing Board, set up under the Racing Board and Racecourses Act, 1945 (No. 16 of 1945) to assist in the better breeding of race-horses. Corporations of various types regulate other aspects of Irish life from tourism to shipping and seafisheries.

These references to Irish public corporations indicate how the Belfast and Dublin parliaments have developed distinctive techniques for the solution of the problems with which they were faced. The former has varied the British nationalization pattern by the introduction of independent boards to organize various social services, and the latter has combined statutory authority and the use of the ordinary companies legislation to form its commercial undertakings. Once again, the possibilities for comparative research are hopeful. As the recent study of *The Public Corporation*[9] edited by Professor W. Friedmann has shown, the comparisons and contrasts between the types of public corporation used in different parts of the world are illuminating. Thus, for example, the Irish transport legislation could be compared with that in force in Australia and New Zealand, Canada, and South Africa. Again, the Irish boards for the production of electricity could be compared with similar bodies in the Commonwealth, and the Irish Republic's air lines could be examined in conjunction with corresponding Commonwealth corporations. For the lawyer and the political scientist the interest of comparative studies of this kind lies in such matters as the status and control of the corporate bodies,[10] while their operation and effect concern the economist. But whatever the standpoint of the investigator may be, the material is abundant and the Irish experience is extremely relevant.

JUDICIAL SCRUTINY AND CONTROL

Before 1921 the courts in Ireland, like their counterparts in England, had fairly frequent opportunities of considering both the legislative activities of subordinate bodies and the judicial activities of administrative tribunals and similar bodies.

One of the British decisions which fell to be considered in the Irish courts was the leading case of *Institute of Patent Agents v. Lockwood*, [1894] A.C. 347, in which it was held that rules which were to have "the same effect as if they were contained in [the parent

---

[9] *University of Toronto Comparative Law Series No. 1* (London, 1954).

[10] *Cf.* Patrick Philip O'Donoghue, "The Relations of Statutory Corporations with the Government and the Oireachtas," *Public Administration in Ireland* (Dublin, 1949), II, 18; Frederick Basil Chubb, "Public Control of Public Enterprise," *Administration*, II (1954), 21; Michael Scully, "Parliamentary Control of Public Corporations in Eire," *Public Administration*, XXXII (1954), 455-462.

act]" could not be examined by the courts. Both Sir William Graham-Harrison and Professor John Willis have analyzed this case, but for the present purpose it is significant that the Irish Lord of Appeal who sat in that case, Lord Morris (a former Lord Chief Justice of Ireland) did not assent to the general proposition. In *R. (Conyngham) v. Pharmaceutical Society of Ireland*, [1899] 2 I.R. 132 a similar statutory provision was considered. Palles C. B. distinguished *Lockwood's* case on the grounds that there wide powers had been given to a government department, but parliament had retained the power of annulling the subordinate legislation; in *Conyngham's* case neither of these two elements appeared. O'Brien J., on the other hand, held that the rule challenged in *Conyngham's* case was entirely outside the scope of the parent act, which he regarded as qualifying the general effect of *Lockwood's* case. Again, in *Commissioners of Public Works v. Monaghan*, [1909] 2 I.R. 718 the validity was challenged of a fishery by-law which, if approved by two judges of the superior courts, was to be 'binding upon and observed by all persons whatsoever, and sufficient in all courts of justice and equity to justify all persons who shall act under the same." Dodd and Andrews JJ. (with whom Palles C. B. concurred) held that they were not precluded from declaring ultra vires a by-law clearly outside the scope of the parent act, while Johnson J. distinguished *Lockwood's* case on the ground that there an element of parliamentary control remained. On the other hand, Lord O'Brien L. C. J. followed *Lockwood's* case. In *Mackey v. Monks*, [1916] 2 I.R. 200, 241 a question arose as to the validity of some factories' regulations which could be annulled by parliament but which were not to have effect as if they were contained in the parent act. In the Court of Appeal in Ireland O'Brien L. C. (not to be confused with his namesakes, the judge and the Lord Chief Justice) and Molony L. J. distinguished *Lockwood's* case by reference to the wording of the legislation, and Ronan L. J. drew the distinction between the parliamentary power of annulment and the judicial function of scrutiny for validity. The House of Lords ([1918] A.C. 59) overruled the Irish courts on the substance of the case, but did not advert to *Lockwood's* case. Finally, in *Corporation of Waterford v. Murphy*, [1920] 2 I.R. 165 the Irish High Court declared invalid a local by-law imposing a fee, although a copy of the subordinate legislation was to be "conclusive evidence of the validity of such by-laws." *Lockwood's* case was distinguished on the ground that there the powers were wider than in the *Waterford* case, where the by-law was clearly outside the scope of the act. In sum, the Irish courts were not enamored of *Lockwood's* case and distinguished it wherever possible, following the lead of the Irish member of the House of Lords who originally dissented.

As for the control of subordinate courts and tribunals, the Irish reports during the nineteenth century and the early part of the twentieth century furnish many examples of the way in which the prerogative writs were used to curb excess of jurisdiction and to cure injustices. Round these cases there was spun much of the web of fine distinctions which comprises so much of administrative law.

A frequent litigant on these occasions was the Local Government Board for Ireland, which exercised general control over the hierarchy of local authorities. Some of the cases in which this board was involved must suffice to illustrate the courts' methods of using the prerogative writs. For example, in *R. (Dixon) v. Local Government Board*, (1878) 2 L.R. Ir. 316 certiorari was sought against the board because they had constituted an area as a township when it did not contain the number of inhabitants required by statute. It was contended that the board's action was ministerial rather than judicial, but the Queen's Bench Division held that the board had made decisions of a judicial character which could properly be reviewed by the court. Seven years later, in *In re the Local Government Board, ex parte Commissioners of Kingstown*, (1885) 16 L.R. Ir. 150 the Exchequer Division had to consider the effect of an inquiry held by an inspector of the board as to the propriety of making a provisional order relating to a water supply. Prohibition was sought to prevent the holding of the inquiry, and it was argued that this should not lie, since the inquiry was not a judicial one. Palles C. B. pointed out at p. 157 that the fact that proceedings were not ministerial did not make them judicial, since they might be quasi-legislative, that is, "proceeding towards legislation," and prohibition was refused; the decision was upheld on appeal (18 L.R. Ir. 509). In another local government case, *R. (Porter) v. Omagh Union Guardians*, (1890) 26 L.R. Ir. 619, certiorari was sought to quash the certificate of an auditor employed by the Local Government Board. It was held that a general examination of the accounts of a poor law union was not a judicial act, and that certiorari would not lie, though Holmes J. pointed out that the writ might be sought in respect of certain certificates which did involve a judicial determination. Again, in *R. (Wexford County Council) v. Local Government Board*, [1902] 2 I.R. 349, the question for decision was whether the board was acting judicially in determining the rates of remuneration for certain local authority officers. The Court of Appeal rejected the contention that the board was exempt from control by certiorari on the ground that it was "a Government administrative department." Since the decision in question purported to be binding, it was judicial, but since it was made by an inferior body in excess of jurisdiction, certiorari lay to quash the decision. The board's method of reaching certain decisions was queried in *R. (Cairns) v. Local Government Board*, [1911] 2 I.R. 331 but Madden J. pointed out that "the Local Government Board is one of several great administrative bodies who find themselves, in the course of administration, performing duties which this court regards as judicial" and that "it is impossible to lay down any hard and fast rule as to the requirements of natural justice in such a case. It was never contemplated, and it would be unreasonable to hold, that a formulated procedure, such as that which has come into use in Courts of Justice, should be adopted." Certiorari was accordingly refused. Again, in *R. (Bryson) v. Lisnaskea Union Guardians and Local Government Board*, [1918] 2 I.R. 258 certiorari was sought to determine the validity of a decision of a local authority approved by the board to grant certain superannuation allowances to local government officers. It was alleged that the poor law guardians had acted with insufficient evidence, and that the board was in excess of jurisdiction in approving the action of the guardians. The King's Bench Division held that the guardians were acting in a judicial or quasi-judicial capacity, and that certiorari should issue.

Commenting on the first two cases which have been summarized, Professor W. A. Robson pointed out that the Irish judges differed from their English brethren in holding that finality, rather than discretion, was the test for distinguishing between judicial and administrative acts.[11] The later cases show how the Irish judges

[11] *Justice and Administrative Law* (3d ed.; London, 1951), 12-13.

evolved a method reconciling the judicial or quasi-judicial decisions of subordinate bodies with their administrative functions, insuring that "natural justice" was observed, and that decisions which did not observe this principle, or were in excess of jurisdiction, were quashed. The cases cited were only a few examples of this process in its application to local government. For instance, *R. (McKenney) v. Antrim Justices*, [1901] 2 I.R. 133 is frequently cited on the right to issue mandamus against a decision where an alternative method of appeal lies. And the unsettled state of Ireland in the early 1920's gave rise to a number of decisions on the inability of the courts to interfere with decisions of military tribunals while a state of martial law exists. Thus in *R. v. Allen*, [1921] 2 I. R. 241 it was held that the civil courts could not interfere *durante bello* with the decision of a military court sitting in an area where martial law had been proclaimed, though in *Egan v. Macready*, [1921] 1 I.R. 265 habeas corpus was granted on the ground that only a court-martial, not a military court, had power to impose the death sentence under the Restoration of Order in Ireland Act, 1920 (10 & 11 Geo. 5, c. 31). In *Re Clifford and O'Sullivan*, [1921] 2 A.C. 570 prohibition was sought against a military court, but the Court of Appeal in Ireland held that they had no jurisdiction in a criminal cause or matter. The House of Lords overruled the Irish court on this point but held that a military court was not the kind of tribunal to which prohibition would lie, and in any event the functions of the court were spent once the proceedings which had been challenged were completed.

A study of the use of the prerogative writs in Ireland is long overdue, but perhaps the cases which have been cited have shown something of the ranges of the activities of the Irish courts in this respect, and the fact that they were prepared on occasion to take action on lines differing from the English decisions relating to judicial control of inferior tribunals.

THE ATTITUDE OF THE NORTHERN IRELAND COURTS

Since their constitution in 1921 the courts in Northern Ireland have continued the process of investigation into the validity of delegated legislation and of the activities of inferior tribunals. In the chapter on Constitutional Developments since 1920 (*supra*) reference was made to the case of *R. (O'Hanlon) v. Governor of Belfast Prison*, (1922) 56 I.L.T.R. 170 where it was held that certain regulations were within the powers conferred by the Civil Authorities (Special Powers) Act (Northern Ireland), 1922 (12 & 13 Geo. 5, c. 5). The learned editors of the title "Northern Ireland" in the second edition of Halsbury's Statutes[11a] have contended that *R. v. Halliday, ex parte Zadig*, [1917] A.C. 260, on which the Northern Ireland court relied in *O'Hanlon's* case, was not exactly parallel, and that the test of validity should be objective rather than subjective. If the point should ever be discussed further in the Northern Ireland courts the application of the principle of the classic decision in *Liversidge v. Anderson*, [1942] A.C. 206 (1941) would obviously be relevant.

A more recent example of the control exercised by the Northern Ireland courts over the validity of legislation occurred in *Minister of Agriculture v. McCartney*, [1948] N.I. 1. The regulation queried in that case obliged a person claiming allegedly smuggled cattle to prove that they had not been smuggled; it further debarred him from raising any further defense or objection in forfeiture proceedings. In the Court of Appeal Black J. reserved the question of the validity of the regulation, but Babington and Porter L. JJ. both held that the regulation was invalid, on the ground that the parent act did not authorize interference with court procedure. Babington L. J. further held that a Minister, in making regulations, must recognize the right of the subject to appeal to the courts and present his case free from arbitrary limitations. The English decision in *Chester v. Bateson*, [1920] 1 K. B. 829 was expressly followed by this judge in holding that certain basic principles underlie the making of subordinate legislation, and that the courts will be reluctant to construe an instrument as infringing these principles.

The extent to which the courts will refuse to interfere with the decisions of administrative authorities is illustrated by a trio of Northern Ireland cases in which the writ of mandamus was refused. In *R. (Quinn) v. Portadown Urban Council*, [1938] N.I. 1 a local authority failed to give to an applicant for the renewal of a license the statutory notice relating to an objection, but nevertheless decided to hear the objection and refuse the renewal. The applicant asked for mandamus to compel the renewal of the license, but the issue of the writ was refused on the ground that the applicant had an alternative remedy, since he could appeal to the county court. This was also

[11a] London, 1950, vol. 17, 169.

the basis of the decision in *R. (Hendron) v. Northern Ireland Road Transport Board*, [1944] N.I. 48. In that case an act of the Northern Ireland parliament had laid down a procedure for the settling of disputes between the Board and its employees. A similar procedure was later provided under wartime emergency legislation and, since the court held that this was not less beneficial, convenient, and effective, mandamus to compel the use of the earlier procedure did not issue. Then in *R. (Diamond and Fleming) v. Warnock*, [1946] N.I. 171, mandamus was sought to compel the release of a prisoner on hunger strike but it was refused on the grounds, inter alia, that the writ would not issue to a Minister of the Crown and that, in any event, the statutory powers of the Minister were discretionary and not mandatory.

In dealing with these problems of substantive ultra vires and the activities of administrative authorities, the courts in Northern Ireland were, of course, dealing with problems which confronted the courts in other parts of the Commonwealth. For example, in *R. (Sloan) v. Lord Mayor of Belfast*, (1923) 57 I.L.T.R. 71 the Northern Ireland King's Bench Division held that when a local authority licensed a motor to ply for hire, the authority was acting in a quasi-judicial capacity and that certiorari would lie to quash a license granted in contravention of local by-laws. With this may be contrasted the recent English decision (which has been the subject of some criticism[12]) in *R. v. Metropolitan Police Commissioner, ex parte Parker*, [1953] 1 W.L.R. 1150, where it was held that certiorari would not lie to quash a decision to revoke a cab-driver's license, since that act was neither judicial nor quasi-judicial. If the point should arise again in the Northern Ireland courts both this case and the decision of the Privy Council in the Ceylon case of *Nakkuda Ali v. Jayaratne*, [1951] A.C. 66 (1950) would clearly be material.

THE ATTITUDE OF THE DUBLIN COURTS

A couple of cases decided on the validity of instruments made under the Emergency Powers Act, 1939 (No. 28 of 1939) must serve to illustrate the activities of the Dublin courts in inquiring into the validity of delegated legislation. Thus in *Attorney-General v. Duff*, [1941] I.R. 406 it was argued that the penalties imposed

[12] D. M. Gordon, "The Cab-Driver's Licence Case," *Law Quarterly Review*, LXX (1954), 203-213.

by an Emergency Powers Order were greater than those specified in the parent act, which could not be amended by a subordinate instrument. The High Court held, however, that it was legitimate for an Emergency Powers Order to apply the provisions of an earlier statute which in turn attracted the penal provisions of customs legislation; the validity of this piece of subordinate legislation by reference was accordingly upheld. Again, in *Minister for Agriculture v. O'Connell*, [1942] I.R. 600 it was contended that the annual perpetuation of the emergency legislation prevented the making of any subordinate legislation which referred to a period after the next renewal of the legislation. In the Supreme Court, Sullivan C. J. rejected this contention, referring to the circumstances in which the emergency legislation was passed and remarking, at p. 607, that

. . . in making the Order in question the Government was entitled to have regard to what was obviously the intention of Parliament, and to make an Order which would be operative so long as the Act should continue to be in force, whether by virtue of the then existing statutory provisions or of any subsequent legislation.

It is noteworthy that counsel cited in argument the cases of *R. v. Halliday, ex parte Zadig*, [1917] A.C. 260 and *Liversidge v. Anderson*, [1942] A.C. 206 (1941) in support of the contention that the strict rule of construction to be adopted in the case of penal statutes does not apply to statutes passed to deal with a public emergency or with a public danger. Although this was not referred to in the judgment it is clear that in the Irish Republic, as in other jurisdictions, the maxim *inter arma leges silent* was given a limited application; although not completely silenced, some diminution of the law's voice was necessary in exceptional circumstances.

In considering the judicial control of administrative tribunals by the Irish courts,[13] it is necessary to remember Art. 37 of the 1937 Constitution, which provides that nothing

. . . shall operate to invalidate the exercise of limited functions and powers of a judicial nature, in matters other than criminal matters, by any person or body of persons duly authorised by law to exercise such functions or powers, notwithstanding that such person or such body of persons is not a judge or a court appointed or established as such under this Constitution.

[13] *Cf.* Vincent Grogan, "Administrative Tribunals," *Public Administration in Ireland* (Dublin, 1954), III, 32.

With this must be read Art. 34, 3, (1), which gives the High Court power "to determine all matters and questions whether of law or fact, civil or criminal." This provision, which is similar to Art. 64 of the 1922 Constitution, prevents any prohibition of the review by the courts of inferior judicial decisions, but it does not, of course, mean that the courts will necessarily make such a review or take action as a result; the principles on which the courts will act are to be found in the decided cases.

Here it may be noted that in 1926 the Irish Free State by High Court rules substituted court orders for the former prerogative writs. In this respect Dublin preceded London by some twelve years, for it was not until the passing of s. 7 of the Administration of Justice (Miscellaneous Provisions) Act, 1938 (1 & 2 Geo. 6, c. 63) that the Westminster parliament took similar action. A very few of the cases decided by the Dublin courts during the past three and a half decades must suffice to indicate the attitude of the judges towards the use of the prerogative writs and orders. Two early decisions were the product of the unsettled circumstances which surrounded the birth of the Irish Free State. In R. (Childers) v. Adjutant-General, [1923] 1 I.R. 5 it was held that habeas corpus would not issue to a military court, on the ground that while a state of war existed the civil courts had no jurisdiction over the acts of the military authority. Then, as mentioned in the chapter on Legal History (supra), in R. (Kelly) v. Maguire and O'Sheil, [1923] 2 I.R. 58 it was held that prohibition would not lie against the courts which had been set up by Dáil Eireann in 1920 and which continued to function until they were suspended in 1922 by the Provisional government.

In more settled circumstances the courts were able to determine the extent of their jurisdiction over more regularly constituted bodies. For instance, in a 1927 case, R. (Spain) v. Income Tax Commissioners, reported at [1934] I.R. 27, the High Court held that mandamus did not lie to compel a quasi-judicial body to alter its decision when that decision had already been reached as a result of a hearing and determination. On the other hand, in O'Driscoll v. Cork County Council, [1931] I.R. 92 it was held that a statutory appeal was an additional remedy, not an alternative one which would prevent the issue of mandamus to a local authority to determine the amount of compensation for loss of office suffered by a local authority solicitor. But the great bulk of the cases were decided on applications for certiorari to quash the decisions of tribunals.

A statutory attempt to prevent the questioning of a compulsory purchase order "by prohibition or certiorari or in any legal proceedings whatsoever" was considered in *The State (Wood) v. West Cork Board of Health*, [1936] I.R. 401, where a majority of the High Court construed the relevant statute in favor of the issuing of certiorari. Again, in *The State (McCarthy) v. O'Donnell and the Minister for Defence*, [1945] I.R. 126 the decision challenged was a referee's report which was to be "final and conclusive and binding on all persons and tribunals whatsoever." The Supreme Court held that a provision of this kind was not applicable "where an imperative condition regulating the functions and duty of the tribunal had been disregarded" so that certiorari would lie since the quasi-judicial body had acted in excess of jurisdiction. Another indication of the scope of judicial review was given by Gavan Duffy J. in *Murren v. Brennan*, [1942] I.R. 466 when he said at p. 476:

The question of the finality of the Minister's decision is not directly before me; but I may point out that, while a court of law would be slow to interfere with any decision clearly entrusted by statute to a Minister of State, the phrase "whose decision shall be final" in the sub-section cannot exclude the constitutional jurisdiction of the High Court in a case deemed by the High Court to call for interference.

The pre-1921 principles that certiorari would issue only to curb excess of jurisdiction or lack of natural justice, and not to correct erroneous decisions taken within an inferior tribunal's jurisdiction, continued in use after 1920. Thus in *Walsh v. Minister for Local Government and Public Health*, [1929] I.R. 377 the question arose of the validity of an order confirming the action of a local government auditor. It was held that the order was not a "speaking order" since it did not state any views on points of law which could be challenged in the courts; Murnaghan J. put the point succinctly when he stated in the Supreme Court, at p. 404, that the Minister "had jurisdiction to decide the matters raised, and if he made an erroneous determination in a matter of law in arriving at his decision, his order cannot be questioned for want of jurisdiction." On the other hand, in *The State (Ryan) v. Revenue Commissioners*,

[1934] I.R. 1, certiorari was brought to challenge an assessment to tax which had been made by a single Revenue Commissioner. The High Court held that to accord with the statutory provisions the assessment should be made by two commissioners, and that it should be quashed since it was clear on the face of it that it was made in excess of jurisdiction. Again, *McCarthy's* case showed that failure to comply with a specified statutory procedure can constitute an excess of jurisdiction against which certiorari will lie.

Another decision relates to the fundamental question in all certiorari cases—whether there is a judicial decision which can properly be reviewed by the courts. In *The State (Conlan) v. Referee appointed under the Military Service Pensions Act, 1934,* [1947] I.R. 264 certiorari was sought to quash a request by the Minister for Defence for the reviewing by a referee of a report on a pensions claim. The respective functions of these two persons were put briefly by Murnaghan J. at p. 271 when he pointed out that under the relevant enactment the referee was required to hear any additional evidence and that in his opinion "the Minister did not exercise any judicial authority in requesting a review and it was incumbent on the referee to decide whether the evidence on which the review was requested was of the type required by the statute." Looking back to the pre-1920 cases, it is clear that the relevant consideration is still whether or not a decision purports to determine rights and duties; in *Conlan's* case this was the function of the referee rather than the Minister, whose actions might truly be described as ministerial. In this way the judges in the Four Courts today, like their Victorian predecessors and their counterparts in Belfast, London, and elsewhere in the Commonwealth, still classify the distinguishing features of administrative processes.

These random examples of the way in which the Irish courts scrutinize administrative legislation and decisions indicate yet another field for comparative study. The succeeding sections relate to a different branch of administrative law and show something of the legal position of the different Irish governments.

THE LEGAL POSITION OF THE CROWN IN IRELAND

Since, as explained in the chapter on Constitutional History (*supra*), the de facto King of England was also the de jure King of

Ireland, the legal position of the Crown was the same on both sides of the Irish Sea. When the extension of English law throughout Ireland was completed at the beginning of the seventeenth century, the Dublin courts had occasion to examine the extent of the prerogative in putting a value on money (*The Case of Mixed Money*, (K.B. 1605) Dav. Rep. 18, 80 Eng. Rep. 507) and in claiming royal rights to the navigable waters of rivers (*The Case of the Royal Fishery of the Banne*, (K.B. 1610) Dav. Rep. 55, 80 Eng. Rep. 540); not unnaturally, the judges pronounced in favor of the prerogative power.

Again, the reports of Irish cases in the nineteenth century contain many examples of the privileged position of the Crown. Because of the Lord Lieutenant's position as Viceroy, it was held that he could not be sued in respect of an official action, though this immunity did not extend to injuries caused, or debts contracted, by the Lord Lieutenant in his personal capacity (*Luby v. Lord Woodhouse*, (1865) 17 Ir. C.L.R. 618; *Sullivan v. Earl Spencer*, (1872) I.R. 6 C.L. 173). As for Crown property, the Irish courts held that it could be affected only by express and clear enactment, not by inference or implication, and that such property was therefore not liable to pay the form of local taxation known as "grand jury cess" (*Earl of Lonsdale v. Wilson*, (1886) 8 Ir. Law Rep. 412; 13 Ir. Law Rep. 438). The "shield of the Crown" (in the phrase current in Australian law) was extended to protect the Commissioners of Public Works in Ireland from an action for negligence in respect of the Phoenix Park, Dublin, which was a Royal park (*Murphy v. Soady* (1886), reported [1903] 2 I.R. 213 n.); but twenty years later it was held that these Commissioners had been incorporated by a special act of parliament in respect of Stephen's Green, Dublin, and were consequently liable for negligence arising out of their duties in that connection (*Wheeler v. Commissioners of Public Works in Ireland*, [1903] 2 I.R. 202). Proceedings against the Crown by way of petition of right in Ireland were regulated by statute, and required the royal fiat as did petitions against the Crown in the English courts; the Petitions of Right (Ireland) Act, 1873 (36 & 37 Vict. c. 69) extended to Ireland the Petitions of Right Act, 1860 (23 & 24 Vict. c. 34). The Irish reports during the succeeding fifty years show how this procedural device was used by local authorities in disputes with the government, as in *Kildare County Council v. the King*, [1909] 2 I.R. 199, as well as by individuals who considered themselves aggrieved, as in *Wheeler's* case.

In matters relating to the procedure of litigation, the Crown enjoyed privileges in such matters as costs (which were discussed in *R. (Byrne) v. Lord Mayor of Belfast*, [1919] 2 I.R. 143) and limitation of actions, for the Crown could rely on the statutes governing these when it was a defendant, but was not bound by these rules when suing as plaintiff. So, for instance, a Crown debt could be recovered "out of time" (*Attorney-General v. Howley*, [1914] 1 I.R. 124). Also, it was always possible for a public authority within the meaning of the Public Authorities Protection Act, 1893 (56 & 57 Vict. c. 61) to plead as a defense to a tort action that it had not been brought within six months from the cause of action. For example, this was successfully pleaded by the Resident Commissioner for National Education in an action brought against him by a teacher (*Newell v. Starkie*, [1917] 2 I.R. 73, 83, 621). Thus in matters ranging from the details of law suits to the powers and immunities of the sovereign's representative the legal position of the Crown was the same in Ireland as in England.

By 1920 the various Dominions had advanced beyond the United Kingdom in making the Crown liable to be sued. In New Zealand the Crown Suits Act, 1881 allowed a petition of right to be brought for breach of contract and for wrongs or damages arising from public works; in 1910 the Crown Suits Amendment Act (No. 54 of 1910) extended the liability in tort to actions which would lie between private persons. In Australia, s. 56 of the Judiciary Act, 1903 (No. 6), made the Crown in right of the Commonwealth liable in tort. And the first Act of the Union Parliament, the Crown Liabilities Act, 1910, made the Crown in South Africa liable for torts and breaches of contract committed by its servants in the same way as an ordinary employer would be liable. However, the close association between Ireland and England had prevented anything in the nature of an Irish experiment of this kind.

THE POSITION IN NORTHERN IRELAND SINCE 1921

The continuation of Northern Ireland in the United Kingdom has resulted in a continuation of the legal position of the Crown.

By s. 4(1) of the Government of Ireland Act, 1920 (10 & 11 Geo. 5, c. 67), the Crown is one of the matters which is ultra vires the parliament of Northern Ireland, and by s. 8(1) the executive power continues to be vested in the Crown, but is delegated to the Governor. Decisions such as that of the House of Lords in *Duncan v. Cammell Laird & Co.*, [1942] A.C. 624, relating to the privilege which the Crown may claim for documents in evidence, apply in Northern Ireland. For this reason Northern Ireland authorities on the Crown's legal position are sparse, but three may be taken as indicative of the trend of parallelism with English law.

In *In re Orr*, [1924] 2 I.R. 120 Wilson J. upheld the priority in bankruptcy proceedings of a claim for arrears of income tax, on the ground that this was a Crown debt. Again, in *In re Lindsay*, [1926] N.I. 128, Brown J. gave a similar priority, for the same reason, to a claim for arrears of health insurance contributions. (He also held that the Ministry of Labour for Northern Ireland was suing as Insurance Commissioners rather than as a government department, so that it could be ordered to pay costs.) The interesting feature of these two decisions is that the first related to revenue accruing to the United Kingdom exchequer, while the second concerned monies which the Northern Ireland government was entitled to collect, a distribution of executive functions which became important when the question arose of the Crown's liability in tort.

Another decision which illustrates the continuity of the Northern Ireland law relating to the Crown was *Morton v. Air Ministry*, [1946] N.I. 136. In that case Black J. had to consider the effect of s. 6 of the Trade Disputes and Trade Unions Act (Northern Ireland), 1927 (17 & 18 Geo. 5, c. 20), under which "any local or public authority" was forbidden to make trade union membership a condition of employment. The learned judge held that certain employees in Northern Ireland of the Royal Air Force were Crown servants, and he followed English authorities in holding that the 1927 Act did not bind the Crown. He also made the point that since the Royal Air Force was a matter excepted from the Northern Ireland Parliament's jurisdiction by s. 4(3) of the Government of Ireland Act, the Northern Ireland statute of 1927 would not affect the employment in Northern Ireland of Royal Air Force personnel for, as he said at p. 141:

It might seriously hamper the efficiency of the Air Force if the Parliament of Northern Ireland could by its legislation import terms into the conditions of employment by the Air Force of civilian personnel in Northern Ireland which were unacceptable to the Department of State responsible for the maintenance of the Force or which raised difficulties or impossibilities of administration.

The extent to which a local legislature may bind the executive of a government with powers to legislate on a particular topic is a problem which has arisen in other jurisdictions. Thus in Canada it has been held that speed rules may be enforced against customs officers (*R. v. McLeod*, [1930] 4 D.L.R. 226) but that provinces cannot require licenses for motor cars carrying troops on official duties (*R. v. Anderson*, (1930) 39 Man. R. 84; *R. v. Rhodes* [1934] O.R. 44 (1933)), while in Australia it has been held that state law relating to motor cars applies to a Commonwealth military officer (*Pirrie v. McFarlane* (1925) 36 C.L.R. 170). Professor Geoffrey Sawer has, however, pointed out that it is heretical

to stress the elements of juristic individuality in the personality of the seven Australian governments. Majority decisions tend to treat the dogma of Crown unity as the primary rule to be disregarded only where the operation of the Constitution Acts and of Australian Statutes necessarily requires that each government be treated as a separate juristic person; this empirical approach has so far been adequate to deal with such questions as the ability of the governments to sue each other and to have "separate property" notwithstanding their mystical legal unity within the Crown.[14]

In Northern Ireland this device of referring to the Crown "in right of" different governments has been adopted, but the traditional doctrine that statutes bind the Crown only by express statement of necessary implication has been modified. S. 7 of the Interpretation Act (Northern Ireland), 1954 (c. 33), provides that

No enactment passed or made after the commencement of this Act shall bind or affect in any manner whatsoever Her Majesty or Her Majesty's rights or prerogatives, unless it is stated therein that Her Majesty is bound thereby to the full extent authorised or permitted by the constitutional laws of Northern Ireland or to such less extent as is specified in the enactment.

[14] "Constitutional Law" in G. W. Paton (ed.), *The Commonwealth of Australia: The Development of Its Laws and Constitution* (London, 1952), 38, 78.

This section does not apply to pre-1955 Northern Ireland Acts (to which the former rules of interpretation will continue to apply), but as respects post-1954 enactments of the Northern Ireland parliament the doctrine of necessary implication has been abolished. The reference to "the constitutional laws of Northern Ireland" does no more than state the law in force, for any unauthorized attempt by the parliament of Northern Ireland to bind the Crown would be ultra vires. The constitutional laws mentioned are defined in s. 46(2) of the Interpretation Act to include the Government of Ireland Act, 1920, subsequent amending or extending acts, and statutes "otherwise relating to or affecting the legislative powers of the Northern Ireland Parliament." From the delegation of executive power to the Governor, to be exercised by the departments of the government of Northern Ireland, it follows that the Belfast legislature can make laws affecting what is colloquially referred to as "the transferred Crown," *i.e.*, the authorities administering matters within the scope of the Northern Ireland parliament's legislative powers.

In providing for the future, Northern Ireland acts must state specifically if, and how, the Crown is to be bound: the Northern Ireland parliament here followed the lead given by the Privy Council when in *Province of Bombay v. Municipal Corporation of Bombay*, [1947] A.C. 58 (1946) it stated at p. 63 that "if it be the intention of the legislature that the Crown shall be bound, nothing is easier than to say so in plain words." The Northern Ireland section followed the precedent of s. 16 of the Canadian Interpretation Act (*Revised Statutes of Canada* 1927 c. 1, as amended), so that the consideration of that section by the Privy Council in *Nisbet Shipping Co. Ltd. v. The Queen*, [1955] 1 W.L.R. 1031 is directly relevant.

The distinction between the Crown "in right of" various governments was adopted in the application to Northern Ireland of the Crown Proceedings Act, 1947 (10 & 11 Geo. 6, c. 44). It has already been mentioned that under s. 8 of the Government of Ireland Act, 1920 the executive power continues to be vested in the Crown but is delegated to the Governor of Northern Ireland and exercised by the various Northern Ireland government departments. This triple combination of vesting, delegation, and exercise militates against any theory of the divisibility of the Crown, though it undoubtedly results in a division of functions in practice; but in theory these are "aspects" of the Crown's power rather than divisions. The Northern Ireland government departments were constituted by executive action, a "Notification" by the then Lord Lieutenant of Ireland. By s. 2 of the Ministries of Northern Ireland Act, 1921 (12 Geo. 5, c. 6), the new parliament constituted the newly created departments bodies corporate, and provided that they could sue and be sued as such. In so doing Irish precedents were being followed, for such organs of Irish administration as the Department of Agriculture and Technical Instruction and the Local Government Board had been constituted as bodies corporate.

But the incorporation of government departments, while providing potential plaintiffs with a defendant who could be brought into court, did not alter the substantive position of those departments. Over a quarter of a century after the setting-up of the new jurisdiction, this situation was altered by the extension of the Crown Proceedings Act, 1947 to Northern Ireland. S. 53 provided for the making of an Order in Council "amending the law both in its application to the Crown in right of His Majesty's Government in the United Kingdom and in its application to the Crown in right of His Majesty's Government in Northern Ireland." These two aspects of the Crown's functions were emphasized by s. 53 (6) of the 1947 Act, containing the usual "pre-appointed day" provision which, as explained in the chapter on Constitutional Developments since 1920 (*supra*), preserves the powers of the parliament of Northern Ireland in relation to matters within its competence. However, the Order in Council authorized by s. 53 contemplated a single adaptation of the Act in relation to both the United Kingdom and Northern Ireland governments, and this was done by the Northern Ireland (Crown Proceedings) Order, 1949 (No. 1836), which came into force on January 1, 1950.

The Order applied the whole of the 1947 Act to Northern Ireland in relation to the Crown in right of the United Kingdom government. Because such matters as the postal services, the armed forces, and aircraft are outside the powers of the Northern Ireland parliament, the provisions of the Act dealing with these topics were excluded from its application in relation to the Crown in right of the Northern Ireland government. Additional provisions were inserted in the Act by the Order to deal with cases where doubt might arise as to which was the appropriate government department to be sued, or which government should be made a defendant; in such cases the Attorney-General for Northern Ireland is to be sued, and if in the second type of doubtful case the liability established is that of the United Kingdom government, the Treasury will recoup the Northern Ireland Ministry of Finance.[15]

With these variations the Crown in Northern Ireland, in both its "aspects," is now suable in the Northern Ireland courts in the same way as it is liable on the other side of the Irish Sea. As regards limitation of actions, the law at present in force in Northern Ireland is contained in a miscellaneous collection of statutes, for there is no equivalent of the English Limitation of Actions Act, 1939 (2 & 3 Geo. 6, c. 21); but it is still the law in both jurisdictions that the Crown is not bound by statutes of limitations, though it may take advantage of them. By s. 7 of the Northern Ireland Act, 1947 (10 & 11 Geo. 6, c. 37), the Westminster parliament conferred on the Northern Ireland legislature power to deal with limitation of actions by and against the Crown, so that any further developments in Northern Ireland could be achieved by local legislation. Here it may be noted that s. 9 of the Law Reform (Miscellaneous Provisions) Act (Northern Ireland), 1951 (c. 7) extended to twelve months the period during which tort actions had to be brought against public authorities, and by s. 3 of the Law Reform (Miscellaneous Provisions) Act (Northern Ireland), 1954 (c. 26) this protection was completely abolished, as it has been in the rest of the United Kingdom.

Summing up the development during the past thirty-five years of the law of Northern Ireland relating to the Crown, we find a considerable similarity with the English law. The Northern Ireland courts have followed the English decisions in such matters as the priority in bankruptcy proceedings of Crown debts and the extent to which the Crown is bound by local statutes. The link with Great Britain extends to legislation and is shown in the adaptation of the 1947 Crown Proceedings Act for Northern Ireland. It is perhaps significant that the only major departure from the British law—the requirement that future Northern Ireland Acts should state clearly

[15] *Cf.* [W. A. Leitch], "Civil Proceedings by and against the Crown," *Northern Ireland Legal Quarterly*, VIII (1950), 223.

whether, and in what way, the Crown is to be bound—followed a Canadian precedent, and it will be interesting to see whether this practice of looking further afield is extended to other topics. So far as the legal position of the Crown is concerned, the empiricism described by the learned Australian commentator has certainly held sway in Northern Ireland.

THE LEGAL POSITION OF THE IRISH FREE STATE GOVERNMENT

As explained in the chapter on Constitutional Developments since 1920 (*supra*), Art. 51 of the 1922 Constitution of the Irish Free State vested executive authority in the King, exercisable in accordance with the Canadian precedent. Under Art. 73 the laws in force in 1922 were continued and by Art. 80 the Irish Free State government was, as regards departmental property, assets, rights, and liabilities, to be regarded as the successors of the Provisional government and, so far as departmental functions were concerned, as the successors of the British government. This Article was considered by the House of Lords in *Attorney-General v. Great Southern & W. Ry. Co. of Ireland*, [1925] A.C. 754; so far as the British courts were concerned, it was clear that the Irish Free State government stood in the shoes of the British government. For the Irish courts, however, the matter was more complicated, as different aspects of the problem arose in various cases.

First, two Irish Free State enactments may be noted. By s. 2 of the Ministers and Secretaries Act, 1924 (No. 16 of 1924) the members of the Executive Council were constituted corporations sole, with perpetual succession and a common seal; they were empowered to hold land and to sue in their official names and, subject to the fiat of the Attorney-General, they could be sued. Thus Ministers in Dublin are in a different position from their opposite numbers in Belfast, who are the heads of incorporated departments but are not themselves bodies corporate. But Dublin Ministers and Belfast Ministries resembled each other in that both could plead the Public Authorities Protection Act, 1893 (56 & 57 Vict. c. 61) as a defense. In *Corrigan v. Biddulph*, [1938] I.R. 610 it was held that the protection of the 1893 Act extended to the driver of a post office van, who was doing so in the performance of a duty which the Minister for Posts and Telegraphs owed to the public, and who was engaged in the direct execution of a statute. The second relevant statutory provision was s. 38(2) of the Finance Act, 1924 (No. 27 of 1924), which provided that

Moneys due or payable to or for the benefit of the Central Fund shall have and be deemed always to have had attached to them all such rights, privileges, and priorities as have heretofore attached to debts due to the Crown.

This statutory attraction of Crown privileges for certain purposes reinforced the general principle of legal continuity.

As happened in Northern Ireland, a number of cases which came before the Dublin courts turned on the priority of debts in bankruptcy proceedings. That the Irish Free State government was entitled to claim the same priority for moneys due to it as the Crown had formerly possessed was recognized in a trio of cases decided between 1925 and 1927—*In re Maloney*, [1926] I.R. 202; *In re Reade*, [1927] I.R. 31; *In re K.*, [1927] I.R. 260. This principle had become well established by 1931 when a question arose of the priority to be accorded in bankruptcy to a claim for arrears of unemployment insurance contributions, which were recoverable "as debts due to the Crown." In *In re Hennessy*, [1932] I.R. 11 the Dublin Supreme Court affirmed the priority of the government's claim, rejecting an argument that Crown priority was inconsistent with the Constitution. This was in line with the Northern Ireland case, *In re Lindsay*, [1926] N.I. 128. An interesting feature of these Dublin bankruptcy decisions was the fact that they considered the situation in other parts of the Commonwealth, particularly Canada, and indeed in *In re Reade* Kennedy C.J. at p. 50 specifically advanced the doctrine of different "aspects" of the Crown's functions in different parts of the Commonwealth. Again, in *In re Maloney* Johnston J. stated (at p. 206):

. . . that branch of the prerogative on which the present claim is based— namely, that the Crown, as representing the Government and people of the country, is not bound by a statute unless it is expressly or by necessary implication referred to therein—can be resorted to in the present case by the Land Commission acting for and on behalf of the Minister for Finance.

The extent to which a statute binds the executive power was to arise under the Irish Constitution of 1937, but the continuity of the exemption under the 1922 Constitution is clear from Johnston J's dictum.

There were also other indications of this continuity of the previous law, a good example of this being the contractual liability of the government. In *Leydon v. Attorney-General*, [1926] I.R. 334 a schoolteacher brought an action to declare his salary rights; in so far as the Minister for Education was concerned it was argued that the classic decision of *Churchward v. The Queen*, [1865] L.R. 1 Q.B. 173 made the contract unenforceable, since it would require an appropriation by the Oireachtas for its fulfilment. The Supreme Court, however, held that a declaration of the plaintiff's rights was possible, and assumed that the government would take note of these. *Churchward's* case was also considered in *Kenny v. Cosgrave*, [1926] I.R. 517, which raised several interesting points. This was an action brought against the President of the Executive Council for damages for alleged breach of an indemnity agreement; it was claimed that the plaintiff had suffered loss as a result of a trade dispute and that he had not been recompensed as he had been promised. The Supreme Court followed the 1786 decision in *Macbeath v. Haldimand*, (K.B.) 1 T.R. 172, 99 Eng. Rep. 1036 in holding that the President was not liable in his official capacity for breach of contract; the court relied on *Dunn v. Macdonald*, [1897] 1 Q.B. 555 and held that the President, as a public servant, could not be made personally liable for an implied warranty of authority; and *Churchward's* case was followed in holding that the contract would not be enforceable against the Executive Council, since it would require an appropriation by the Oireachtas. The contrast between *Leydon's* case and *Kenny's* case was brought into relief by the decision in *Leen v. President of the Executive Council*, [1928] I.R. 408, where a claim was made for payment of compensation for malicious damage, which had been valued at £4,000 by a commission set up by agreement between the Provisional government and the British government in 1922. In the Supreme Court, Kennedy C. J. and Fitzgibbon J. held that there was no way of enforcing this claim (for which no sum had been specifically appropriated) either by way of contract or estoppel or by mandamus. Dissenting, Murnaghan J. would have allowed the plaintiff's right to have been declared, following *Dyson v. Attorney-General*, [1911] 1 K.B. 410 (1910). Five years later, *Leen's* case was distinguished in *Galway Co. Council v. Minister for Finance and Attorney-General*, [1931] I.R. 215, in which the Council sought a declaration that they were entitled to certain payments from the Minister (who had assumed liability for them) in respect of malicious injuries.   Johnston J. followed *Leen's* case in regard to certain payments for which only general appropriation of money had been made, stating that an alternative decision would weaken the responsibility of the executive to parliament; but as regards other payments he held that there had been an express acknowledgment by the Minister of the County Council's right, and that this supplied the element lacking in *Leen's* case.   While the general principles of the former law were followed, the facts might justify some variation in their application.

A similar continuity of principle is to be found in relation to the executive's liability in tort.   In *Carolan v. Minister for Defence*, [1927] I.R. 62 damages were claimed for the negligence of a soldier. The plaintiff contended that the maxim that "the King can do no wrong" did not apply to Irish Free State Ministers, who had been specially incorporated by the Ministers and Secretaries Act, 1924. But in the High Court Sullivan P., at p. 66, summarized the basis of the English cases (starting with *Lane v. Cotton*, (K.B. 1701) 1 Ld. Raym. 646, 91 Eng. Rep. 1332) as follows:

The reason why a public officer having the management of some branch of the Government business is not responsible for the wrongful acts of a subordinate in the same employment as himself is that the relationship of master and servant does not exist between them, both being servants of the public.

The High Court further held that neither the 1922 Constitution nor the Ministers and Secretaries Act, 1924 (No. 16 of 1924) altered the exemptions and liabilities of Ministers of State, who continued to enjoy immunity both for their public acts and from vicarious liability. In this conection it may be noted that s. 170 of the Road Traffic Act, 1933 (No. 11 of 1933) gave a right of action against the Minister for Finance for the negligent driving of a vehicle owned by the state.   For this limited purpose the Minister was placed in the same position as an ordinary employer.

Another aspect of the legal position of Irish Free State Ministers was illustrated in earlier proceedings in *Leen's* case, reported as *Leen v. President of the Executive Council,* [1926] I.R. 456. Here interrogatories were served on, and discovery of documents claimed against, the defendant, who claimed privilege. At p. 463 Meredith J. summed up this claim and the principle underlying it in the following way:

> . . . the defendants object to answer on the ground of privilege, and that the disclosure would be detrimental to the public interest and service, and is contrary to public policy. If the defendants are entitled to the privilege that the Crown would have, I cannot go behind this objection. It is contended, however, by the plaintiff that the privilege can only be claimed by the Crown as such. I can find nothing, however, in the authorities on this privilege in respect of discovery to suggest that the rule of law which has always been in force, and which has to be administered as heretofore under the Constitution of the Irish Free State, is dependent upon the magic of any particular nomenclature. On the contrary, it appears to me to be broadbased upon the public interest. . . . The principle has its roots in the general conception of State interests and the functions of Courts of Justice, which make it independent of the particular type of constitution under which the body of law which recognises that principle is administered.

In grappling with these problems of the priority of state debts, the liability of the state in contract and tort, and the privileged position of the state in procedural matters, the Irish courts were coping with difficulties confronting courts in other parts of the Commonwealth.[16] The courts of what was then the youngest Dominion relied on earlier authorities, but it is noteworthy that they emphasized the principles on which their decisions were based. It was as if the judges, anxious for the proper development of the fledgling Constitution, were determined to fortify precedent with principle, so that continuity was insured not only by reliance on pre-1922 decisions, but also by stating principles suitable for the smooth working of the new regime.

THE LEGAL POSITION OF THE IRISH REPUBLICAN GOVERNMENT

In the chapter on Constitutional Developments since 1920 (*supra*) reference was made to the popular origin of executive power

[16] *Cf.* Wolfgang Friedmann, *Principles of Australian Administrative Law* (Melbourne, 1950).

which, like legislative and judicial power, is declared by Art. 6 of the 1937 Constitution to "derive, under God, from the people"; by Art. 28, 2, the executive power is to be exercised by or on the authority of the government. (In this respect Art. 53 of the Indian Constitution and Art. 39 of the Pakistan Constitution differed from the Irish precedent, since they vested executive authority in the respective presidents.) An indication was given of the concept of the state in the 1937 Constitution, an aspect of that document which must surely be the subject of further judicial scrutiny. As for the present legal position of the government of the Irish Republic, this provides a further illustration of the continuity of legal principles. The basis for this continuity was laid by Art. 49 of the 1937 Constitution, which provided that

All powers, functions, rights and prerogatives whatsoever exercisable in or in respect of Saorstát Eireann immediately before the 11th day of December, 1936, whether in virtue of the Constitution then in force or otherwise, by the authority in which the executive power of Saorstát Eireann was then vested are hereby declared to belong to the people.

Art. 49 went on to provide that the powers and rights thus transferred were to be exercised only by or on the authority of the government, which in its turn was to be the successor of the Irish Free State government "as regards all property, assets, rights and liabilities." Coupled with this article was Art. 50, continuing the laws in force at the coming into operation of the Constitution. In this way the new government stepped into the shoes of its predecessor, and was given the power of exercising, or directing the exercise of, prerogatives attaching to the Crown before its elimination from the 1922 Constitution in December, 1936.

In comparison with Art. 49 of the Irish Constitution, Art. 223 of the Burmese Constitution provides a close parallel, since it transferred "all rights, authority, jurisdiction and prerogative heretofore belonging to His Britannic Majesty." The two succeeding articles transferred rights, assets, and liabilities, and allowed the Union to sue and be sued by the name of the Union of Burma. Both the Union of India (1950 Constitution, Art. 300) and Pakistan (1956 Constitution, Art. 136) may sue and be sued as such, but neither the Indian Constitution, in transferring rights, liabilities, and property

(Arts. 294-296), nor the Pakistan Constitution, in dealing with similar matters (Arts. 133, 231) made any reference to prerogatives. In this respect the Irish and Burmese Constitutions differ from those of the Indian subcontinent, but in the Irish Republic no specific provision was made for actions against the state as such.

As for the recent Irish cases, the problem of bankruptcy priorities necessitated judicial pronouncements on the position of Irish Ministers. Thus in *In re Irish Aero Club,* [1939] I.R. 204, Gavan Duffy J. had to consider Ministerial claims to priority for aerodrome license fees and aeroplane inspection charges; he construed s. 38(2) of the Finance Act, 1924 (No. 27 of 1924) narrowly, holding that it related only to taxes and duties, not to fees, so that there was no statutory provision for the priority of the charges in question. The same learned judge had to consider the priority of claims for income tax, unemployment insurance contributions, and telephone charges in *In re P.C.,* [1939] I.R. 306. For the first two claims he relied on the 1924 Finance Act and on the decision in *In re Hennessy,* [1932] I.R. 11, which has been mentioned. On the third claim, Gavan Duffy J. examined Art. 49 of the Constitution, but he distinguished between a Royal Exchequer (for which prior rights might be claimed) and the Central Fund for the Eire revenues, holding that in the latter case statutory authority was necessary to give priority to claims in bankruptcy. The "kingless constitution" to which the learned judge referred may require to be supplemented by statute to preserve every vestige of former royal authority.

The position of the Irish government in relation to tort actions was illustrated by a claim made for loss of the services of a member of the police force, the Gárda Siochána, who had been injured. In *Attorney-General and Minister for Justice v. Dublin United Tramways Co. Ltd.,* [1934] I.R. 590 the Dublin High Court followed *Carolan v. Minister of Defence,* [1927] I.R. 62 and held that a policeman, like a soldier, was a servant of the public; the Attorney-General could properly represent the public who had been deprived of the Civic Guard's services, so that damages could be awarded for the impairment of the master and servant relationship. A very similar case from New South Wales was recently decided by the Privy Council in *Attorney-General for New South Wales v. Perpetual*

Trustee Co., [1955] A.C. 457. There an *action per quod servitium amisit* was brought by the New South Wales government in respect of an injury to a police constable. The Judicial Committee considered the comparable position of a soldier, pointing out that the Supreme Court of Canada had been considering the effect of a Canadian statute when they held, in *R. v. Richardson,* [1948] S.C.R. 57 that the Crown could sue for the loss of a soldier's services. In *The Commonwealth v. Quince,* (1944) 68 C.L.R. 227 the Australian High Court had held that the Crown could not bring an action of this kind, and in *United States v. Standard Oil Co.,* (1947) 332 U.S. 301, the court had pointed out that the government-soldier relationship differed materially from the ordinary relationship between master and servant. In the 1955 decision the Irish case of 1939 was dismissed, at p. 489, as giving too little weight to the distinction between the domestic relation of servant and master and that of the holder of a public office and the state which he serves. Thus the Irish case differs from Commonwealth decisions, and it will be interesting to see what line is taken if the matter should come before the Dublin Supreme Court.

The most exhaustive examination of the distribution of the Crown's former powers in the Irish Constitution took place in *Cork County Council and Burke v. Commissioners of Public Works and Others,* [1945] I.R. 561. In that case a claim was made for the payment to the local authority of rates on premises let by two departments of the Dublin government. On the one hand it was argued that the relevant statutes were of general application and cut down any vestige of prerogative right; on the other it was contended that government departments were in the same position as the Crown had been, and that special words or a necessary implication were necessary to bind the state. Thus the case presented the issues in concise form.

Murnaghan J. did not answer the general question of governmental succession to the Crown's prerogative, since it was admitted that the prerogative privileges extended to the premises under consideration. He held, however, that a rating enactment was of general application, but that, following the Supreme Court's decision in *Fitzsimons v. Menkin,* [1938] I.R. 805 government departments were not bound by a rent restriction statute. On the latter point O'Byrne J. and Black J. agreed, but they differed from their colleague in holding that the rating enactment did not bind the state. These two judges both indicated their view of the continuity of prerogative rights (at pp. 578 and 588 respectively), and all three judgments paid attention to the legal position in the Commonwealth and the United States. All the judges referred to *United States v. Hoar*, (C.C. Mass. 1821) 26 Fed. Cas. 329, No. 15,373, and O'Byrne J. quoted the reasoning of Story J. who stated the relevant principle in the following words:

In general, acts of the legislature are meant to regulate and direct the acts and rights of citizens; and in most cases the reasoning applicable to them applies with very different, and often contrary force to the government itself. It appears to me, therefore, to be a safe rule founded in the principles of the common law, that the general words of a statute ought not to include the government, or affect its rights unless that construction be clear and indisputable upon the text of the act.

The same learned judge also referred to the position in Australia, Canada, and New South Wales, citing *Roberts v. Ahern*, (1904) 1 C.L.R. 406; *The Liquidators of the Maritime Bank of Canada v. The Receiver-General of New Brunswick*, [1892] A.C. 437; and *Attorney-General for New South Wales v. Curator of Intestate Estates*, [1907] A.C. 519. The Irish decision was fortified by both American principle and Commonwealth precedent.

These Irish cases give further proof of the continuity in the Irish Constitution of the legal principles relating to the crown prerogative. As for legislative action, it is noteworthy that the Oireachtas and the Northern Ireland parliament both repealed the Public Authorities Protection Act in the same year, 1954. The Dublin enactment was the Public Authorities (Judicial Proceedings) Act (No. 27 of 1954), and as well as removing the protection of the 1893 Act it abolished certain other procedural privileges. As for property, Art. 10 of the Constitution vested the Irish Free State's property in the new state, and provided that its management could be regulated by law. This was done by the State Property Act, 1954 (No. 25 of 1954) which, amongst other things, by s. 27 declared that the rights and prerogatives of the people under Art. 49 of the Constitution were, in relation to property, to be exercised by the government through the

Minister for Finance. In this way the 1937 Constitution is supplemented "in accordance with law."

As yet no Dublin equivalent of the 1947 Crown Proceedings Act has been forthcoming. If such an Act is eventually placed on the Irish statute book, it should provide interesting comparisons both with the Westminster legislation and with the United States Federal Tort Claims Act, 1946 (28 U.S.C. §§ 1291, 1346, 1402, 1504, 2110, 2402, 2411, 2412, 2671-2680).

SUMMARY

The Crown in two "aspects" is still very much a part of the Constitution of Northern Ireland and, as such, occupies a legal position comparable to that which it enjoyed in Ireland in 1921. The devolution of power effected by the Government of Ireland Act, 1920 has placed the Crown in the dual position which it occupies in Australia and Canada, but the constitutional changes have not diminished the effect of the legal rules, which continue to be applicable. In the 1922 Constitution of the Irish Free State the position assigned to the Crown was that which it held in Canada, and case law pointed definitely to the continuation of the former rules though, as has been noted, the judges buttressed references to precedent by reliance on principle. Similarly, the "kingless constitution" of 1937 made specific provision for the continuation of prerogative rights. In this the Irish precedent was followed in Burma, but not in India or Pakistan. The post-1937 Irish cases have shown how the surviving prerogative powers have been applied in the working of a republican regime, where Commonwealth precedents may still be relevant. In sum, the courts both in Belfast and Dublin have reached substantially similar conclusions in widely different constitutional circumstances.

CONCLUSION

The preceding sections of this chapter have sought to show something of the scope of delegated legislation in both Northern Ireland and the Irish Republic, and the methods of judicial and parliamentary control used in Belfast, Dublin, and London. As Sir Cecil Carr has shown, such topics are eminently suited to comparative study. The references to administrative tribunals have sketched the ways in which Northern Ireland and the Irish Republic have traveled on parallel and divergent lines in constructing the administrative apparatus of a modern state; reference has also been made to the varying forms of public corporation used in the two areas. The range of different topics with which these tribunals and corporations deal provides material for the comparative examination of the techniques and control of social services and other activities. Finally, the third section of the chapter indicated the legal position of the respective governments in Belfast and Dublin, the former deriving authority from a Westminster statute, the latter regulated by two successive self-contained constitutions. Here again there is material for the comparison of the Irish position with corresponding situations in the two main types of Commonwealth constitution—those which still retain the statutory form given by Westminster, and those which have adopted new forms.

In sum, it is hoped that this bird's-eye view of Irish administrative law may be of assistance to those interested in this important sector of modern public law.

6

Land Law

IN THE FRAGMENTARY pattern of the history of Irish private law the subject of land law provides the thread with the greatest continuity. From the first grant of land by Henry II to the latest developments in the law of the devolution of property the land law of Ireland has been the legal topic with the most direct influence on the history of the people. A full study of the economic effects of Irish land law has yet to be written, though various writers have treated this subject in relation to different periods. For the comparative lawyer, the development of Irish land law shows the parallel evolution of the English system in the country to which it was first transplanted; it is only in more recent centuries that comparisons with Commonwealth systems become relevant.

In the chapter on Legal History (*supra*), some indication was given of the need for investigation of the former Irish legal system, the so-called *brehon* law, and of the gradual development of the common law in Ireland. Land law provides a particularly good example of the way in which such studies could be carried out. Such topics as the tribal method of landholding and the law of elective succession to the kingship await authoritative elucidation; other interesting fields for study are the interrelations of the English and Irish systems, the possible feudalization of the Irish law, and the way in which, despite prohibitions on the use of Irish law, disputes were referred to Irish *brehons* for determination.

With the extension of the common law to the whole of Ireland in James I's reign came the final elimination of Irish land law from the legal system. In the *Case of Gavelkind*, (K.B. 1605) Dav. Rep. 49, 80 Eng. Rep. 535 the Dublin judges held that equal devolution of land could not be regarded as a customary part of the common law applicable in Ireland. In the *Case of Tanistry*, (K.B. 1607) Dav. Rep. 28, 80 Eng. Rep. 516 a similar disapproval was expressed of the method of succession by choice rather than descent, so that all formal trace of the Irish law disappeared. Yet even to-day, in the West of Ireland, there are holders of strips of arable land, the successors of those who formerly held under the Irish system of rundale, whereby a right of pasturage was held in common and yearly divisions of arable land made between those participating; no more remains of the Irish system.

THE INTRODUCTION OF ENGLISH LAND LAW

Land law figured prominently in the process, described in the chapter on Legal History (*supra*), of the introduction of the common law into Ireland. The story commenced with Henry II's visit in 1172, when after being recognized by some Irish rulers he proceeded to give grants of land to certain Norman barons, who were to hold it as tenants in chief of the king. In the succeeding centuries the making of grants of Irish land, and adjudging such land forfeit for insurrection, was to form a recurrent pattern. Not until the end of the seventeenth century, following the confiscations and settlements after the Williamite wars, was the land law of Ireland to be permitted to develop in any kind of settled atmosphere. The inauguration of the feudal system meant the introduction of the machinery of English real property law. An early case recorded in 1199 shows that William of Naas in county Kildare gave John (who at that time was lord of Ireland as well as king of England) one hundred marks for a writ of *mort d'ancestor* against the abbot and the monks of Baltinglass in county Wicklow.[1] The litigious William was among the first of a very long line of those who have enriched the Irish law reports in the course of prosecuting their claims to land.

Again, in the thirteenth century when the writs used in London were transmitted to Dublin for use there, and the statutory changes in the law of England were ordered to be observed in Ireland, the land law played an important part. The form and limitation of writs in real actions, the institution of quo warranto, the prohibition on the evasion of feudal services by gifts to the Church, the limita-

---

[1] H. S. Sweetman, *Calendar of Documents relating to Ireland 1171-1307* (London, 1875-1886), I, No. 89.

tion of the descent of conditional fees, the ban on the subinfeudation of a fee simple—all these became part of the Anglo-Irish law. The great statutory pillars of English land law were also built on the other side of the Irish Sea to support the Anglo-Irish structure.

There were two aspects of this application of the feudal system to Ireland, a legal one and a practical one. The enactments forming the framework of English land law were applied in Ireland while they were relevant to the circumstances prevailing in at least a part of the island. There was no question of a mortmain statute being held inapplicable because it was political rather than legal, as was held in *Attorney-General v. Stewart*, (Ch. 1817) 2 Mer. 143, 35 Eng. Rep. 895 to be the case in relation to a mortmain statute in Grenada. Recently Lord Asquith of Bishopstone referred to the application of Charles II's Statute of Military Tenures (12 Car. 2, c. 24) in what is now Canada, and pointed out that the North American Indians there in 1660 would hardly have appreciated the niceties involved in turning all tenures into common socage (*Attorney-General for Alberta v. Huggard Assets Ld.*, [1953] A.C. 420, 442). Similarly in Ireland such comparatively recent cases as *R. (Moore) v. O'Hanrahan*, [1927] I.R. 406; *Moore v. Attorney-General*, [1934] I.R. 44; and *Little v. Cooper*, [1937] I.R. 1 turned on the application in county Donegal of Magna Carta, which was observed in Ireland long before that particular county came under the jurisdiction of the common law. However, this problem arose from the extension of English law throughout Ireland, not from the original application there of the document. In practice, the effect of the feudal system in Ireland was very different from that which it had in England, the reason being the differences between the English landholders and the Irish tenants. As a nineteenth century Irish lawyer-economist put it:

> In both countries the law is based on the feudal system, which gave the landlord a certain superiority over his tenants. But the feudal relation, with its reciprocal rights and duties, never existed in Ireland. Here the landlord never led his tenants to battle; if they fought on the same field, it was on different sides. They had no traditions of common victories or common defeats. The relations that existed between them were hostile.[2]

[2] Mountifort Longfield, "The Tenure of Land in Ireland," J. W. Probyn (ed.), *Systems of Land Tenure in Various Countries* (London, 1870), 1.

This hostile landlord-tenant relationship is relevant to any consideration of landholding in Ireland.

METHODS OF LAND SETTLEMENT

In the four centuries following Edward I's land legislation the land of Ireland, while still remaining under the theoretical lordship of the kings of England, passed through many hands. The fluctuating area of Anglo-Irish authority naturally limited the extent of the development of English land law. The Black Death left its mark on fourteenth-century Ireland, and the landowners commenced the practice of absenteeism which moved the Irish parliament to protest by legislation, though the practice persisted into the nineteenth century and was one of the causes of the land troubles and the ultimate land reforms. The area of the Pale shrank, and it was not until the time of the Tudors that the policy of the reconquest of Ireland began. Three methods were used to achieve this aim.

The first, commenced in the 1540's, was the policy of "Surrender and Re-grant," under which the Irish chiefs submitted to the English king and received their lands from the king in return. This was inaugurated concurrently with the redistribution of church lands confiscated at the Reformation.

A second method was that of composition, under which inquisitions were held to determine the ownership of large areas of land, as distinct from individual agreements for surrender and re-grant. This had the advantage of preserving the rights of smaller landholders whereas the method of surrender and re-grant left large areas in the domain of an overlord. It is, however, typical that the one attempt at large-scale composition, undertaken in Connaught in 1585, failed because it was not ratified by the Irish parliament.

The third method—that of settlement—was the most successful. Attempted in Leix and Offaly (renamed King's County and Queen's County) in 1556, it was more successful in Munster thirty years later, but it was most successful in the Province of Ulster in James I's reign.

THE SEVENTEENTH CENTURY

In James I's reign minute inquiries into defective Irish titles helped to establish the English system in particular cases, so that titles were confirmed by the Crown and did not depend on the *brehon* law. It was in this atmosphere that the plantation of Ulster was undertaken. On the "Flight of the Earls" in 1607, indictments for treason were returned against the O'Neill of Tyrone and the O'Donnell of Donegal, their lands escheated to the Crown, and Acts of Attainder were passed. In 1609 the "Articles of Plantation" were issued under which large tracts of land were offered to English and Scottish settlers. The London livery companies took part in this venture, and today the Irish Society (the Society of the Governors and Assistants, London, of the New Plantation in Ulster within the Realm of Ireland) still has interests in the city and county of Londonderry, which were renamed to include the English capital as a prefix to the original Irish title.[3]

The scheme of the plantation was that grants of land were made in fee farm, subject to a rent payable to the Crown, on terms which included the building of fortified dwellings (or "bawns," which may still be seen in Ulster) and the settling of the land by tenants. The plantation of Ulster had a considerable effect on the general history of the country, for under it a considerable part of the North was settled by those of English and Scottish stock, though many native Irish were given direct grants from the Crown and others became tenants of the planters. Plantations on a smaller scale were also carried out in the Irish midlands, but that in Ulster was the largest and most enduring.

The method of settlement by plantation did not, however, lead to the peaceful development of Irish land law. In Charles I's reign the Irish equivalent of the Star Chamber—the Court of Castle Chamber—and the activities of a Commission for Defective Titles authorized by the Irish Parliament (10 Car. 1, c. 3; 10 Car. 1, Sess. 3, c. 2) combined to place the titles to much Irish land in the melting-pot. Even the charter granted to the Irish Society in Londonderry was forfeited for breach of the conditions on which it had been granted. Then came the rising of 1641, in the causes of which the land policy of the Dublin and London governments was a main factor. The English parliament intervened and in 1642 the Long Parliament passed a series of acts (16 Car. 1, cc. 33-35, 37)

---

[3] For a full discussion of this settlement see Theodore William Moody, *The Londonderry Plantation, 1609-41* (Belfast, 1939).

forfeiting the estates of the rebels and providing for the apportioning of their lands among "adventurers" who were prepared to subscribe for these.

Following the campaign conducted by Cromwell and Ireton in 1649-1652, an Act of Settlement was passed by the Commonwealth Parliament in 1652 and an Act of Satisfaction the following year. Under these most of the lands of those Irish Catholics and Protestant royalists who had not supported the Commonwealth were forfeited and distributed among the 1642 adventurers and the Cromwellian soldiers. The larger proprietors and tenants were transplanted to lands across the river Shannon, an incident which survives in the grim Cromwellian statement that the Irish could go "To Hell or Connaught."

On the restoration of Charles II more changes were made in the proprietorship of Irish land. By Acts of the Irish parliament passed in 1662 (14 & 15 Car. 2, c. 2) and 1665 (17 & 18 Car. 2, c. 2) one third of the settlers' land was forfeited, and a Court of Claims established to allot land to those who claimed restoration. But there was not sufficient land to satisfy all these claims, and while the 1641 position was in a large measure restored, claims to land were a main grievance of those who supported James II when he held the Patriot Parliament in Dublin in May, 1689, which purported to repeal Charles II's Acts of Settlement. But the resettlement of Ireland which James II's followers projected was superseded by the Williamite victory and the signing of the Treaty of Limerick in 1691. Yet it was not until 1697 that the Irish parliament confirmed the Treaty, and then in modified form. Meantime another Court of Claims had adjudged forfeit the estates of certain Jacobites, and William had both restored certain forfeitures and made further grants. In the result, an English statute of 1699 (11 Will. 3, c. 2) resumed most of the royal grants and vested them in trustees for the sale of confiscated land. With the Williamite settlement the long series of Irish confiscations came to an end.

Pausing here, and looking back over the five centuries separating Henry II's first grants of Irish land from William III's settlement, the general pattern of Irish land law begins to emerge. It was an offspring of the English law, with a strong family resemblance to its parent; but whereas in England the parent had unchallenged domination, in Ireland the child had a much more difficult life. The thirteenth-century legislation fashioned the Irish law on English lines, but for the next three centuries it had to compete with the Irish system, the *brehon* law. Of the various attempts made at consolidating the reconquest of Ireland, the method of plantation was the most successful, but the upheavals of the seventeenth century did not make for orderly development, despite the various settlements in different parts of the country. Incidentally, there are echoes of these settlements in modern Irish legal practice, for there are still payable certain of the quit rents reserved on grants of land under these seventeenth-century settlements.

While, therefore, the history of Irish land law is longer than that of other common law systems, it is as turbulent as the general history of the country. In the colonies land grants might have to be established in defiance of physical difficulties;[4] in Ireland the difficulties were of a different kind, for the title to land often depended on the political activities of the landholder.

SOME LEGAL POINTS

In the period covered by this brief sketch there are some points of specifically legal interest. One is that by the time English land law was finally extended throughout Ireland the feudal system on which it was based had become obsolete, though the feudal rules remained. The Irish parliament was therefore able, after a two-year interval, to follow the English parliament when in 1662 military tenures were abolished in Ireland (14 & 15 Car. 2, c. 19). Another interesting feature of the Irish law is that apparently copyhold tenure did not take root in Ireland, perhaps because the unsettled state of the country militated against the claiming of customary tenure by copy of the court roll of a manor.

Again, the process of bringing Irish land law into line with that in England had its difficulties. For example, it was not until 1634 that the Irish parliament passed the statute 10 Car. 1, Sess. 2, c. 1, being its version, and an identical copy, of the English Statute of Uses, (27 Hen. 8, c. 10), and insured that the creation of a use passed both the legal and the equitable interest to the beneficiary. But it was also in 1634, in the English case of *Sambach v. Dalston*, (Ch.)

[4] *Cf.* John Spencer Bassett, "Landholding in Colonial North Carolina," *Law Quarterly Review*, XI (1895), 154-166.

Toth. 188, 21 Eng. Rep. 164, that it was held to be legitimate to create "a use upon a use" in which the legal and equitable interests would be separated. It is interesting to speculate whether the Irish statute operated as such, or whether it was virtually nullified by the citation of the English decision. Also, a recent Northern Ireland decision—*In re Sergie*, [1954] N.I. 1—revealed an interesting fact about the Irish Statute of Uses. This enactment was combined with a reproduction of the English Statute of Enrolments (27 Hen. 8, c. 16) under which the transactions of bargain and sale of land had to be formally enrolled to prevent the legal interest in freehold estates from being conveyed secretly. The effect of combining the Irish enactments may have been to require that a use would itself have to be enrolled to be effective; but it is fortunate that this three-hundred-year-old conundrum could be left unsolved by finding another basis for the decision.

Then the plantation period produced two interesting variations of English law. Many of the Crown grants made about this time contained a provision allowing the tenants in chief to make subgrants in fee simple *non obstante* Quia Emptores, and these were later confirmed by legislation, such as the Irish statute 10 Car. 1, Sess. 3, c. 3. Thus it was possible to create the tenurial relationship between the Crown grantee and the subgrantee, although the practice of subinfeudation had been prohibited by the English parliament in 1290, and by the statute Quia Emptores which appears to have been used in Ireland at the time when it was made and then confirmed in its application there when, as mentioned in the chapter on Constitutional History (*supra*), the Irish parliament passed Poynings' Law. The result is that fee farm grants, as they are called, are extremely common in Ireland, whereas in England they did not create the tenurial relationship and have been used mainly for the purpose of building leases in the industrial north. This remarkable use of the Crown's dispensing power in dealing with Irish land thus provided Ireland with a special type of land grant.

The second legal matter originating at the beginning of the seventeenth century is that to the plantation of Ulster has been ascribed the origins of the Ulster tenant-right custom, under which, as will be mentioned later, it was claimed that the interests of tenants were expanded by the inclusion of special rights of renewal and compensation. This custom became a controversial issue in Irish politics in the nineteenth century, when the descendants of the seventeenth-century settlers sought, and eventually obtained, recognition of this extension of their interests.

THE EIGHTEENTH CENTURY

It is both appropriate and convenient to commence a sketch of the substantive details of Irish land law with the eighteenth century. The Williamite settlement insured the stability of titles and on this foundation it was possible for the law to develop in normal fashion, subject of course to the various economic influences which made the Irish land problem both so distinctive and so important. Also, at the commencement of the century there were in force certain enactments of major importance to Irish land law.

An Irish version (7 Will. 3, c. 12) of the Statute of Frauds had been passed in 1695 providing, like its English model of twenty years before (29 Car. 2, c. 3), for the evidencing in writing of certain transactions relating to land. The Irish parliament also enacted a Statute of Distributions (7 Will. 3, c. 6), making the same provision for the descent of the personal property of an Irish intestate (after payment of debts) as had been made in England by the statutes of 1670 (22 & 23 Car. 2, c. 10) and 1685 (1 Jac. 2, c. 17). The acts were further evidence of the practice of keeping Irish law in line with English law, though with a legislative time-lag.

In one respect the Irish parliament went further than Westminster. Henry VIII's attempt to introduce a system of registration of deeds relating to land had not been successful, and the system was introduced only locally, in Yorkshire in 1703 (2 & 3 Anne c. 4) and Middlesex in 1708 (7 Anne c. 20). The Irish Registration of Deeds Act, 1707 (6 Anne c. 2) provided for the voluntary registration of transactions relating to land and gave priority to those which were thus registered. The Irish system, which will be considered comparatively in a later section of this chapter, extended throughout the country, and it is still a feature of Irish conveyancing practice.

In the development of the substantive law, economic factors played an important part. The larger landholders—those who held grants from the Crown subject to a rent—were often absentee landlords, who preferred life in London to that on their Irish estates.

This led to the creation of a race of middlemen, who in their turn made grants of short duration; the middlemen were often able to make more profit from the land than the landlords, whose remedy against the fee farm grantee was the common law one of distress. In consequence the practice developed of granting long leaseholds, which gave the landlord two advantages; in addition to a rent he could charge a fine for renewal of the lease when it expired, and he had too the remedies of distress on the land for nonpayment of rent and, if necessary, ejectment from the land. To achieve this aim there was devised the perpetually renewable lease, which was rare in England but became very common in Ireland. This involved the granting of a lease for the lives of three persons, with a convenant for perpetual renewal as the lives died. Since the renewal involved the payment of a fine, the landlord could expect an additional source of income, albeit necessarily a sporadic one. This type of grant involved the passing of a freehold estate which was virtually a perpetuity. Another type of renewable leasehold was regarded as a chattel interest, since it took the form of a lease for years determinable on the expiration of three lives. It is possible that this particular form of chattel interest was devised to evade the provisions of one of the penal laws, for by an Irish statute of 1703 (2 Anne c. 6) Catholics were debarred from purchasing land, or taking a longer lease than thirty-one years.

As for the power to grant leases, it was possible for land held subject to a settlement (that is, descending in tail) to be leased for three lives or forty-one years under an Irish act of 1634 (10 Car. 1 Sess. 3, c. 6). A special leasing power was that used to create what became known as "bishops' leases." Under another act of 1634 (10 & 11 Car. 1, c. 3) bishops were prevented from conveying the lands of their sees but were permitted to lease them for periods not exceeding twenty-one years. Although there was no obligation to do so, it became the practice to renew these leases when they expired for periods of one, two or three years. In turn, the holder of a bishop's lease often sublet at a profit, convenanting with the sublessee to renew the sublease *toties quoties*, that is for as long as the bishop renewed the head lease. The sublessee had to pay a portion of the renewal fine and a proportion of any increase in rent which the bishop imposed. The granting of "tot. quot." leases became so well recognized that the renewal fine imposed by the bishop was calculated as a proportion of the profit which the lessee would make by subletting after he had paid the bishop his due. In most dioceses this fine was fixed at one-fifth of the profit rent but in the diocese of Armagh (perhaps because of its associations with the archbishopric of Ireland), the renewal fine charged was one-eighth of the profit rent. Trinity College, Dublin, also had power to grant leases on similar lines.[5] There were other extensions of the power to make leases, but perhaps the most distinctively Irish were those statutes— 12 Geo. 1, c. 10 and 11 & 12 Geo. 3, c. 21—which permitted the making, for reclamation purposes, of sixty-year leases of bog lands.

Given the power to make leases, and assuming that this power was exercised in one of the ways which have been mentioned, it must be stated that the statutory provisions governing the relationship between the Irish landlord and his tenant in the eighteenth century were heavily weighted in favor of the landlord. If he had granted a lease for lives, and any question arose as to the continued existence of one of the *cestuis qui vie,* the landlord could rely on the Irish statute 7 Will. 3, c. 8, under which, until it was proved to the contrary, a "life" was presumed to be dead if he was abroad or absent elsewhere in the realm for more than seven years. In particular, a series of acts passed by the Irish parliament in the eighteenth century, commencing with the statute 11 Anne c. 2, made the formalities of the remedy of ejectment easier for the landlord. In 1745 the remedies of ejectment and distress were, by the Irish statute 25 Geo. 2, c. 13, made available where agreements for leases had been made, although no formal lease had been signed; and at the beginning of the next century, in 1816, the statute 56 Geo. 3, c. 88 made it possible to bring ejectment proceedings in the civil bill courts held locally in the counties, instead of suing in the superior courts in Dublin. Against this the tenant could only set the Tenantry Act of 1780 (19 & 20 Geo. 3, c. 30), under which an interest was not to be forfeited merely because of neglect to renew it, unless it could be proved that there was a demand for the renewal fine, coupled with subsequent failure or refusals to pay the fine. Also the tenant could claim the property in trees which he had planted, by virtue of a

[5] *Cf.* Thomas De Moleyns, *The Landowner's and Agent's Practical Guide* (8th ed.; Dublin, 1899).

series of acts passed to encourage afforestation, for the country had been shorn of the riches of her medieval forests.

But it would be misleading to suggest that questions concerning the refinements of leasehold interests occupied the minds of the majority of occupiers of land. The smaller tenants had often very small holdings indeed, and held them in an extremely tenuous way. The small farmer, perhaps holding a yearly tenancy, had no incentive to improve that holding, because he might find that the rent was increased because of the improvements which he had made, and this applied also to the renewal of a thirty-one year lease. Further there developed the custom known as the "hanging gale" whereby the rent was always paid six months in arrear, so that the threat of ejectment always hung over the tenant's head, for a notice to quit might be set out on the back of the demand for rent.

Two interesting points may be noted here about the agricultural practices of the eighteenth century. One of these was the system of taking land in "conacre." This involved the granting of the right to enter on land and take one crop from it. It did not mean that the person making the "letting" parted with possession of the land; conacre consisted merely of a license to take a crop from the land. It has been suggested that the origin of this practice lay in the fact that poorer people could obtain a crop of potatoes by making a conacre agreement with a farmer who could afford to keep the land fertilized.[6] Whatever its origin, the system has survived to the present time, when it enables the small farmer to enlarge his agricultural operations without the expenditure of capital on the acquisition of an interest in land.

The second feature of agricultural practice was the "burning of land"—setting fire to the topsoil to increase its fertility temporarily. Since this was ultimately harmful to the land, it was prohibited by the Irish parliament.

Added to the precariousness of the "hanging gale" and the conacre letting, and the ban on fertilizing by fire, the small holder was also liable to pay tithe to the established church on any land which he tilled. When clergymen sold their rights to tithe farmers, who in turn employed tithe proctors to collect the tithes, the tithe farmer

[6] William Dwyer Ferguson and Andrew Vance, *The Tenure and Improvement of Land in Ireland considered with reference to the relation of Landlord and Tenant and Tenant Right* (Dublin, 1851), 200.

naturally looked for profit over and above the purchase price of the right and the expenses of collection. In short, the position of Irish tenants was such that what are euphemistically called "agrarian disturbances" were almost bound to come.

In the latter part of the eighteenth century the Whiteboys (who wore white shirts over their clothes) began to object forcibly to the payment of tithe and to attempts at enclosure which destroyed the grazing and turf-cutting (turbary) rights to which they had been accustomed. Outbursts of violence occurred sporadically and the Irish parliament legislated to repress them. In Ulster discontent with the agrarian system was focused on one incident in 1771, when the Marquis of Donegall evicted tenants who refused to pay greatly increased fines for the renewal of their leases. For two years bands of men known as "The Hearts of Steel" upset the tenor of life in the two northeast counties, Antrim and Down. The Hearts of Steel not only championed the cause of tenants in Ulster; many emigrated to America and helped in another struggle for the assertion of rights which was then taking place.

In brief, a backward glance over eighteenth-century Ireland shows that the main legal feature of Irish land law is the emphasis on leasing powers and limited interests, whether freehold or chattel real; the main economic feature was the effect of the method of land holding on smaller tenants, whose dissatisfaction was expressed in agrarian disturbances. Both these elements were to recur during the nineteenth century; in the eighteenth century the pages of the Irish statute-book bore eloquent testimony both to the increasing complexity of the law and the economic condition of Irish land.

THE NINETEENTH CENTURY

A rise in population at the end of the eighteenth century and the beginning of the nineteenth was accompanied by an increase in the subdivision of holdings into even smaller holdings. The economic distress in the period following the Napoleonic wars was not much alleviated by the introduction of a poor law system, based on the English workhouse method, in 1838. Famine was a recurring threat (as in 1817 and 1822) and in the years 1845-1847 the failure of the potato crop caused what is known in Ireland simply as "the Famine." Much emigration followed and during the succeeding sixty years the population of Ireland was halved, falling from eight million to four million. This did not, however, appease the land hunger and throughout the century there were sporadic agrarian disturbances, an agitation for the legalization of the Ulster custom (which gave tenants security in their holdings and compensation for improvements made on them) and, in the 1880's, the "Land War." Drastic remedies were needed, and eventually they were introduced. At the beginning of the century the Irish farmer was the tenant of a small holding which he had no incentive to improve; by the end of the century he was well on the way to becoming the absolute owner of his own holding.

EXTENSION OF LEASING POWERS

The general policy of the nineteenth-century land legislation was a typically Victorian one of expansion. This is especially apparent in the extension of the powers of those holding large estates. In 1834 there was passed for Ireland a Fines and Recoveries Act (4 & 5 Will. 4, c. 92) by which the tenant in tail under a settlement could bar the entail, when he became of full age and obtained the consent of the tenant for life, by enrolling a deed. Later, when general powers were given for the compulsory purchase of land for the construction of public works, both English and Irish owners of limited interests in land were given power to convey these, as, for example, by the Lands Clauses Consolidation Act, 1845 (8 & 9 Vict. c. 18). In 1849 by the statute 12 & 13 Vict. c. 77 Incumbered Estates Commissioners were appointed to authorize sales for the purpose of discharging incumbrances on land, and to give the purchaser an indefeasible title. This jurisdiction was transferred to the Landed States Court in 1858 (21 & 22 Vict. c. 72), which became a branch of the Chancery Division of the High Court under the Supreme Court of Judicature (Ireland) Act, 1877 (40 & 41 Vict. c. 57). A series of Settled Estates Acts commencing in 1856 extended the powers of persons holding under settlements to make leases and to sell land. These acts were followed by the Settled Land Acts, 1882-90 (45 & 46 Vict. c. 38 to 53 & 54 Vict. c. 69), which applied in Ireland as in England, and enabled life tenants under settlements to make leases for thirty-five years, building leases for ninety-nine years, and sales subject to the trusts of the settlement.

The effect of these latter acts was to import into all settlements the wide powers of dealing with land which would have been con-

ferred by a settlement drafted in generous terms. The individual
caprices of settlors were not to be allowed to interfere with the
management of the land in the best possible way.

EXTENSION OF LEASEHOLDERS' INTERESTS

Other examples of the policy of expansion are to be found in
enactments giving leaseholders a larger interest in land. First in
the series is a set of acts, beginning with the statute 3 & 4 Will. 4,
c. 37, passed in William IV's reign to deal with church temporalities.
Under these, holders of the bishops' leases, which were a feature
of Irish land holding in the eighteenth century, were enabled to
purchase a fee simple interest, subject to a perpetual fee farm grant.
Holders of *toties quoties* leases were also enabled to purchase fee
farm interests in certain cases. The rent was regarded as a rent
service not a rent charge, so that the relation of landlord and tenant
subsisted. On the disestablishment of the Church of Ireland by the
Irish Church Act, 1869 (32 & 33 Vict. c. 42) church property was
vested in commissioners, who were empowered to sell estates in fee
to tenants, and to this day the Ministry of Finance for Northern
Ireland derives revenue from the payment of purchase rents of former
ecclesiastical property.

A more general measure for the creation of interests in fee
was the Renewable Leasehold Conversion Act, 1849 (12 & 13 Vict.
c. 105). This authorized the substitution of one distinctive form
of Irish landholding—the fee simple subject to a rent, or fee farm
grant—for another, the perpetually renewable lease, whether for
lives, years, or years and lives. A new type of statutory fee, the
fee farm conversion grant, was created and the rent was calculated
by reference to the old rent, the renewal fines, and the better terms
attaching to the new interest; for the grantor the remedies of distress
and ejectment were made available. At this time a private act (14
& 15 Vict. c. cxxvii) enabled Trinity College, Dublin, to grant
similar perpetuity interests to its long lessees and sublessees. Thus
a general act and a private one gave legislative sanction for the
transmutation of leasehold interests into fee farm grants, but usually
only the larger landholders benefited, although there are still in-
stances of small holdings held on conversion grants.

Towards the end of the nineteenth century the Redemption of
Rent (Ireland) Act, 1891 (54 & 55 Vict. c. 57) gave general powers

to fee farm grantees and long leaseholders to redeem their rents, thus freeing their interests from payment. Failing agreement on the terms, a fair sum might be fixed—a provision very far removed from the detailed and limited authority for expansion of interests given in the early part of the century.

THE LANDLORD-TENANT RELATIONSHIP

Another aim of the nineteenth-century legislation relating to Irish land was the alteration of the relationship between landlord and tenant. This was brought about by direct amendment, and by the Irish land purchase scheme; the latter subject will be treated separately.

The first act dealing with the legal relationship was the Landlord and Tenant Law Amendment Act Ireland, 1860 (23 & 24 Vict. c. 154), called Deasy's Act after its sponsor in the House of Commons. This Act had a long struggle to reach the statute-book. The Royal Commission on Irish Land under the chairmanship of the Earl of Devon had reported in 1847, and following this two members of the Irish Bar, Ferguson and Vance, had prepared their *Tenure and Improvement of Land in Ireland* (*supra* note 6) as a private report on the legal changes necessary to bring the Irish law of landlord and tenant into line with then existing conditions. Bills for this purpose were introduced into the House of Commons in 1852 and 1854, but it was not until 1860 that these efforts eventually received legislative approval.

The crux of Deasy's Act is contained in s. 3, which provided that the relation of landlord and tenant was to be based on an express or implied contract, not upon tenure or service, that a reversion was not to be necessary, and that the relationship was to subsist "in all cases in which there shall be an agreement by one party to hold land from or under another in consideration of a rent." The prima facie meaning of the section is clear enough—that a new conception of the landlord-tenant relationship was introduced, to be created in certain circumstances and to subsist without the necessity, imposed by the common law rules, of the landlord retaining a reversionary interest in property granted to the tenant. This requirement had been insisted on in 1832 when the House of Lords, overruling the Court of Exchequer Chamber in Ireland, held in *Pluck v. Digges*, 5 Bligh N.S. 31, 5 Eng. Rep. 219 that a reversion was necessary to support a rent in a case where a landlord granted all his interest to a tenant. The existence of the middleman has been put forward as the reason for s. 3 of the 1860 Act, since his tenants would regard him as their landlord, though he might have only a limited interest in the land and might have granted away all that interest in return for a rent. If he had no reversion he would not have been able to distrain for rent unless he had specifically created a rent charge. Linked with this view of the origin of s. 3 is the suggestion that, apart from the abolition of the necessity for a reversion, the section did not create a revolution in the landlord-tenant relationship so as to allow the contractual creation of any relationship to be called that of landlord and tenant; on this argument the section merely set out the circumstances in which the known relationship of landlord and tenant would be contractually created.[7] Among the cases decided by the Irish courts after 1860 may be found authorities to support both the wide and the narrow view of the effect of s. 3 of Deasy's Act, but at the present time the matter has become one of academic argument rather than judicial decision, for subsequent developments in Irish landholding turned attention away from the landlord-tenant relationship.

Deasy's Act did, however, set out a number of aspects of that relationship—the formalities of its creation, the convenants to be implied, the law as to fixtures and waste, the position of assignments and subletting, and the procedure to be followed on ejectment—so that the Act is now the foundation for the Irish law of landlord and tenant, although its immediate economic effect appears to have been small. When the Royal Commission on Irish Land under the chairmanship of the Earl of Bessborough reported in 1880, it remarked on the slight effect of the 1860 Act; in practice middlemen provided themselves with the necessary powers to recover rent when they were creating their subleases, so that there was no need to rely upon the general law. It has also been alleged that the 1860 Act, with its emphasis on contract, cut down the operation of the Ulster custom, so it is appropriate to consider next an aspect of the landlord-tenant relationship which emphasized the rights of the tenant rather than the remedies of the landlord.

[7] For a discussion of Deasy's Act, see James Louis Montrose, "Fee Farm Grants," *Northern Ireland Legal Quarterly*, II (1938), 194; III (1939), 40, 81, 193; IV (1940), 40, 86.

THE ULSTER CUSTOM

A writer from the North of Ireland may perhaps be pardoned for drawing particular attention to the existence of the Ulster custom. As previously mentioned, its origin has been attributed to the English and Scottish settlers who came to Ireland at the time of James I's plantation of Ulster. The emphasis in the plantation terms on the husbandry of farms, together with the determination of the settlers to make a success of their venture, are thought to have combined to produce the better agricultural conditions which in the eighteenth century prevailed in Ulster in comparison with the rest of Ireland. At all events, there grew up a distinct feeling among the Ulster tenants that their rights amounted to something more than occupation of their lands for a definite or indefinite period. Because the validity of the custom as such does not appear to have been tested in the courts, the sources of judicial opinion as to the nature of the custom are to be found only in cases decided after 1870, but the 1847 report of the Devon Commission on Irish Land contains valuable information on the operation of what was called "tenant right."

While the operation of the custom varied in different parts of the province, the main elements were said to be the right to continue in possession, with a reasonable limit on increases of rent for improvements made by the tenant; the right to sell and to have the purchaser recognized by the landlord as tenant in the seller's place; and the right to compensation on eviction or determination of the tenant's interest. Apart from questions as to the limit of legal memory and variations in the operation of the custom, it would seem that the courts would not have recognized tenant-right as a valid custom in the common-law sense, although the practice was much more widespread than English estate usages. Agitation for legalization of the custom was, naturally, particularly strong in Ulster, where a Tenant Right League was formed in 1847, and one of the aims of the League of North and South which was formed in 1850 was the legalizing of the custom and its extension throughout the rest of the country. Legalization of the Ulster custom by the United Kingdom parliament was a personal aim of a land owner in county Down, Sharman Crawford, who campaigned for this by introducing tenant-right bills into the House of Commons in 1850 and 1852. The

Devon Commission had recommended the payment to tenants of compensation for improvements, but this did not take into account the existing value of their tenant-right to those who held under the custom, which was, of course, much wider. The practices on different estates tended to cut down the operation of the custom which had contributed much to the agricultural prosperity of the province of Ulster by giving tenants incentive to cultivate their holdings as well as possible. But it was not until Gladstone made his first attempt to deal with the Irish land problem in 1870 that the custom was legalized.

THE LANDLORD AND TENANT (IRELAND) ACT, 1870

The Landlord and Tenant (Ireland) Act, 1870 (33 & 34 Vict. c. 46) took the form, unusual for Westminster legislation, of a direct legalization of the Ulster custom. In the words of s. 1:

> The usages prevalent in the province of Ulster, which are known as, and in this Act included under, the denomination of the Ulster tenant-right custom, are hereby declared to be legal, and shall, in the case of any holding in the province of Ulster proved to be subject thereto, be enforced in the manner provided by this Act.

The use of the plural "usages" instead of the singular has been criticized on the ground that it did not recognize the essential elements of the custom but left the operation of the section open to restrictive construction by the courts, to the detriment of tenants. But it is difficult to see how the custom could have been legalized in any other fashion, apart from some form of definition, which itself would probably have been criticized as not being all-embracing. The fact that the custom had varied in its effect from estate to estate inevitably militated against uniformity of the custom when it was made legal. In any event, in the years following 1870 various judicial pronouncements on the nature of the custom were marked by a certain dissimilarity in their statements of the nature of the custom.

As well as legalizing the Ulster custom, the 1870 Act also legalized similar tenant-right customs in other parts of the country. But tenants of holdings not subject to these beneficial practices were not forgotten by the Act, which made certain alterations which tenants of all holdings (whether or not they were subject to tenant-right customs) could use to their advantage. Compensation was provided for tenants for two reasons—disturbance and improvements. Without removing the landlord's right to evict his tenant, the Act provided that the tenant could refuse to give up possession until he had been compensated for his loss of the holding. The Act laid down maxima (scaled according to the rateable valuation of the holding) within which the courts were to work, but in no case was this compensation to exceed two hundred and fifty pounds. This method was replaced in 1881 under the Land Law (Ireland) Act of that year (44 & 45 Vict. c. 49) by one which calculated compensation according to the rent payable. The second type of compensation—that for improvements—aimed at paying the tenant quitting his holding, or ejected for nonpayment of rent, a sum for the works done by him, or his predecessors in title, which increased the letting value of the holding, together with a sum towards the tillage, manures, etc. unexhausted at the time the tenant left the holding. Certain improvements, such as those made before 1850, were excluded, but there was a general presumption that improvements had been made by the tenant, which put him in a favorable position. The criterion was the effect of the expenditure of money, not the expenditure itself.

The principle of the 1870 Act was the alteration of the relationship between landlord and tenant so that the tenant would have some assurance that his work on his holding would not be in vain; it differs from the principle of "extension of interests" which has been previously postulated in that it did not convert the tenant's interest into a greater one; it merely provided a monetary compensation in certain circumstances. The main defect in the economics of the 1870 Act was that it did not prevent landlords from raising rents; it merely ordered the making of certain payments in cases where the tenant's interest determined.

"THE THREE F'S"

The question of rents had an important place in the campaign for what were known as the "Three F's"—Fair Rent, Free Sale, and Fixity of Tenure. The Tenant Right Leagues had campaigned for the acceptance of these ideas, and in the 1870's increasing economic distress caused by the raising of rents and poor harvests created a favorable atmosphere for the foundation of the Land League in 1879, with the dual objects of the reduction of rents and the initiation of a scheme whereby the tenants would be enabled to purchase their holdings. This flourished particularly in the south and west of the country. Their action in refusing to work for a certain Captain Boycott on his estate in county Mayo gave a new word to the English language. In the North various associations with tenant-right objects advocated legislation for the "Three F's" and the 1880 Commission on Irish Land, under the chairmanship of the Earl of Bessborough, reported in favor of these. Accordingly the Land Law (Ireland) Act, 1881 (44 & 45 Vict. c. 49) enshrined the principle of the "Three F's" in legislative language.

A Land Commission was constituted, with judicial and lay members, which was given wide powers for the operation of the Act. Fair rents subcommissions throughout the country determined the judicial rents of holdings or of year-to-year tenancies. Fixity of tenure was achieved by granting tenants a statutory term of fifteen years, subject to statutory conditions; this was virtually a perpetual interest subject to revision of rent at fifteen-year intervals. The right of free sale was conferred directly on tenants, subject to the landlord's right to buy the holding himself, and to object to the purchaser, in which case the reasonableness of the objection was to be judicially determined. The resemblance between this system and the method of selling tenant-right under the Ulster custom is a marked one. As did the 1870 Act, the 1881 Act allowed tenants of holdings subject to tenant-right customs to choose whether they would rely on their customary rights or proceed under the statute. Despite the "No Rent Manifesto" issued by the Land League, the Fair Rent Act was put into operation, but agricultural prices became further depressed and in 1886, by the Irish National League's "Plan of Campaign," tenants on estates were encouraged to make a lump-sum offer to their landlord for their rents, and if he refused these were to be withheld. The Land Law (Ireland) Act, 1887 (50 & 51 Vict. c. 33) accordingly provided for the determination of all rents fixed before 1886, and extended the provisions of the 1881 Act to cover leaseholders, who were not forced to wait until the expiration of their leases but were enabled to anticipate their rights.

In 1896 another Irish Land Law Act (59 & 60 Vict. c. 47) provided a uniform system of determining fair rents, by fixing the rental value of holdings deducting improvements allowances. Three-quarters of the tenants took advantage of the 1881 Act when it was first introduced, but on the expiration of the statutory terms progressively fewer tenants had judicial rents fixed. The reason is a simple one—the gradual replacement of the principle of dual ownership in land (in which both landlord and tenant shared fixed rights) to one of owner-occupation, which was brought about by the operation of the Irish land purchase scheme.

REGISTRATION OF TITLE

There are, however, other interesting aspects of Irish land law in the past sixty or seventy years which may be mentioned before considering the land purchase scheme in some detail.

One of these features is the method of registration of title. In 1891 the Local Registration of Title (Ireland) Act (54 & 55 Vict. c. 66) established a central registry, and one in each county, for the registering of titles to land. (The Record of Title (Ireland) Act, 1865 (28 & 29 Vict. c. 88) had introduced this system for such titles as those made by the Landed Estates Court, but this had not been widely used.) The land purchase scheme has a direct connection with the registration of title, since this is compulsory in cases where tenants have purchased their holdings under the scheme, and voluntary in other cases. Owners in fee are registered as full owners, while tenants in tail or for life are registered as limited owners. Certain burdens affect land without being registered, and others take priority as they are registered. The fee simple is registered in the owner or owners, and backed by a guarantee fund for those who may be affected by any mistake in the investigation of title. Transfers and devolutions of, and charges on, the land must appear on the register to be effective. Generally, the Irish system of registration of title resembles the voluntary system introduced in England by the Land Transfer Act, 1875 (38 & 39 Vict. c. 87) and the Torrens system, which by 1891 had been introduced in Australia, spread to New Zealand and Canada, and was shortly to be introduced into the United States.

The 1891 Act did not, however, confine itself to these matters. In Part IV it provided that land compulsorily registered—that is, land acquired under the Land Purchase Acts—was to descend on death as if it were personalty rather than realty, being held by the personal representatives for distribution according to the owner's will or in accordance with the rules of intestate succession to personalty. The old law—the widow's right to dower, the husband's tenancy by the curtesy, and the rules of distribution—was repealed in relation to such land. In this assimilation of real and personal property for the purpose of devolution the Irish Registration Act of 1891 preceded the English "Birkenhead" legislation by three decades.

A SUMMARY OF NINETEENTH-CENTURY DEVELOPMENTS

The turn of the century is a convenient, if somewhat arbitrary, point to consider the revolutionary changes in Irish land law which characterized the nineteenth century. Some reference has been made to economic forces—the land hunger, the poor harvests and famine, the agrarian disturbances—which provided the reason for these changes. The pragmatic approach of the Westminster parliament was shown by its legislation dealing with Irish land, for formal legal changes were followed by measures aimed at the economics of the situation only when pressure was so great that it could not be resisted.

From the procedural changes of the Irish Fines and Recoveries Act, 1834 to the Settled Land Acts, 1882-1890, the Irish owner of limited interests, like his English counterpart, was empowered to exercise wide powers over his interest. Similarly, what has been termed the principle of "expansion of interests" was applied throughout the century in dealing with the problems of landholding peculiar to Ireland. From the Church Temporalities Acts, passed just before the beginning of Victoria's reign, to the Redemption of Rent Act, enacted when her reign was drawing to its close, the idea of converting leasehold interests in land into fees was carried out, and the fee farm grant which had been a feature of landholding in the seventeenth century was recognized by the legislative creation of statutory fees. The whole relation of landlord and tenant was recast, and the important question of agricultural improvements was regulated. The legalization of the Ulster custom and similar tenant-right practices was another legislative recognition of Irish land problems, though it was not entirely satisfactory in its operation, as was shown by the introduction of legislation embodying the principles of the "Three F's." Attention then shifted to the problem of converting tenants into owners, by the granting of fee simple estates subject to annuities, and to assist in this the system of registration of title was applied in Ireland, as it had been in different ways in other parts of the Commonwealth. In sum, special statutory provision was made to deal with the Irish land question in the nineteenth century, just as the Irish law proceeded along its own course in the two preceding centuries.

PRESENT-DAY PROVISIONS RELATING TO THE USE OF LAND

This sketch of the development of Irish land law in the nineteenth century may have given the impression that the distribution of agricultural land is of sole importance in Ireland. While agricultural land predominates in area, developments in urban areas have also been the subject of legislation. For example, the Town Tenants (Ireland) Act, 1906 (6 Edw. 7, c. 54) gave to the occupiers of residential and business premises the right to compensation for improvements; the Act also gave compensation for unreasonable disturbance to occupiers of premises in urban districts used for trade or business purposes. In this way the town tenant was placed in a position rather similar to that of his country cousin under the Landlord and Tenant (Ireland) Act, 1870, though the 1906 Act has not been widely used. In Northern Ireland the problem of extending tenancies of business premises has been tackled by direct legislation in the period of scarcity following the Second World War. Under Business Tenancies (Temporary Provision) Acts (Northern Ireland), 1952 (c. 2) and 1954 (c. 36), tenants have been given the opportunity, for a temporary period, of having their leases extended by a court, which also fixes the rent for the statutory term. In the Irish Republic this problem has been dealt with by the Landlord and Tenant Acts, 1931 (No. 55 of 1931) and 1943 (No. 10 of 1943) setting out the circumstances in which a leasehold interest may be extended.

The scarcity of housing accommodation which led to the introduction of Rent Restriction Acts in the middle of the First World War also resulted in the application of this legislation to Ireland. The Increase of Rent and Mortgage Interest (Restrictions) Act passed by the Westminster parliament in 1920 (10 & 11 Geo. 5, c. 17) contained adaptations providing for its application in Ireland, and this forms the basis of the legislation at present in force in Northern Ireland. There the system of control was extended by the Rent and Mortgage Interest (Restrictions) Act (Northern Ireland), 1940 (4 & 5 Geo. 6, c. 7) to houses to which the 1920 Act did not apply, in order to deal with problems of scarcity arising in the Second World War. Despite the fact that this legislation was originally described as temporary it has remained in force for as long as Northern Ireland has been in existence. In the Irish Republic the Westminster Act of 1920 was replaced by an Act passed by the Irish Free State parliament in 1923 (No. 19 of 1923), which was amended during the emergency period in 1939-1945 by delegated legislation. This system was replaced by the Rent Restrictions Act, 1946 (No. 4 of 1946) which (despite the complexities with which it had to deal) is a model of concise legislation in comparison with the tangled legislation in force in Northern Ireland and Great Britain.

Another, and extremely important, aspect of present-day property law is the planning legislation which governs the use and development of land. Neither Belfast nor Dublin has followed London into the complexities of the Town and Country Planning Act, 1947 (10 & 11 Geo. 6, c. 51). As has been mentioned in the chapter on Administrative Law (*supra*), the system of planning used in Northern Ireland is a moderate one with a carefully graduated system of safeguards and appeals to protect the citizen from oppressive decisions of planning authorities preventing him from making a reasonable use of his property. Similarly, in the Irish Republic a series of planning acts has regulated the general principles of building development. An interesting aspect of the Dublin legislation is that in *The State (Modern Homes (Ireland) Ltd.) v. Dublin Corporation*, (1954) 88 I.L.T.R. 79 the court intervened to order the preparation of planning schemes regarded as being unduly delayed by a local authority.

Thus Irish land law has made provision for the town dweller as well as the country man; and further, that provision is in substance much the same on both sides of the land frontier.

A SUMMARY AND SOME COMPARISONS

In other parts of the Commonwealth, notably Australia and New Zealand, the distribution of land has been a major problem during the past century or so, and in modern India it is an especially urgent problem. In Ireland, as will be seen, the chief problem has been the expansion of the rights of occupiers of land into full ownership. But both in Ireland and overseas the doctrines of English real property law were subject to certain modifications.

For example, by the time English law was extended throughout Ireland in the seventeenth century, feudalism had ceased to have much meaning, although the feudal doctrines, such as escheat to mesne lords and forfeiture to the Crown, remained. Incidentally, the plantation practice of making grants of land "as of our Castle of Dublin" was similar to those grants of land in the American colonies held "our Manor of East Greenwich."[8] Thus in Northern Ireland, as in the rest of the Commonwealth, the theory of tenure survives and all land is held of the Crown, absolute ownership being impossible. In the Irish Republic, tenure has not been abolished (as happened in some American states after the Revolution) and the doctrine of estates in land was specifically recognized by Art. 11 of the 1922 Constitution and Art. 10 of the 1937 Constitution, so that this common law conception is now enshrined in a fundamental constitutional document.

Some further points arise on the application of this doctrine of estates in Ireland. In the first place, the seventeenth-century practice of allowing grants in fee to be made *non obstante* Quia Emptores led to the emergence of a common method of holding Irish land— the fee farm grant, or fee simple subject to a rent. Thus, when in the nineteenth century the Westminster parliament began to extend the interest of certain Irish landholders, the statutory fee subject to a rent was a convenient means for doing this. Next, the Conveyancing Act, 1881 (44 & 45 Vict. c. 41) applied both in England and Ireland, so that the rules for the creation of a fee simple were relaxed simultaneously in both countries. Then the existence in Ireland of large estates subject to settlements meant that the fee tail was of considerable importance. It was not turned into a fee simple or other outright grant (as was done in New South Wales and Victoria, since the fee tail is rare in Australia)[9] or abolished altogether, as was done in New Zealand in 1951.[10] Such doctrines as the Rule in Shelley's Case and the Rule against Perpetuities are still

[8] *Cf.* Sir Cecil Thomas Carr, "Our Manor of East Greenwich," *Law Quarterly Review*, XXIX (1913), 349-353.

[9] P. M. Fox, "Real Property" in G. W. Paton (ed.), *The Commonwealth of Australia: The Development of Its Laws and Constitution* (London, 1952), 118.

[10] E. J. Haughey, "The Historical Development of the Civil Law: Property," in J. L. Robson (ed.), *New Zealand: The Development of its Laws and Constitution* (London, 1954), 276-292.

part of the law of Ireland, for the activities of Lord Birkenhead in Irish affairs did not extend to a reform of the property law such as is associated with his name in England.

As for the creation of new kinds of estates, much may depend on the interpretation placed upon s. 3 of Deasy's Act, making contract rather than tenure the basis of the landlord-tenant relationship. No provision of comparable breadth appears to exist, and one cannot predict how far the present-day Irish judges will follow their predecessors of a century ago in attempting to struggle out of the rigorous confines of the common law doctrines. Perhaps some day the courts in Belfast or Dublin will be faced with the attempted creation of a lease, say, "for the duration of the war"; no doubt the shade of Serjeant Deasy will wait anxiously for the decision!

Again, the legalization of the Ulster custom was unique, as was the custom itself. Those claiming tenant-right in Ireland were not mere squatters, for they already had an interest in the land. Nor were they merely claiming compensation for improvements, like English tenants invoking the benefit of estate customs. The origin and generality of Irish tenant-right were such that those claiming under it sought a declaration of a right in addition to their legal interest. Variations in the custom and its recent origin prevented it from being recognized at common law, but the legislature stepped in to protect specifically this and similar tenant-right customs.

The question of the improvements for which a tenant was entitled to compensation was also important in Irish land law. In this connection it is of interest to note that as recently as 1941 a New South Wales Agricultural Holdings Act gave tenants rights similar to those given to Irish tenants in 1870, and also gave landlords there the statutory right to waste which their counterparts in Ireland had been given over seventy years before.[11] Again, the principle of compensation for improvements has been applied in cases where Crown grants of land in Australia[12] and South Africa[13] are resumed.

In the realm of conveyancing a remarkable similarity can be

[11] S. M. Wadham, "Law and Legal Institutions Affecting the Rural Economy" in G. W. Paton (ed.), *The Commonwealth of Australia: The Development of Its Laws and Constitution* (London, 1952), 224.

[12] Wadham, *op. cit. supra* note 11 at 225.

[13] Gilbert William Frederick Dold and Christian Petrus Joubert, *The Union of South Africa: The Development of its Laws and Constitution* (London, 1955), 396.

found throughout the Commonwealth in the law relating to registration of deeds and registration of title. After several experiments the Scottish parliament established in 1617 the Register of Sasines, which is still kept at Register House, Edinburgh. The American colonists favored a system of registration of deeds, which was established in Plymouth Colony in 1626 and in Virginia and Connecticut in 1639. A system of recording transactions relating to land was established in South Africa in 1685, and in 1703 there came the establishment of the Yorkshire Registry, followed in 1707-1708 by the establishment of registries in Middlesex and Dublin. The system was extended as English law was carried to different parts of the world so that in some form or another it was prevalent in the nineteenth century. Its difficulties were that it was cumbersome and merely formed a record of dealings in land. While these were given priority over unregistered transactions (a principle first applied in the United States in 1634) they did not constitute a complete title to land and consequently did not eliminate the difficulties of tracing title. It was because of these difficulties that the Torrens system of registration was introduced into South Australia in 1858, from where it soon spread to the other Australian states, to New Zealand, and to Canada. Under this system the title to land is investigated and recorded, and the person registered as owner had full title to the land. This system is often spoken of as being compulsory, but with two exceptions it is compulsory only in the sense that Crown grants made after the introduction of the system must be recorded; for other types of transaction it remains voluntary. An exception to this principle came with the enactment in New Zealand in 1924 of the Land Transfer (Compulsory Registration of Titles) Act (No. 32), and another example is provided by the provisions for compulsory registration in South Australia, where the Torrens system originated.[14] New Zealand has gone further and amalgamated her two systems of registration by the Land Transfer Act, 1952 (No. 52).[15]

The similarity between the Torrens system and the system introduced into Ireland by the Local Registration of Title Act, 1891 lies not only in the method of operating the registration system, but also in the fact that all holdings purchased under the Irish Land

[14] Fox, *op. cit. supra* note 9 at 125-126.
[15] Haughey, *op. cit. supra* note 10 at 279-280.

Purchase Acts must be registered, in just the same way as Crown grants are registered in other parts of the Commonwealth. The Irish system differs from the Torrens system in that it permits the registration of both full and limited ownership, and has a separate register for leaseholds, while under the Torrens system there is a single register and only absolute ownership is recorded. A single idea, transplanted to different parts of the world, has been molded by legislation to provide similar assistance for those seeking evidence of their rights to land.

Mention of the Irish Act of 1891 leads naturally to the question of devolution of property on intestacy, since the 1891 Act provided that realty subject to the Irish Land Purchase code was to descend as if it were personal property. The assimilation of realty to personalty for this purpose had been carried out in other parts of the Commonwealth before the reforms made by the Birkenhead legislation in England in 1925. While the Australian states rely on modifications of the Statute of Distributions to regulate the descent of all types of property on intestacy, in 1944 New Zealand went further and devised a scheme based on the English Administration of Estates Act, 1925 (15 & 16 Geo. 5, c. 23).[16] In 1955 the Parliament of Northern Ireland passed an Administration of Estates Act (c. 24) similar to the English Act of 1925, abolishing primogeniture, the wife's right to dower, and the husband's tenancy by the curtesy, and providing that real and personal property will on intestacy descend in the same way to the surviving spouse, issue, or specified next of kin or, failing that, will go to the Crown as *bona vacantia*. It will be interesting to see whether Dublin follows the lead set by Belfast in this matter.

There is one respect in which Ireland has not followed the lead set by the Commonwealth in altering the law of real property. The testator's family maintenance legislation introduced by New Zealand in 1900 and now part of the family protection code enables a court to decide whether a man has made reasonable provision for his family: if it thinks he has not, the court may override the terms of the will. This has been followed in Australia and Great Britain, but so far it has not made its appearance on the statute-book either

---

[16] P. E. Joske, "Succession" in G. W. Paton (ed.), *The Commonwealth of Australia: The Development of Its Laws and Constitution* (London, 1952), 159; Haughey, *op. cit. supra* note 10 at 290-291.

in Belfast or Dublin, though a committee set up in Northern Ireland in 1954 reported by a majority in favor of the introduction of legislation on the lines of the Westminster Inheritance (Family Provision) Act, 1938 (1 & 2 Geo. 6, c. 45). For the moment, the Irish testator retains freedom of choice as to the provision he may make by will for his family.

This brief comparative survey has concentrated on the doctrine of estates, the landlord-tenant relationship and some of its incidents, registration methods, and succession; but even such technical matters as these show how the English law of real property, in the process of transplantation, both acquires new features and retains identifiable marks of its origin. If, however, the economic problems and solutions differ considerably from those in England, does the English law retain its capacity for alteration, or is it forced into statutory channels vastly different from the original course? A partial answer to this question may be found in a description of the Irish land purchase scheme, and a short comparison with methods of land settlement used in other parts of the Commonwealth.

THE IRISH LAND PURCHASE SCHEME

In considering the land problem in Ireland in the nineteenth century we are fortunate in having Elizabeth R. Hooker's economic survey *Readjustments of Agricultural Tenure in Ireland,* published in Chapel Hill, North Carolina in 1938. The problem was very different from, say, that in Australia and New Zealand. In these newly populated and rapidly developing countries large tracts of land had to be apportioned among settlers so that the land could be worked. In Ireland the settlements had ended two centuries previously, and the problem was that of the equitable division of land among the tenants of small holdings. An additional complication was that the population exceeded the productive capacity of the land, leading to agricultural depression, famine, and emigration; direct legislative action was necessary to bring about an agricultural revolution. But while Crown grants could be freely made of stretches of uncultivated land in the antipodes, in Ireland many interests lay between the rights of the Crown and the interest of the small farmer, so that some means had to be found of acquiring these intervening interests and transferring to the tenant a full estate in his holding. For the lawyer interest lies in the methods used, while the

economist's concern is with the effects of the land purchase scheme;
but this is a subject in which law, economics, and history merged to
change the pattern of Irish life in three-quarters of a century, and to
govern much of it today.

The idea of assisting the tenant in the expansion of his interest
first appeared in the Irish Church Act, 1869 (32 & 33 Vict. c. 42)
under s. 52 of which the Church Temporalities Commissioners were
empowered to sell church lands to tenants by making an advance of
three-quarters of the purchase price, repayable on a thirty-two year
mortgage.   Less than seven thousand tenants benefited by these
powers, but their originator, the economist and politician John Bright,
saw his ideas carried further by the introduction of land purchase
provisions into the 1870 Landlord and Tenant Act (33 & 34 Vict.
c. 46).   Under these provisions, certain sales could be made in the
Landed Estates Court, and tenants could receive two-thirds of the
purchase money from the Board of Public Works, this sum being
secured by the charging on the land of a five per cent annuity repayable in thirty-five years.   Under the Land Law (Ireland) Act,
1881 (44 & 45 Vict. c. 49) the newly constituted Land Commission
was given the powers of the Board of Works under the 1870 Act,
and the amount of the purchase price which might be advanced to a
tenant was increased to three-quarters.   In addition, the Land Commission was empowered to purchase estates on which a proportion
of the tenants were willing to buy their holdings.

While these provisions introduced the method of land purchase,
first on mortgage and then by means of an annuity, and although the
giving of assistance to prospective tenant-purchasers was vital to the
success of these schemes, only about fifteen hundred availed themselves of the facilities provided by the 1870 and 1881 Acts.   More
attractive terms were necessary if the tenants were to become proprietors of the interest in fee of their holdings.   Accordingly, the
principle of annuity payments instituted by the 1870 Act and the
machinery of the Land Commission set up by the 1881 Act were used
in a series of acts passed at the end of the nineteenth century and
the beginning of the twentieth, with the avowed aims of abolishing
the system of "dual ownership" in land and of placing the agricultural
land of Ireland in the hands of those who worked it.

The first of these acts, the Purchase of Land (Ireland) Act,
1885 (48 & 49 Vict. c. 73) was known as the "Ashbourne Act,"

after its sponsor, the then Lord Chancellor of Ireland. By this Act a sum of five million pounds was provided for the purchase of land by agreement between landlords and their tenants: the Land Commission was given power to pay the whole of the purchase price charged to the tenant, but retained a "guarantee deposit" of one-fifth, which was not paid over to the landlord until the annuities paid by the tenant amounted to the same sum; the rate of interest on the annuity was fixed at four per cent and the repayment period was extended from thirty-five years to forty-nine; the method of carrying out sales was changed from that of the ordinary conveyance to one of making vesting orders by the Land Commission; and the Commission was enabled to buy estates in the Landed Estates court for resale to tenants. Under the 1885 Act, an amending Act passed in 1887 (50 & 51 Vict. c. 33), and one of 1888 (51 & 52 Vict. c. 49) which provided another five million pounds for the scheme, over twenty-five thousand tenants acquired holdings, a considerable advance on the few hundreds of tenants who had become owners under the pre-1885 legislation.

Further advances were made by the passing of two Acts called the Balfour Acts after the then Chief Secretaries for Ireland, one of whom, A. J. Balfour, later became Prime Minister. The Purchase of Land (Ireland) Act, 1891 (54 & 55 Vict. c. 48) introduced methods of financing the Irish land purchase scheme by the issue of guaranteed stock, and of insuring the repayments of annuities by varying the amount of interest and providing for additional payments. The operation of the complicated provisions of this Act slowed down the progress of the scheme, and the 1891 Act was replaced by the Land Law (Ireland) Act, 1896 (59 & 60 Vict. c. 47) simplifying the procedure, increasing the period for repayment by the tenant to seventy-three years, and reducing the amount of the annuity at the end of each of the first three decades of repayment. In the result, over forty-six thousand tenants acquired holdings, almost double the number under the Ashbourne Acts.

A part of the 1891 Act which remained unrepealed was that which constituted the Congested Districts Board. By a combined test of population and rateable value, certain counties were regarded as "congested" in that the population was too large to be properly supported on the land. The counties which were so designated stretched from Donegal in the northwest of the country to Cork and Kerry in the southwest. The Congested Districts Board was given one and a half million pounds of the funds left after the disestablishment of the Irish Church under the 1869 Act, and given powers to deal with small holdings, to assist migration and emigration, and to develop agriculture and industries. The Board was also authorized to purchase certain estates and to sell holdings to tenants, who obtained advances from, and repaid annuities to, the Land Commission. The Board's activities were, of course, much wider in scope than those of the Commission, which was concerned only with the land purchase scheme. The Board's fostering of industry and development of agriculture were important factors in the life of the areas over which it had jurisdiction, and today its work is being continued, for the Irish Republic is still concerned with the economic difficulties of these areas, especially the Irish-speaking districts, the Gaeltacht.

The next important development came in 1903, when another Chief Secretary for Ireland, George Wyndham, sponsored the Irish Land Act, 1903 (3 Edw. 7, c. 37) which dealt with the problem of the redistribution of land on a much broader basis than any of its predecessors. Cash payments to landlords were reinstituted, they were granted an additional bonus of twelve per cent of the purchase price, and the retention of the "guarantee deposit" was abolished. A new principle, that of sale of estates, appeared. Under this method, whole estates were sold directly to tenants (through the agency of the Land Commission's Estates Commissioners) at "zone" prices whose range was fixed by the Act. Landlords could sell their estates to the Estates Commissioners for resale to tenants or could repurchase certain areas for their own use. As for the tenants, the amount of the annuity could be reduced in certain cases (replacing the 1896 Act system of ten-yearly reductions), and the average period during which the annuity (at three and one-quarter per cent) was to run was sixty-eight and a half years. To finance this project one hundred and fifty million pounds was to be raised by guaranteed two and three-quarter per cent stock. The Wyndham Act achieved by far the most spectacular results of any piece of land purchase legislation, since almost two hundred and twenty thousand holdings were acquired in accordance with its terms. Yet the basis of the scheme was still agreement between landlord and tenant on the desirability of selling. The aim of the United Irish League founded by William O'Brien in 1898 was the compulsory acquisition of all agricultural land. This proposal was hardly calculated to endear itself to Edwardian landlords and, as usual, was at first introduced only for specific purposes. The Evicted Tenants Act, 1907 (7 Edw. 7, c. 56) gave the Land Commission's Estates Commissioners power to acquire compulsorily land for the reinstatement of former tenants who had been evicted, or the sons of such tenants. And by the Irish Land Act, 1909 (9 Edw. 7, c. 42) (once again popularly called after the then Chief Secretary, Augustine Birrell) the congested districts were extended, and power was given to acquire compulsorily land within these districts, and also congested estates in other parts of the country. The Birrell Act also created a new three per cent stock for the financing of the scheme (which had broken down in the course of operating the Wyndham Act) and increased the rate of interest for annuities to three and one-half per cent, reducing the average period of repayment to sixty-five and a half years. The Act operated mainly in the congested districts, and resulted in the transfer of some fifty thousand holdings.

In 1913 the principle of compulsory acquisition was embodied in a bill which failed to master the hazards of the parliamentary course at Westminster in the period of the Home Rule crisis. The all-party Irish Convention reported in 1918 in favor of automatic acquisition of the agricultural land remaining unpurchased in Ireland, but a bill for this purpose introduced in 1920 failed to pass, another victim of a constitutional crisis. After the setting up of the two new governments in Ireland the land purchase scheme was carried out in the two areas in ways similar in general principles but differing in details and effect. It is worth noting at this juncture the fact that up to 1921 over three hundred and fifty thousand holdings had been created out of almost twelve million acres, or almost two-thirds of the agricultural land of Ireland. This was a considerable feat by any standard, but more especially remarkable when it is remembered that the half-century before 1920 was concerned with resettlement, not, as in the newer parts of the Commonwealth, with the original settlement.

COMPLETION OF LAND PURCHASE IN NORTHERN IRELAND

To take first the completion of the land purchase scheme in Northern Ireland, it may be noted that the Westminster parliament was not finished with the problems of Irish landholding, since land purchase was one of the "reserved" matters under the Government of Ireland Act, 1920. A separate Land Purchase Commission for Northern Ireland was constituted in 1923, and a departmental committee recommended the adoption of the Irish Convention's plan of 1918 and the Land Bill of 1920. By 1925 almost thirty-nine thousand holdings had been created under the Land Purchase Acts out of two-thirds of the tenanted land of Northern Ireland. Under the Northern Ireland Land Act, 1925 (15 & 16 Geo. 5, c. 34) the remaining "tenanted land" was vested in the Northern Ireland Land Purchase Commission. This was to be transferred to purchasers as soon as possible. A standard price and standard annuities were fixed by reference to the rent, the average period for repayment being sixty-six and a half years. After an extension of time given by the Northern Ireland Land Act, 1929 (19 & 20 Geo. 5, c. 14), the Northern Ireland Land Purchase (Winding-Up) Act was passed in 1935 (25 & 26 Geo. 5, c. 21), and in 1937 the Northern Ireland Land Commission was wound up, the Westminster parliament's interest in the land of Northern Ireland became restricted to such matters as the collection of the annuities, and the general subject matter of land purchase came within the scope of the Northern Ireland parliament's powers. As Sir Arthur Quekett put it, "The Northern Ireland Parliament are not precluded by the Constitution from embarking upon a new policy of land settlement, should they wish to do so."[17] Some thirty-nine thousand further holdings had been created under the 1925 Act, so that ninety per cent of the agricultural land, or eighty per cent of the total area of Northern Ireland was vested in owners who had formerly held only tenancies but were now owners of a fee simple, subject to a terminable annuity. The shades of Bright and Gladstone, to say nothing of the doughty Ulster fighters for tenant-right and land ownership, must have been particularly pleased at the statistics of this result in part of the island whose land problems had given so much trouble. It remains to be seen whether, when the annuities expire or have been redeemed, any further complications arise towards the end of the present century.

LAND PURCHASE IN THE IRISH REPUBLIC

In the Irish Republic events have taken a different course, mainly

[17] "The Completion of Land Purchase in Northern Ireland," *Northern Ireland Legal Quarterly*, IV (1940), 26, 74.

because of the use of an additional method of dealing with the land. In Northern Ireland it was possible to provide for the automatic sale of tenanted land and its vesting in the tenants in a comparatively short space of time. In the Irish Republic the existence of the congested districts and the necessity of insuring that holdings are economic ones has resulted in the slower operation of the land purchase scheme.

The position was for a time complicated by the existence of the Dáil courts, exercising an effective jurisdiction in certain areas to deal with land matters; as has been mentioned in the chapter on Legal History (*supra*), the ordinary courts refused to recognize the existence of illegal tribunals. In 1923 the Irish Free State parliament passed a Land Act (No. 42 of 1923) known as the Hogan Act because it was sponsored by the then Dublin Minister for Agriculture. By that time the working of the land purchase scheme had resulted in the creation of over three hundred and ten thousand holdings covering seven-tenths of the agricultural land of the Irish Free State. Under the 1923 Act, land held under a contract of tenancy with less than sixty years to run ("tenanted land") was to vest automatically in the Land Commission, as were other classes of land ("untenanted land") in the congested districts. In addition, such other untenanted land as the Commission might need was to vest in it. Provision was made for the fixing of a standard price and standard annuities, and later legislation provided for the revision of these, though the period for repayment remained at sixty-six and a half years. These annuities were halved by the Land Act, 1933 (No. 38 of 1933) and it is on this basis that present-day purchases take place. The 1933 Act also placed certain matters (other than appellate or judicial questions) within the exclusive jurisdiction of the Commission, and these were increased by the Land Act, 1950 (No. 16 of 1950), which also altered the composition of the Commission. Within the administrative framework, and subject to appeals to the courts on questions of law, the Commission exercises wide powers.

The fact that the Commission is also the successor to the Congested Districts Board accounts for the scope of its control over land affairs; the general aim of its activities is that set out in Art. 45, 2 (v), of the 1937 Constitution, under which the state has to direct its policy to secure that "there may be established on the land in economic security as many families as in the circumstances shall be practicable." Thus, the Commission (which, on the vesting of land, takes the place of the landlord) has been authorized to resume tenancies, which it may amalgamate in order to create economic holdings. By the Land Act, 1939 (No. 26 of 1939) the purposes for which tenancies may be resumed are the relief of congestion, the increase of food supplies, and the allotment of holdings under the Hogan Act to persons entitled to such holdings; the market value was prescribed as the compensation to be paid for holdings resumed in this way.

As for untenanted land, the Commission has power, under the Land Acts of 1933 and 1936 (No. 41 of 1936) to acquire this compulsorily for allotment or the relief of congestion, with safeguards for efficient farmers who could claim an alternative holding in certain circumstances. In this way large grazing lands and the properties of the "new landlords" (who had bought out the holdings of tenant purchasers) could be acquired for redistribution among those tenants who had to be removed from uneconomic holdings. Thus the Land Commission not only has power to acquire land compulsorily but it has also to exercise its judgment on the agricultural efficiency of farmers. As one of the present Commissioners puts it, the fact that inquiries are made into the working of many farms means that "Acquisitions of this kind have, and are, being strenuously opposed on technical and legal grounds."[18]

Again, both as successors to the Congested Districts Board, and as "interim landlords" of properties in process of being vested in tenants, the Land Commission has the task of making improvements. It has consolidated numerous small holdings in the west of the country and has provided tenants who could not be accommodated there with holdings in the fertile midlands. As a result of its activities, tenanted land has been turned into over one hundred and twenty thousand holdings, while holdings for over one hundred thousand persons from congested districts and other persons have been created from untenanted land. It has been estimated that over one hundred and thirty thousand tenants have yet to become full owners of their lands, and that some twenty-eight thousand of these have strip holdings of the "rundale" kind, which will involve consolidation of holdings for some persons and transfer of others to new

[18] Kevin Roantree O'Shiel, "The Changes Effected in Recent Land Commission Legislation," *Public Administration in Ireland* (Dublin, 1954), III, 299.

holdings.[19] The problem is a formidable one, further complicated by the existence of the "landless men," but by the time it is finally solved the greater part of the land in the Irish Republic will be in the hands of over five hundred thousand owners of land in fee simple where seventy years ago there were only fifteen thousand such owners.

A SUMMARY AND SOME COMPARISONS

It is over three-quarters of a century since the Irish land purchase scheme was put into operation and the changes in land holding which have been brought about during that period have been revolutionary. From the first tentative measures under the Irish Church Act the scheme gathered rapid momentum, aided by social conditions and political agitation which led to the supersession of the fair rent plan and the eventual abolition of the system of "dual ownership." In 1903 Wyndham's Act gave new impetus to the scheme by placing the acquisition proposals on a wider basis. The system of automatic acquisition used in the Irish Free State's Act of 1923 and the Northern Ireland Act of 1925 was the logical conclusion of the proposals which John Bright had first put forward in the 1860's. The fact that in Northern Ireland the scheme has been completed, while in the Irish Republic the Land Commission is still in operation, is explained by the existence of the congested districts in the west of the country.

The essence of the Irish method was the vesting in the tenant of a fee simple subject to a terminable annuity; the methods of achieving this varied, but the underlying principles are acquisition and compensation, followed by transfer and repayment. It is instructive to compare this system with those of making Crown grants of land in the Commonwealth. In Australia, for example, the "conditional purchase lease" was developed as a means of enabling persons to acquire interests in land.[20] This transaction is similar to the Irish fee and annuity, but the interest which the Australian tenant takes is at most a fee simple conditional. The lease is made subject to conditions to insure the working and improving of the land, and on completion of the periodical payments the tenant is entitled to obtain a Crown grant of the fee simple. In the Irish case the fee is vested subject to the annuity; in the Australian case the fee vests

---

[19] Kevin Roantree O'Shiel, "The Work of the Land Commission," *Public Administration in Ireland* (Dublin, 1949), II, 73.

[20] Fox, *op. cit. supra* note 9 at 120-123.

when the final payment is made. Another type of Australian interest bears a strong resemblance to an Irish one. The Australian perpetuity lease, a statutory interest, may be subject to conditions and in any event requires the payment of a perpetual rent. The analogous Irish interests are the fee farm grant—the fee simple subject to a rent, created in licensed breach of feudal rules—and the fee farm conversion grant, whose creation was authorized by statute. In origin the Irish and Australian interests differ, for the former were originally created as, or expanded from, common law interests, while the latter derived entirely from legislation; but the net result—a perpetuity subject to a rent—is the same.

Similarly in South Africa, five-year leases with an option to purchase are granted, and if the option is taken up the purchase price is payable by a series of annual instalments. A Crown grant is issued when the full purchase price is paid.[21] The similarity with the Australian system, and the analogy with the Irish land purchase scheme, are clear.

In New Zealand, various methods of creating Crown interests have been used. Different types of leaseholds were granted, one of these being a long lease for nine hundred and ninety-nine years subject to a fixed rent. Later legislation enabled the holders of leasehold interests to convert them into fee simple interests.[22] Similar in principle to the Irish scheme, this New Zealand method also resembled the Irish one in its provision for deferred purchase. In so far as the New Zealand legislation authorized the expansion of a tenant's interest, it also resembled an earlier trend of the Irish law, in which expansion was preferred to acquisition.

The emphasis on leasehold interests has been pointed out by an Australian commentator:

It is somewhat paradoxical that while Australian jurisprudence made a start free from the anomalous incidents of feudal tenures, in the short space of a century her land laws became complicated by the introduction of a species of leasehold tenure of which the different types far outnumbered those of the early English feudal tenures, and which exhibit a far greater degree of variety in their incidents.[23]

In New Zealand also Crown leaseholds were varied and numerous,

---

[21] Dold and Joubert, *op. cit. supra* note 13 at 395.
[22] Haughey, *op. cit. supra* note 10 at 281.
[23] Fox, *op. cit. supra* note 9 at 120.

but in Ireland the field for experimental types of Crown grant was thoroughly worked over in the seventeenth century. The aim of the Irish tenant was the acquisition of the fee simple, and by the end of the twentieth century he will largely have achieved this aim.

As for the administration of land schemes, a parallel may be drawn in general terms between the continuing work of the Minister for Lands and the Land Commission in Dublin and the functions of the different Ministers for Land and Land Boards in the Commonwealth, since all are concerned in differing degrees with the allotment of holdings and dealings with them. The power to resume holdings, which has already been mentioned, is a specific example of the similarity of function, and an examination of the way in which similar functions are discharged in relation to land in different parts of the Commonwealth would undoubtedly prove valuable.

Thus while different areas in which English land law has been applied must adapt that law to different types of economic problems, the principles, and some of the details, of some of the Commonwealth schemes which have been mentioned bear a strong resemblance to those used in Ireland. Once again the common source of the legal system has led to the proposition of similar solutions for problems arising in jurisdictions far apart from each other.

THE PERSONALITIES OF THE LAND LAW

In connection with this Commonwealth comparison it is apposite to mention the name of W. F. Massey, sometime New Zealand premier, for it was his Reform party government which in 1912 initiated the policy of granting freeholds to Crown tenants. Now Massey was an Ulsterman, so perhaps it is not too fanciful to surmise that knowledge of the Irish land problem, and its personalities, had some influence on developments in New Zealand, for the nineteenth century was an era when men of strong character grappled with the problems of Irish land. At the outset Daniel O'Connell protested against the tithe system, and Sharman Crawford campaigned for the legalization of tenant right; then the Attorney-General for Ireland, Napier, and later Serjeant Deasy sought to unravel the complexities of the Irish law relating to landlord and tenant; later still John Bright devised land purchase schemes which Gladstone's government introduced and extended, and Isaac Butt and after him Charles Stewart Parnell linked the problems of Irish tenants with the necessity for constitutional as well as economic changes, such as Ashbourne and Balfour introduced. In all, it is an imposing gallery of Victorian political figures. And when the court of the Land Commission sits for the last time, and the final annuity is paid to turn the last tenant purchaser into a full and unrestricted owner, the work of those Victorian figures will, at long last, be complete, and ripe for final comparison with similar schemes elsewhere in the Commonwealth.

BIBLIOGRAPHY

THE BOOKS and periodical literature mentioned in these lists proved extremely useful in the writing of the present work, but this bibliography lays no claim to being exhaustive. For published books, Volume IV of Sweet and Maxwell's *Legal Bibliography* (2nd ed.; London, 1957) and supplemental volumes are invaluable in discovering printed material. Ireland, however, still lacks a work equivalent to Sir William Searle Holdsworth's *Sources and Literature of English Law* (Oxford, 1925) or Sir Percy Henry Winfield's *Chief Sources of English Legal History* (Harvard, 1925).

For convenience, this bibliography has been divided into sections to correspond with the chapter headings, and further divided into lists dealing with books and articles. It should, however, be noted that many of the works mentioned also contain material relevant to another heading. Thus, for example, some of the books mentioned in the list of works on Constitutional History would also be useful in dealing with Legal History.

It is hoped that this bibliography will be of assistance to those seeking information about these various branches of Irish law.

I. LEGAL HISTORY

PART I

BALL, FRANCIS ELRINGTON. *The Judges in Ireland, 1221-1921.* 2 vols., New York, 1927.

MacNEILL, EOIN. *Early Irish Laws and Institutions.* Dublin, 1935.

MILLS, JAMES. *Calendar of the Justiciary Rolls, Ireland, XXIII to XXXI years of Edward I.* Dublin, 1905.

MILLS, JAMES. *Calendar of the Justiciary Rolls, Ireland, Edward I, Part II, XXXIII to XXXV years.* Dublin, 1914.

SWEETMAN, H. S. *Calendar of Documents relating to Ireland 1171-1307.* 5 vols., London, 1875-86.

THURNEYSEN, RUDOLF. *Studies in Early Irish Law.* Dublin, 1936.

WOOD, HERBERT. *A Guide to the Records Deposited in the Public Record Office of Ireland.* Dublin, 1919.

WOOD, HERBERT, LANGMAN, ALBERT E., AND GRIFFITH, MARGARET C. *Calendar of the Justiciary Rolls, Ireland, I to VII years of Edward II.* Dublin, 1956.

PART II

AMOS, SIR MAURICE SHELDON. "The Common Law and the Civil Law in the British Commonwealth of Nations," *Harvard Law Review*, L (June, 1937), 1249-1274.

ANON. "The Anomalous Position of Our Courts of Justice," *Irish Law Times and Solicitors' Journal*, LXXXV (April 7, 1951), 83-85.

ARTHURS, JOHN BRENDAN. "Early Irish Law," *Bulletin of the Committee of Irish Historical Sciences, No. 61* (1952).

BINCHY, DANIEL ANTHONY. "The Linguistic and Historical Value of the Irish Law Tracts," *Proceedings of the British Academy*, XXIX (1943), 195-227.

CURTIS, EDMUND. "Notes on Betagh Tenure in Mediaeval Ireland," *Proceedings of the Royal Irish Academy, Section C*, XLIII (1936), 62.

JOHNSTON, WILLIAM JOHN. "The First Adventure of the Common Law," *Law Quarterly Review*, XXXVI (January, 1920), 9-30.

JOHNSTON, WILLIAM JOHN. "The English Legislature and the Irish Courts," *Law Quarterly Review*, XL (January, 1924), 91-106.

MACDERMOTT OF BELMONT, LORD. "Law and Practice in Northern Ireland," *Northern Ireland Legal Quarterly*, X (1953), 47.

MACDERMOTT OF BELMONT, LORD. "The Supreme Court of Northern Ireland—Two Unusual Jurisdictions," *Journal of the Society of Public Teachers of Law* (New Series), II (1954), 201-213.

MAITLAND, FREDERIC WILLIAM. "The History of the Register of Original Writs," *Harvard Law Review*, III (October, November, December, 1889), 97-115, 167-179, 212-225.

MAITLAND, FREDERIC WILLIAM. "The Introduction of English Law into Ireland," *Collected Papers* (3 vols.; Cambridge, 1911), II, 81-83.

NEWARK, FRANCIS HEADON. "Notes on Irish Legal History," *Northern Ireland Legal Quarterly*, VII (1947), 121.

NEWARK, FRANCIS HEADON. "On Appealing to the House of Lords," *Northern Ireland Legal Quarterly*, VIII (1949), 102.

NEWARK, FRANCIS HEADON. " The Case of Tanistry," *Northern Ireland Legal Quarterly*, IX (1952), 215.

Ó BUACHALLA, LIAM. "Some Researches on Ancient Irish Law," *Journal of the Cork Historical and Archaeological Society* (Second Series), LII (1947), 41, 135; LIII (1948), 11, 75.

OTWAY-RUTHVEN, ANNETTE JOCELYN. "The Request of the Irish for English Law, 1277-80," *Irish Historical Studies,* VI (September, 1949), 261-270.

OTWAY-RUTHVEN, ANNETTE JOCELYN. "The Native Irish and English Law in Medieval Ireland," *Irish Historical Studies,* VII (March, 1950), 1-16.

RICHARDSON, HENRY GERALD. "English Institutions in Medieval Ireland," *Irish Historical Studies,* I (September, 1939), 382-392.

WOOD, HERBERT. "The Court of Castle Chamber or Star Chamber in Ireland," *Proceedings of the Royal Academy, Section C,* XXXII (1914), 152.

II. CONSTITUTIONAL HISTORY

PART I

ATWOOD, WILLIAM. *The History and Reasons of the Dependency of Ireland upon the Imperial Crown of the Kingdom of England.* London, 1698.

BALL, JOHN THOMAS. *Historical Review of the Legislative Systems operative in Ireland from the Invasion of Henry the Second to the Union (1172-1800).* 2d ed., London, 1889.

BECKETT, JAMES CAMLIN. *A Short History of Ireland.* London, 1952.

BERRY, HENRY FITZPATRICK. *Statutes and Ordinances, and Acts of the Parliament of Ireland. King John to Henry V.* Dublin, 1907.

BERRY, HENRY FITZPATRICK. *Statute Rolls of the Parliament of Ireland, Henry VI.* Dublin, 1910.

BERRY, HENRY FITZPATRICK. *Statute Rolls of the Parliament of Ireland, First to Twelfth Years of Edward IV.* Dublin, 1914.

COUPLAND, REGINALD. *The American Revolution and the British Empire.* London, 1930.

CURTIS, EDMUND. *A History of Medieval Ireland From 1086 to 1513.* 2d ed., London, 1938.

CURTIS, EDMUND. *A History of Ireland.* 5th ed., London, 1945.

DICEY, ALBERT VENN. *England's Case against Home Rule.* London, 1886.

DICEY, ALBERT VENN. *A Leap in the Dark, or Our New Constitution.* London, 1893; 2d ed., London, 1911.

DICEY, ALBERT VENN. *A Fool's Paradise.* London, 1913.

DILLON, MYLES, ed. *Early Irish Institutions.* Dublin, 1954.

DUFFY, SIR CHARLES GAVAN, ed. *The Patriot Parliament of 1689* by Thomas Davis. London, 1893.

HARRIS, WALTER. *Hibernica.* Dublin, 1750. Part II contains the seventeenth-century works by Darcy and Mayart on English authority over Ireland.

HYDE, HARFORD MONTGOMERY. *Carson: The Life of Sir Edward Carson, Lord Carson of Duncairn.* London, 1953.

KEITH, ARTHUR BERRIEDALE. *Constitutional History of the First British Empire.* Oxford, 1930.

LECKY, WILLIAM EDMUND HARTPOLE. *A History of Ireland in the Eighteenth Century.* New ed., 5 vols., London, 1892.

LECKY, WILLIAM EDMUND HARTPOLE. *The Leaders of Public Opinion in Ireland.* New ed., 2 vols., London, 1912.

MACARDLE, DOROTHY. *The Irish Republic.* 4th ed., Dublin, 1951.

MACDONALD, J. A. MURRAY, AND CHARNWOOD, LORD. *The Federal Solution.* London, 1914.

McDOWELL, ROBERT BRENDAN. *Irish Public Opinion, 1750-1800.* London, 1944.

McDOWELL, ROBERT BRENDAN. *Public Opinion and Government Policy in Ireland, 1801-1846.* London, 1952.

McILWAIN, CHARLES HOWARD. *The American Revolution: A Constitutional Interpretation.* New York, 1924.

MACNEILL, EOIN. *Celtic Ireland.* Dublin, 1919.

MACNEILL, JOHN GORDON SWIFT. *The Constitutional and Parliamentary History of Ireland till the Union.* London, 1917.

MOLYNEUX, WILLIAM. *The Case of Ireland's being bound by Acts of Parliament in England, stated.* Dublin, 1698.

MOODY, THEODORE WILLIAM, AND BECKETT, JAMES CAMLIN, eds. *Ulster since 1800.* London, 1954.

MORGAN, JOHN HARTMAN, ed. *The New Irish Constitution: An Exposition and some Arguments.* London, 1912. (This is a survey by various authors of the Government of Ireland Bill, 1912, and the surrounding circumstances.)

MORLEY, HENRY, ed. *Ireland under Elizabeth and James the First.* London, 1890. (This contains Sir John Davies' writings on Ireland at the beginning of the seventeenth century.)

MORRISSEY, J. F. *Statute Rolls of the Parliament of Ireland, Twelfth to Twenty-Second Reigns of Edward IV.* Dublin, 1939.

O'HEGARTY, PATRICK SARSFIELD. *A History of Ireland under the Union, 1801 to 1922.* London, 1952.

ORPEN, GODDARD HENRY. *Ireland under the Normans, 1169-1216.* 4 vols., Oxford, 1911.

PHILLIPS, WALTER ALISON. *The Revolution in Ireland, 1906-1923.* London, 1923.

PORRITT, EDWARD. *The Unreformed House of Commons.* Cambridge, 1909.

RICHARDSON, HENRY GERALD, AND SAYLES, GEORGE OSBORNE. *The Irish Parliament in the Middle Ages.* Philadelphia, 1952.

SCHUYLER, ROBERT LIVINGSTON. *Parliament and the British Empire.* New York, 1929.

PART II

ANSON, SIR WILLIAM. "The Government of Ireland Bill and the Sovereignty of Parliament," *Law Quarterly Review,* II (October, 1886), 423-443.

BECKETT, JAMES CAMLIN. "The Irish Parliament in the Eighteenth Century," *Proceedings of the Belfast Natural History and Philosophical Society,* IV (1955), 17.

BINCHY, DANIEL ANTHONY. "Secular Institutions" in *Early Irish Society* (Dublin, 1954), 52.

CURTIS, EDMUND. "The Acts of the Drogheda Parliament, 1494-5, or Poynings' Law" in Agnes Conway, *Henry VII's Relations with Scotland and Ireland.* (Cambridge, 1932), 118.

EDWARDS, ROBERT DUDLEY, AND MOODY, THEODORE WILLIAM. "The History of Poynings' Law: Part I, 1494-1615," *Irish Historical Studies,* II (September, 1941), 415-424.

HOWARD, C. H. D. "Joseph Chamberlain, Parnell and the Irish 'Central Board' Scheme, 1884-5," *Irish Historical Studies,* VIII (September, 1953), 324-361.

KENNEDY, BRIAN ALOYSIUS. "Sharman Crawford's Federal Scheme for Ireland" in *Essays in British and Irish History in Honour of James Eadie Todd.* (London, 1949), 235.

JOHNSTON, WILLIAM JOHN. "The Parliament of the Pale," *Law Quarterly Review,* XXXIV (July, 1918), 291-303.

LYONS, FRANCIS STEWART LELAND. "The Irish Unionist Party and the Devolution Crisis of 1904-5," *Irish Historical Studies,* VI (March, 1948), 1-22.

McDOWELL, ROBERT BRENDAN. "The Irish Executive in the Nineteenth Century," *Irish Historical Studies,* IX (March, 1955), 264.

MOODY, THEODORE WILLIAM. "The Irish Parliament under Elizabeth and James I," *Proceedings of the Royal Irish Academy, Section C,* XLV (1939), 41.

O'CONNOR, THERESA MARGARET. "The Conflict between Flood and Grattan, 1782-3" in *Essays in British and Irish History in Honour of James Eadie Todd.* (London, 1949), 169.

McCRACKEN, JOHN LESLIE. "The Conflict between the Irish Administration and Parliament, 1753-6," *Irish Historical Studies,* III (September, 1942), 159-179.

QUINN, DAVID BEERS. "The Early Interpretation of Poynings' Law, 1494-1534," *Irish Historical Studies,* II (March, 1941), 241-254.

III. IRELAND AND THE COMMONWEALTH: DOMINION STATUS AND INTERNATIONAL LAW

PART I

BROMAGE, MARY C. *De Valera and the March of a Nation.* London, 1956.

EVATT, HERBERT VERE. *The King and His Dominion Governors.* Oxford, 1936.

HANCOCK, SIR WILLIAM KEITH. *Survey of British Commonwealth Affairs,* Vol. 1, *Problems of Nationality, 1918-1936.* London, 1937.

HARVEY, HEATHER JOAN. *Consultation and Co-operation in the Commonwealth: A Handbook on Methods and Practice.* Oxford, 1952.

JONES, JOHN MERVYN. *British Nationality Law and Practice.* Oxford, 1947.

JONES, JOHN MERVYN. *British Nationality Law.* Oxford, 1956.

KEITH, ARTHUR BERRIEDALE, ed. *Speeches and Documents on the British Dominions, 1918-1931.* London, 1932.

MANSERGH, NICHOLAS. *The Commonwealth and the Nations: Studies in British Commonwealth Relations.* London, 1948.

MANSERGH, NICHOLAS. *Survey of British Commonwealth Affairs: Problems of External Policy, 1931-1939.* London, 1952.

MANSERGH, NICHOLAS, ed. *Documents and Speeches on British Commonwealth Affairs, 1931-1952.* 2 vols., London, 1953.

NOEL-BAKER, PHILIP JOHN. *The Present Juridical Status of the British Dominions in International Law.* London, 1929.

STEWART, ROBERT BURGESS. *Treaty Relations of the British Commonwealth of Nations.* New York, 1939.

WHEARE, KENNETH CLINTON. *The Statute of Westminster and Dominion Status.* 5th ed., London, 1953.

PART II

ANON. "Irish Nationality and Citizenship," *Irish Law Times and*

Solicitors' Journal, LXXXVI (March 8, March 15, and March 22, 1952), 65-69, 75-80, 85-89.

BROMAGE, ARTHUR WATSON. "Constitutional Developments in Saorstát Eireann and the Constitution of Éire: I, External Affairs," *American Political Science Review*, XXXI (October, 1937), 842-861.

BROMAGE, MARY C. "De Valera's Formula for Irish Nationhood," *Review of Politics*, XIII (October, 1951), 483-502.

[CALDWELL, JOHN FOSTER] "Reciprocal Enforcement of Judgments and Decrees," *Northern Ireland Legal Quarterly*, II (1938), 188; III (1939), 91, 135; IV (1940), 83.

DOWRICK, FRANK ERNEST. "The Irish Sweep and Irish Law," *American Journal of Comparative Law*, II (Autumn, 1953), 505-515.

GARNER, JAMES WILFORD. "A Question of State Succession," *American Journal of International Law*, XXI (October, 1927), 753-757.

HEUSTON, ROBERT FRANCIS VERE. "British Nationality and Irish Citizenship." *International Affairs*, XXVI (January, 1950), 77-90.

JENNINGS, ROBERT YEWDALL. "The Commonwealth and International Law," *British Year Book of International Law*, XXX (1953), 320-351.

LATHAM, RICHARD THOMAS EDWIN. "The Law and the Commonwealth" in Sir William Keith Hancock, ed., *Survey of British Commonwealth Affairs*, Vol. I, *Problems of Nationality, 1918-1936* (London, 1937), 510-615. Latham's work was reprinted separately. London, 1949.

LATHAM, VALENTINE. "Estate Duty and the Proper Law of a Trust," *International and Comparative Law Quarterly*, (Fourth Series) (July, 1954), 499-502.

MACBRIDE, SEÁN. "Anglo-Irish Relations," *International Affairs*, XXV (July, 1949), 257-273.

MANSERGH, NICHOLAS. "The Implications of Eire's Relationship with the British Commonwealth of Nations," *International Affairs*, XXIV (January, 1948), 1-18.

MANSERGH, NICHOLAS. "Ireland: The Republic outside the Commonwealth," *International Affairs*, XXVIII (July, 1952), 277-291.

MEGAW, JOHN. "British Subjects and Eire Citizens," *Northern Ireland Legal Quarterly*, VIII (1949), 129.

NEWARK, FRANCIS HEADON. "British Nationality and Irish Citizenship," *Northern Ireland Legal Quarterly*, V (1942), 76.

NEWARK, FRANCIS HEADON. " 'Beyond the Seas' from Northern Ireland," *Northern Ireland Legal Quarterly*, XI (November, 1954), 26-31.

O'Connor, Sir James. "Ireland's Money Claim against Great Britain," *Journal of Comparative Legislation and International Law,* (Third Series) VI (1924), Part I, 1-18.

Phelan, Andrew. "The Republic of Ireland and Extradition," *Law Journal,* CVI (January 20, 1956), 39.

Phelan, Edward Joseph. "The Sovereignty of the Irish Free State," *Review of Nations,* I (March, 1927), 35.

Smiddy, Timothy A. "The Position of the Irish Free State in the British Commonwealth of Nations" in *Great Britain and the Dominions* (Chicago, 1928), 105-130.

Webb, P. R. H. "The Twilight of the Doctrine of *Inverclyde v. Inverclyde*," *International and Comparative Law Quarterly,* (Fourth Series) IV (October, 1955), 557-563.

Williams, David Colwyn. "Nullity Jurisdiction in Northern Ireland," *Modern Law Review,* XIX (November, 1956), 669.

IV. Constitutional Developments since 1920

PART I

Figgis, Darrell. *The Irish Constitution.* Dublin, 1922.

Jennings, Sir William Ivor, and Young, Charlotte Mary. *Constitutional Laws of the Commonwealth.* Oxford, 1952.

Keith, Arthur Berriedale. *Responsible Government in the Dominions.* 2 vols., 2d ed., Oxford, 1928.

Keith, Arthur Berriedale. *The Dominions as Sovereign States.* London, 1938.

Kohn, Leo. *The Constitution of the Irish Free State.* London, 1932.

MacNeill, John Gordon Swift. *Studies in the Constitution of the Irish Free State.* Dublin, 1925.

Mansergh, Nicholas. *The Government of Northern Ireland: A Study in Devolution.* London, 1936.

Mansergh, Nicholas. *The Irish Free State: Its Government and Politics.* London, 1934.

Montrose, James Louis, and Newark, Francis Headon. "Northern Ireland," *Halsbury's Statutes of England,* XVII (2d ed., London, 1950), 19-192.

Neill, Desmond Gorman, ed. *Devolution of Government: The Experiment in Northern Ireland.* London, 1953.

O'Sullivan, Donal Joseph. *The Irish Free State and Its Senate.* London, 1940.

Quekett, Sir Arthur Scott. *The Constitution of Northern Ireland.* 3 vols., Belfast, 1928, 1933, 1946.

SHERIDAN, LIONEL ASTOR. "Northern Ireland" in George W. Keeton and Dennis Lloyd, eds., *The United Kingdom: The Development of its Laws and Constitutions.* I (London, 1955), 411-481.

WHEARE, KENNETH CLINTON. *Modern Constitutions.* London, 1951.

WILSON, THOMAS, ed. *Ulster Under Home Rule.* Oxford, 1955.

PART II

ANON. "The Constitution through the Cases," *Irish Law Times and Solicitors' Journal,* LXXXVI (May 17, May 24, May 31, June 7, 1952), 137-139, 143-144, 149-150, 165-166.

BROMAGE, ARTHUR WATSON. Constitutional Developments in Saorstát Eireann and the Constitution of Éire: II, Internal Affairs," *American Political Science Review,* XXXI (December, 1937), 1050-1070.

BROMAGE, ARTHUR WATSON, AND BROMAGE, MARY C. "The Vocational Senate in Ireland," *American Political Science Review,* XXXIV (June, 1940), 519-538.

CHUBB, FREDERICK BASIL. "Vocational Representation and the Irish Senate," *Political Studies,* II (June, 1954), 97-111.

CHUBB, FREDERICK BASIL. "Cabinet Government in Ireland," *Political Studies,* III (1955), 256.

COOK, JOHN IRVINE. "Financial Relations between the Exchequers of the United Kingdom and Northern Ireland" in Desmond Gorman Neill, ed., *Devolution of Government: The Experiment in Northern Ireland.* (London, 1953), 18.

COUTTS, JOHN ARCHIBALD. "The Ejusdem Generis Rule and *O'Neill v. N.I. Transport Board,*" *Northern Ireland Legal Quarterly,* III (1939), 138.

DELANY, VINCENT THOMAS HYGINUS. "Constitution of Ireland," *Irish Law Times and Solicitors' Journal,* XC (April 28, May 5, May 12, May 19, 1956), 101-103, 107-109, 113-115, 119-120.

EDWARDS, JOHN LLEWELYN JONES. "Special Powers in Northern Ireland," [1956] *Criminal Law Review,* 7-18.

GROGAN, VINCENT. "Irish Constitutional Development," *Studies,* XL (1951), 385.

GROGAN, VINCENT. "The Constitution and Natural Law," *Christus Rex,* VIII (1954), 201.

[LEITCH, WILLIAM ANDREW.] "The Northern Ireland Act, 1947," *Northern Ireland Legal Quarterly,* VII (1947), 151.

[LEITCH, WILLIAM ANDREW.] "Civil Proceedings by and against the Crown," *Northern Ireland Legal Quarterly,* VIII (1950), 223.

LEE, GERARD A. "The President of Ireland," *Canadian Bar Review*, XXVIII (December, 1950), 1087-1103.

McWHINNEY, EDWARD. "The Courts and the Constitution in Catholic Ireland," *Tulane Law Review*, XXIX (December, 1954), 69-86.

MONTROSE, JAMES LOUIS. "Legal Aspects of Taxation and Grant under the Northern Ireland System of Devolution" in Geoffrey Sawer, ed., *Federalism: An Australian Jubilee Study* (Melbourne, 1952), 1.

MONTROSE, JAMES LOUIS. "Taking Property without Compensation," *Northern Ireland Legal Quarterly*, XI (1956), 278.

NEWARK, FRANCIS HEADON. "Ejusdem Generis and the Government of Ireland Act, 1920, s. 5," *Northern Ireland Legal Quarterly*, III (1939), 77.

NEWARK, FRANCIS HEADON. "Parliamentary Freedom and the Government of Ireland Act, 1920," *Northern Ireland Legal Quarterly*, IV (1940), 75.

NEWARK, FRANCIS HEADON. "The Taking of Property without Compensation," *Northern Ireland Legal Quarterly*, IV (1941), 168.

NEWARK, FRANCIS HEADON. "The Constitution of Northern Ireland: The First Twenty-five Years," *Northern Ireland Legal Quarterly*, VIII (1948), 52.

NEWARK, FRANCIS HEADON. "The Severability of Northern Ireland Statutes," *Northern Ireland Legal Quarterly*, IX (1950), 19.

NEWARK, FRANCIS HEADON. "Judicial Review of Confiscatory Legislation under the Northern Ireland Constitution," *American Journal of Comparative Law*, III (Autumn, 1954), 552-563.

O'NORMAN, CATHAL. "The Influence of Irish Political Thought on the Indian Constitution," *Indian Year Book of International Affairs*, I (1952), 156-164.

SHERIDAN, LIONEL ASTOR. "Taking Property without Compensation," *Modern Law Review*, XVII (May, 1954), 249-255.

SHERIDAN, LIONEL ASTOR. "Nationalisation and Section 5: Meaning of . . . Take any Property without Compensation," *Northern Ireland Legal Quarterly*, X (1954), 183.

v. ADMINISTRATIVE LAW

PART I

There are no Irish works dealing with administrative law, but there are references to Ireland in the following books.

CARR, SIR CECIL THOMAS. *Delegated Legislation*. Cambridge, 1921.

CARR, SIR CECIL THOMAS. *Concerning English Administrative Law.* New York, 1941.

GRAHAM-HARRISON, SIR WILLIAM MONTAGU. *Notes on the Delegation by Parliament of Legislative Powers.* Privately printed, London, 1931.

ROBSON, WILLIAM ALEXANDER. *Justice and Administrative Law.* 3d ed., London, 1951.

WILLIS, JOHN. *The Parliamentary Powers of English Government Departments.* Cambridge, Mass., 1933.

PART II

CHUBB, FREDERICK BASIL. "Public Control of Public Enterprise," *Administration,* II (1954), 21.

GROGAN, VINCENT. "Administrative Tribunals," *Public Administration in Ireland* (Dublin, 1954), III, 32.

KING, FREDERICK CHARLES. "Administrative Law," *Irish Law Times and Solicitors' Journal,* LXXXV (June 30, July 7, July 14, July 21, 1951), 155-156, 161-163, 167-169, 173-174.

MORTISHED, RONALD JAMES PATRICK. "The Industrial Relations Act, 1946," *Public Administration in Ireland* (Dublin, 1949), II, 75.

O'DONOUGHUE, PATRICK PHILIP. "The Relations of Statutory Corporations with the Government and the Oireachtas," *Public Administration in Ireland* (Dublin, 1949), II, 118.

O'DONOUGHUE, PATRICK PHILIP. "The Citizen Versus the State," *Public Administration in Ireland* (Dublin, 1954), III, 15.

O'SULLIVAN, DONAL JOSEPH. "Delegated Legislation," Chapter XXXI of *The Irish Free State and its Senate.* (London, 1940), 525-544.

SCULLY, MICHAEL. "Parliamentary Control of Public Corporations in Eire," *Public Administration,* XXXII (Winter, 1954), 455-462.

VI. LAND LAW

PART I

CHERRY, RICHARD ROBERT, WAKELY, JOHN AND MAXWELL, THOMAS HENRY. *Irish Land Law and Land Purchase Acts.* 3d ed., Dublin, 1903.

DE MOLEYNS, THOMAS. *The Landowner's and Agent's Practical Guide.* 8th ed., Dublin, 1899.

FERGUSON, WILLIAM DWYER, AND VANCE, ANDREW. *The Tenure and Improvement of Land in Ireland, Considered with Reference to the Relation of Landlord and Tenant, and Tenant-Right.* Dublin, 1851.

FURLONG, JOHN SMITH. *A Treatise on the Law of Landlord and Tenant as Administered in Ireland.* 2 vols., 2d ed., Dublin, 1869.

GLOVER, WILLIAM ERSKINE. *A Treatise on the Registration of Ownership of Land in Ireland.* Dublin, 1933.

HILL, GEORGE. *An Historical Account of the Plantation in Ulster at the Commencement of the Seventeenth Century, 1608-1620.* Belfast, 1877.

HOOKER, ELIZABETH R. *Readjustments of Agricultural Tenure in Ireland.* Chapel Hill, 1938.

LEET, ERNEST F., AND MCCUTCHEON, R. R. *A Sketch of the Law of Property in Land in Ireland.* Dublin, 1937.

LEITCH, WILLIAM ANDREW. *A Handbook on the Administration of Estates Act (Northern Ireland), 1955.* Belfast, 1956.

MADDEN, DODGSON HAMILTON. *A Practical Treatise on the Registration of Deeds, Conveyances and Judgment-Mortgages.* 2d ed., Dublin, 1907.

MAXWELL, THOMAS HENRY. *Outlines of the Law of Landlord and Tenant and of Land Purchase in Ireland.* Dublin, 1909.

MONTGOMERY, WILLIAM ERNEST. *History of Land Tenure in Ireland.* Cambridge, 1889.

MOODY, THEODORE WILLIAM. *The Londonderry Plantation, 1609-41.* Belfast, 1939.

PRENDERGAST, JOHN PATRICK. *The Cromwellian Settlement of Ireland.* London, 1865.

SHERIDAN, LIONEL ASTOR. *Irish Supplement* (London, 1956) to Charles Sweet, *Challis's Law of Real Property.* 3d ed., London, 1911.

SIMMS, JOHN GERALD. *The Williamite Confiscation in Ireland 1690-1703.* London, 1956.

PART II

[LEITCH, WILLIAM ANDREW.] "Quit Rents in Northern Ireland," *Northern Ireland Legal Quarterly,* X (1952), 30.

LONGFIELD, MOUNTIFORT. "The Tenure of Land in Ireland" in J. W. Probyn, ed., *Systems of Land Tenure in Various Countries.* (London, 1876), 1-79.

MONTROSE, JAMES LOUIS. "Fee-Farm Grants," *North Ireland Legal Quarterly,* II (1938), 194; III (1939), 40, 81, 143; IV (1940), 40, 86.

O'SHIEL, KEVIN ROANTREE. "The Work of the Land Commission," *Public Administration in Ireland* (Dublin, 1949), II, 73.

O'SHIEL, KEVIN ROANTREE. "The Changes Effected in Recent Land Commission Legislation," *Public Administration in Ireland* (Dublin, 1954), III, 299.

QUEKETT, SIR ARTHUR SCOTT. "The Completion of Land Purchase in Northern Ireland," *Northern Ireland Legal Quarterly,* IV (1940), 26.

SHEARMAN, HUGH FRANCIS. "State-aided Land Purchase under the Disestablishment Act of 1869," *Irish Historical Studies,* IV (March, 1944), 58-80.

SHERIDAN, LIONEL ASTOR. "The Law of Property" Chapter XX of G. W. Keeton and Dennis Lloyd, eds., *The United Kingdom: The Development of its Laws and Constitutions.* I (London, 1955), 453-481.

INDEX

A

Adams, John, 50
Administrative decisions and tribunals, 192-98; judicial control of, 201-4, 205-6, 207-10
Adoption in Irish Republic, 197
Advowsons, 6
Aer Lingus, 199
Aer Rianta, 199
Agricultural Credit Corporation, 199
Agricultural Wages Board, 187
Allen, Sir Carleton, 192
Andrews, J., 201
Anglo-Irish Agreement, 1921, signing of, 77-78; registration at Geneva, 78; force of, 78; features of, 79, 82; 1925 amendment, 81, 106, 124, 129; Privy Council view of, 86-87; 1938 amendment, 90; option for Northern Ireland, 129; approval of, 137; and 1922 Irish Free State Constitution, 87, 155
Anglo-Irish Agreements, 1938, 90, 100; 1948, 90
Anson, Sir William, 63
Appeals, from Irish Courts to England, 13, 14, 21-22; from Northern Ireland Courts, 19; from Irish Free State Courts, 80-81
Ard-ri (High King), 38
Armagh, Archbishop of, 73; granting of leases, 239
Ashbourne, L. C., 259-60
Asquith, Herbert Henry, 124
Asquith of Bishopstone, Lord, 231
Attorney-General, Ireland, 57; Irish Republic, 160, 191, 218, 224; Northern Ireland, 220, 221
Atwood, William, 48
Australia, High Court, 19, 23, 30, 33, 173; diplomatic representation, 98; on Council of League of Nations, 100; provisions for acquistion of property, 128; prohibition of religious discrimination, 140; trial by jury, 141; Senate of, 141; money bills, 142; joint sittings, 142; amendment of constitution, 145, 171; appeals to Privy Council, 154; constitutional conventions, 160; emergency powers, 176; arbitration, 197; legal position of Crown, 212, 214, 225; registration of title, 250, 256; Crown grants of land, 257; devolution of property, 257; family maintenance legislation, 257; leases, 266-67; mentioned, 4, 56, 65, 70, 77, 90, 108, 125, 126, 129, 133

B

Babington, L. J., 29-30, 205
Balfour, Arthur James, 260
Balfour definition of Commonwealth relationship, 79
Balfour Report on Scottish Affairs, 136
Ball, Francis Elrington, 10, 11, 12
Beckett, James Camlin, 66
Belgium, 104
Bessborough Commission on Irish Land, 245, 249
Betagh, 7
Bills, disallowance of in Canada, 126; reservation of in Northern Ireland, 126; royal assent to in Northern Ireland, 126; money: in Northern Ireland, 125; in Irish Free State, 142, 144, 151; in Canada, Australia, and South Africa, 142; in Irish Republic, 159, 161, 162
Binchy, Professor D. A., 4, 5, 38

Birkenhead property legislation, 112, 131, 255, 257
Birrell, Augustine, 262
Black, J. and L. J. (Northern Ireland), 30, 205, 213
Black, J. (Irish Republic), 32, 177, 226
Black death, 232
Boer War, Irish Brigades in, 67
Bord na Mona, 199
Boundary Commission under Anglo-Irish Agreement, 1921, 81
Bright, John, 259, 263, 266, 268
Brown, J., 213
Bryce, James, 63, 64
Buckingham Palace Conference, 71
Burma, independence, 79, 94; constitution, 223
Butt, Isaac, 58, 60, 66, 268

C

Campbell, Lord, 11
Canada, Supreme Court of, 15, 19, 33, 172; referred to in Anglo-Irish Agreement, 1921, 79, 80-81, 82, 83; appeal to Privy Council, 86, 154; diplomatic representations, 97-98; on Council of League of Nations, 100; Senate, 141; Governor-General, 143; amendment of constitution, 145; constitutional conventions, 160; emergency powers, 175; restrictive practices, 197; legal position of Crown, 214, 215, 225; land tenure, 231; registrar of title, 256; mentioned, 56, 59, 62, 65, 90, 108, 125,126, 128, 129, 130, 134, 139
Carr, Sir Cecil, 227
Castle Chamber, Irish Court of, 9, 233
Catholic emancipation, 54, 57
Censorship of Publications Board and Appeal Board, 196
Ceylon, English law, 8; doctrine of precedent, 27; trade agreement with Eire, 104; constitutional conventions, 143, 160; bicameral legislature, 162; collective responsibility, 163; prohibition of religious discrimination, 167; amendment of constitution, 171; mentioned, 115, 176
Chamberlain, Joseph, 61
Charles I, 233
Charles II, 46, 234
Cheshire, Professor G. C., 112

Chief Justice, Irish Free State, 24; Irish Republic, 26, 196
Chief Secretary for Ireland, 57
Church of Ireland, disestablishment of, 60, 243, 259
Citizenship, Irish, 88, 94, 107, 139; British, 88, 94
Civil Bills, 16
Collective responsibility, in Irish Free State, 143; in Irish Republic, 163; in Ceylon, India, and Pakistan, 163
Colonies, judges in, 17; appeals from, 18; control of legislatures, 43
Colonies, North American, 10, 41, 46, 53, 55, 256
Commission for Defective Titles, 233
Commissioners of Public Works in Ireland, 211, 259
Commonwealth tribunal, proposal for, 85
Conacre, 240
Confederation of Kilkenny, 47, 156
Congested Districts Board, 260-61, 264-65
Connolly, James, 72
Conquest, doctrine of, 46
Consolidated Fund, Ireland, 62; England, 62, 64
Continental Congress, 47
Contract, proper law of, 113
Co-parceners, 6
Copyhold tenure, 253
Coras Iompair Eireann, 195, 199
Cosgrave, William Thomas, 23-24, 84, 96
Costello, John Aloysius, 92, 94
Council of Europe, Eire's membership of, 101; ratification of conventions, 101-2
Council of Ireland, 74, 124
Council of State, Irish Republic, 25; constitution of, 159; functions of, 159, 172
Council of Three Hunded, 58, 67, 73
Courts, Ecclesiastical Courts, 6, 9; Irish Court of Common Pleas, 9, 11; Court of High Commission, 9; Court of Appeal, Ireland, 17, 28-29; decisions of, in Northern Ireland, 29-30; Court of Appeal, Northern Ireland, 19, 29-30; Irish Court of Wards, 9; Irish Court of Chancery, 9, 11, 40, 110; Irish Court of Appeal in Chancery, 17; Irish Court of Exchequer, 9, 11, 18,

19; Irish Court of Exchequer Chamber, 17, 244; Court of Claims, 234; Court of Criminal Appeal, Irish Free State, 24; Court of Criminal Appeal, Northern Ireland, 20-21; Circuit and District Courts, Irish Free State, 24; County Court in thirteenth century, 5-6, 9; in nineteenth century, 18; in Northern Ireland, 21; replaced in Irish Free State, 24. *See also* Appeals; Castle Chamber; Dáil Courts; High Court; High Court of Appeal for Ireland; Judicial Committee of the Privy Council; Justiciar; King's Bench; Petty Sessions; Quarter Sessions; Star Chamber; Supreme Court

Craigavon, Lord, 95

Crawford, Sharman, 246, 268

Cromwell, Oliver, 234

Crossman, J., 112

Crown, link with Ireland, 5, 38, 45; pleas of the Crown, 6; Crown in 1922 Irish Free State Constitution, 78, 88-89; outside powers of Northern Ireland Parliament, 126-27, 212-13; corporation sole, 172; legal position of, in Ireland, 210-11; in Northern Ireland, 212-13

Cumman na nGaedheal, 67

Curtesy, tenancy by, 6, 257

D

Dáil courts, 21-22, 58, 146, 208, 264

Dáil Eireann, 67; constituted, 73, 123, 137; succession to, 96; approval of international agreements, 103; constitution of, in Irish Free State, 141-43, 152-53; constitution of, in Irish Republic, 160-61

Darcy, Patrick, 47

Davies, Sir John, 8, 16

Deasy's Act, 244-45, 255, 268

Declaration of Independence, 1776, 50, 51

Declaratory Act (Ireland—6 Geo. 1, c. 5) 14, 44, 46, 48, 51; (American colonies—6 Geo. 3, c. 12) 46, 49

Defence Regulations (United Kingdom), 186

Defense under Anglo-Irish Agreement, 1921, 82

Delegated legislation in Ireland, 181; in Northern Ireland and Irish Republic, 183-88; emergency provisions, 186-87; Parliamentary control, 188-90; publication, 190-91; judicial scrutiny and control, 200-202, 204-5, 206-8

de Valera, Eamon, 73, 78, 84, 87, 88, 92, 94, 100

Devon Commission on Irish Land, 244, 246

Dicey, Albert Venn, 62, 64-65, 70

Diplomatic recognition and representation of Irish Free State and Irish Republic, 97-98

Dodd, J., 201

Domicil, 112, 113, 115-16

Dominion status of Irish Free State, 79, 82; development of, 83-84; rejected by de Valera government, 87; considered by English courts, 91; and Eire, 92-94; and Northern Ireland, 95

Donoughmore-Scott Committee on Ministers' Powers, 181, 183

Duffy, Gavan, J. and P., 4, 5, 31, 32, 105, 120, 174, 176, 177, 209, 224

Dunraven, Earl of, 67, 73

Durham Report, 56

E

Economic war, 85, 90, 187

Edward VIII, 88

Edwards, Dr. J. LL. J., 130

Electricity Board for Northern Ireland, 198

Electricity Supply Board, 199

Emergency provisions, delegated legislation, 186; in 1937 constitution of Irish Republic, 175

Estonia, 104, 105

European Court of Human Rights, 102

European Customs Union, 104

European Payments Union, 104

European Recovery Programme, 101

Exchequer, Irish, amalgamated with British Exchequer, 56

Executive Committee of Northern Ireland, 126

Executive Council, Irish Free State, 22, 88, 163; approval of titles of honor, 139; constitution, 143; and public safety legislation, 148, 149; alteration, 153; legal position of President, 220

External Affairs, Irish Free State Minister for, 96; Irish Republic's Min-

ister for, 98, 101; Irish and Commonwealth Departments of, 98
External Association, doctrine of, 88
Extradition, 105-6
Eyre, Bills in, 16

F

Fair Trade Commission, 197
Famine, 241-42
Federalism proposed for Ireland, 59, 68; deprecated by Dicey, 70
Fee farm grants, 236
Financial provisions in 1886 Home Rule Bill, 62; in 1893 Home Rule Bill, 64; in Irish Council Bill, 1907, 68; in 1912 Home Rule Bill 69-70; relating to Northern Ireland Parliament, 127
Fine Gael, 92-93
Finland, 104
Fitzgibbon, John (Earl of Clare), 53
Fitzgibbon, J., 87, 220
Fleta, 39
Flight of the Earls, 39, 233
Food and Agriculture Organisation, 101
Four Courts, 11, 30
Fox, Charles James, 53
Foyle Fisheries, 115
France, 104
Franklin, Benjamin, 50
Franks Committee on Administrative Tribunals, 183
Friedmann, Professor W., 200
Fugitive offenders, 120-21
Fundamental rights, in 1922 Irish Free State constitution, 139-41; and public safety legislation, 149; in 1937 constitution of Irish Republic, 164-68, 173, 176-79; in India, 167; in Pakistan, 167-68

G

Gaelic Athletic Association, 66
Gárda Siochána, 184, 224
Gavelkind, case of, 229-30
George III, 53, 54
Germany, 104
Gladstone, W. E., 61, 63, 66, 70, 124, 247, 263, 268
Government of Ireland, 1886 Bill: judicial provisions in, 18; outline of, 61-62; 1893 Bill: judicial provisions in, 18; outline of, 63-64; 1912 Bill (1914 Act): outline of, 68-70;

opposition to, 70-71; suspension of, 71, 123; 1920 Act: outlined, 73-74, 125-26; operation in Northern Ireland, 126-33
Governor of Northern Ireland, 126, 187, 215
Governor-General, Irish Free State, appointment of judges, 22; appointment of, 83; diminution of status, 87; advised by Executive Council, 143; dissolution of Oireachtas, 143; appropriation of money, 143; contrasted with President of Irish Republic, 160; abolition of office, 162
Graham-Harrison, Sir William, 181, 188, 201
Grattan, Henry, 51, 57
Grenada, 231
Griffith, Arthur, 67

H

Habeas Corpus allowed in Ireland, 17, 140; in 1922 Irish Free State constitution, 140; in 1937 constitution of Irish Republic, 164
Haldane, Lord, 86
Hanging gale, 240
Hanna, J., 168, 178
Harris, Walter, 47
Healy, Timothy Michael, 83, 145
Hearts of steel, 241
Henry II, 5, 38, 45, 229, 230
Henry VIII, 45, 181
Hibernicus, 7
High Court, Irish Free State, 22; Irish Republic, 24; Northern Ireland, 19; Southern Ireland, 19
High Court of Appeal for Ireland, 19, 20, 29, 30, 74
Hogan, Patrick, 264
Holmes, J. and L. J., 28, 203
Home Government Association, 60
Home Rule, Isaac Butt and, 58, 60; opposed in Ulster, 63, 66; "Home Rule all round," 68. See also Government of Ireland
Home Rule Confederation of Great Britain, 60
Hooker, Elizabeth R., 258
House of Commons
Westminster, Irish members in, 56; Select Committee on Statutory Instruments, 189; Northern Ireland members of, 128

Ireland, 11, 14; origin, 39-40; composition, 44; Roman Catholics excluded from, 44, 54; declaration of independence, 47; executive not responsible to, 50, 54; office-holders and Crown pensioners in, 54; under Government of Ireland Act, 1914, 69; proposed by Irish Convention, 72

Northern Ireland, 74, 125

Southern Ireland, 74, 137

House of Lords

Westminster, appeals to, 11, 13, 14, 17, 18, 19, 110, 133; force of decisions of, 28; development of, 40; Irish members of, 56; powers curtailed by Parliament Act, 68-69

Ireland, appeals to, 14, 15; development of, 40; episcopal influence in, 50

Hungary, 67

I

Imperial Conference, 1923, 96; 1926, 86; 1930, 85

India, courts in, 8, 15, 25, 33; doctrine of precedent, 27; directives of social policy in 1950 constitution, 103; law-districts, 109; domicil and partition, 121; and Fugitive Offenders Act, 1881, 122; reservation of Bills, 126; compensation for acquisition of property, 128, 135; description of State, 158; President, 159, 160, 223; Prime Minister and Council of Ministers, 160; bicameral legislature, 162; Ministers speaking in both Houses, 163; collective responsibility, 163; fundamental rights, 167-68; social policy, 169; amendment of constitution, 170-71; Supreme Court, 172-73

Industrial Credit Corporation, 199

Initiation of legislation in 1922 Irish Free State constitution, 144, 147

International Bureau of Weights and Measures, 99

International Civil Aviation Organization, 99

International Labor Organization, ratification of conventions by Irish Republic, 99; ratification of conventions for Northern Ireland, 108

International law and 1937 constitution of Irish Republic, 102-3; considered by Dublin courts, 104-6

International Office of Epizootics, 99

Ireton, 234

Irish Citizen Army, 72

Irish Convention (1917-18), 72, 123, 262, 263

Irish Council (1907), 68

Irish Free State (Saorstat Eireann), introduction of phrase, 77; status under Anglo-Irish Agreement, 1921, 79; attitude to Dominion status, 84; power to amend Constitution, 87; area of jurisdiction, 106-7, 138-39; legal position of Government, 218-22; 1922 Constitution: drafting, 137; opening clauses, 138-39; fundamental rights, 139-41; legislature, 141-43; executive, 143-44; referendum and initiation, 144, 147; amendment, 144, 146-47, 149-50; inauguration, 145-46. *See also* Bills; Courts; Dáil Eireann; Diplomatic Recognition; Executive Council; External Affairs; Governor-General; Land Commission; Land Law; Land Purchase Scheme; Ministers and Ministries; Neutrality; Oath; Oireachtas; Provisional Government and Parliament; Senate; Special Powers; Supreme Court; Treaty Practice; Tribunals; University Representation

Irish Home Rule League, 60

Irish Hospitals Sweepstakes, 117, 199

Irish language and 1922 Irish Free State constitution, 139; and 1937 constitution of Irish Republic, 156

Irish Legislative Body (1886), 18, 61, 62

Irish Legislature (1893), 63-64

Irish National League, 249

Irish Nationalist party, 60, 63, 72, 73, 124

Irish Racing Board, 199

Irish Reform Association, 67

Irish Republican Brotherhood, 57, 72

Irish Volunteers, in eighteenth century, 51, 52; in twentieth century, 70-71, 72

Italy, 100

J

Jamaica, 43

James I, 44, 232
James II, 14, 46, 47, 234
Jennings, Professor R. Y., 83
John, 6, 38, 230
Johnston, J., 13, 219, 221
Joint Exchequer Board under Government of Ireland Act, 1914, 69
Judges in Ireland, 10-12; in colonies, 17; independence of Irish, 17; in Northern Ireland, 20; in Irish Free State, 22, 23, 24; in Irish Republic, 26-27
Judgments, extension of, 111-12; enforcement of, 118-19
Judicial Committee of the Privy Council, appeals from Ireland, 13, 15, 19, 23, 81, 86, 89; from colonies, 18; from Australia, 23, 154; decisions of, in Irish Republic, 32; single judgments, 33; validity of Irish legislation, 18-19, 62, 134; and Irish Council Bill, 1907, 68; appeals from Canada, 86, 154
Judicial review in 1886 Home Rule Bill, 18; in 1893 Home Rule Bill, 18; in 1914 Home Rule Act, 19; in 1920 Government of Ireland Act, 19; in Irish Free State, 22; in Irish Republic, 25, 26; of Northern Ireland legislation, 133-35
Justiciar, 5-6, 8-9, 42

K

Keith, Arthur Berriedale, 78, 141
Kellogg Pact, 84
Kennedy, C. J., 146, 151, 157, 191, 219, 220
King's Bench, Irish Courts of, 9, 11, 13, 30; English Court of, 13, 15, 19, 53, 109; King's [Queen's] Bench Division, Ireland, 17, 19; King's [Queen's] Bench Division, Northern Ireland, 20, 31
Kohn, Dr. Leo, 80, 144-45

L

Labour Court, 185, 187, 197
Land Commission
    Ireland, freedom from court orders, 174; constitution of, 249; powers of, 259-62
    Irish Republic, 178-79, 264-66
    Northern Ireland, 263
Land Law, early Irish, 229-30; introduction of English, 230-31, 235-36; leaseholds, 238-40, 242-45; user of

land, 252-53; registration of title, 250-51, 256-57; registration of deeds, 237
Land League, 248-49
Land Purchase Annuities, dispute between Irish Free State and United Kingdom governments, 78
Land Purchase Scheme, in Ireland, 258-62; in Northern Ireland, 262-63; in the Irish Republic, 263-66
Latham, Richard Thomas Edwin, 86
Latvia, 104-5
Law, early Irish (Brehon law), 3-5, 38, 229; to be cited in Dáil Courts, 22
Law, English, introduction into Ireland, 5-8, 230-32; use by native Irish, 6-7
League of Nations and Irish Free State, 83, 96, 100, 106
Liberal party, 61, 63, 65, 68
Limerick, Treaty of, 234
Limitation of actions, 212, 217, 218, 232
Local government, reorganized in Ireland, 56, 66
Local Government Board for Ireland, 202-4, 216
Lord Chancellor, England, 18, 20; Ireland, 11, 19, 20
Lord Chief Justice of Northern Ireland, 19, 20, 191, 196; of Southern Ireland, 19
Lord Lieutenant of Ireland, executive functions under Home Rule proposals, 62, 64, 68, 69, 71; rules for municipal government, 181; setting-up of Northern Ireland government departments, 182, 216; legal position, 211
Lordship of Ireland, 5, 39, 45
Loyal National Repeal Association, 58

M

MacBride, Seán, 101
McDonnell, Sir Anthony, 67
McNair, Lord, 116
MacNeill, Professor Eoin, 3-4, 39, 72
Madden, J., 203
Magna Carta, application in Ireland, 231
Maguire, C. J., 32, 105
Maine, Sir Henry, 3
Maitland, Frederic William, 3, 6
Malta, proposed integration with United Kingdom, 136
Mansergh, Professor Nicholas, 93, 100
Massey, William Ferguson, 268
Master of the Rolls, Ireland, 17

Mayart, Sir Samuel, 47
Meredith, J., 222
Military tenures, 231, 235
Ministers and Ministries of Northern Ireland, 126, 183-88, 216; of Irish Free State, 143-44, 153; of Irish Republic, 163, 183-88
Minute men, 50
Molony, L. J., 201
Molyneux, William, 47-48, 50
Monopolies Commission, 197
Moore, Kingsmill, J., 97, 172
Morris, Lord, 201
Murnaghan, J., 32, 209, 210, 220, 225
Murphy, L. J., 30
Mutiny Acts, 50-51

N

Napoleon, 166
National volunteers, 72
Navigation Act, 46, 47, 50, 51
Neutrality, of Irish Free State under Anglo-Irish Agreement, 1921, 82; of Irish Republic during Second World War, 90, 91, 100
New South Wales, 116, 254, 255
New Zealand, courts in, 8; amendment of constitution, 155; abolition of Legislative Council, 162; arbitration and monopolies, 197; legal position of Crown, 212; fee tail, 254; registration of title, 256; devolution of property, 257; family maintenance legislation, 257; leases, 267; mentioned, 4, 56, 65, 70, 79, 90, 109, 176
Newark, Professor F. H., 8, 16
Noel-Baker, Philip John, 78
North Atlantic Treaty Organization, 102
Northern Ireland, introduction of phrase, 77; opts out of Irish Free State, 81; to remain part of United Kingdom, 93, 106; and United Kingdom treaties, 107-8; power to make agreements, 108-9; area of jurisdiction, 114-15; separate domicil, 115-16; outline of constitution, 123-33; judicial review of legislation, 133-35; summary of constitutional position, 135-36. See also Administrative decisions and tribunals; Attorney-General; Bills; Courts; Crown; Delegated legislation; Dominion status; Governor of Northern Ireland; House of Commons; Land

Commission; Land Law; Land Purchase Scheme; Lord Chief Justice; Lord Lieutenant of Ireland; Ministers and Ministries; Parliament; Plantation of Ulster; Privy Council; Proportional representation; Public Corporations; Senate; Social Services; Special powers; Statutory Rules and Orders; Supreme Court; Ulster; Unionist party; University representation
Northern Ireland bodies: General Health Services Board, 199; Hospitals Authority, 199; Housing Trust, 199; Road Transport Board, 198; Tuberculosis Authority, 198

O

Oath for Irish Free State legislature, 79-80; abolition of, 84, 85-86, 151
O'Brien, J., 201
O'Brien, L. C., 201
O'Brien, L. C. J., 201
O'Brien, William, 261
O'Bryne, J., 150-226
O'Connell, Daniel, Catholic emancipation, 54, 57; repeal of Union, 58, 59, 66, 67, 73; and land law, 268
Oireachtas
Irish Free State, power to elect members of Council of Ireland, 124; constitution of, 141; dissolution of, 143; approval of 1937 constitution of Irish Republic, 155
Irish Republic, constitution of, 160-61; guided by directive principles of social policy, 169
Organization for European Economic Co-operation, 101
Orpen, Goddard Henry, 37-38
O'Sullivan, Dr. Donal, 150

P

Pakistan, courts, 25, 33; doctrine of precedent, 27; directives of social policy in 1956 constitution, 103; compensation for acquistion of property, 128; description of State, 158; President of, 159, 223; Prime Minister and Cabinet of Ministers, 160; unicameral legislature, 162; collective responsibility, 163; social policy, 169-70; amendment of constitution, 171; emergency powers, 176
Palatinate of Ormonds (Tipperary), 9

Pale, English, 38-39, 232
Palles, C. B., 201, 202
Parliament
  Westminster, authority to legislate for Ireland, 40-41; authority challenged, 41, 46-47, 51; authority renounced, 52-53; under Act of Union, 56; and 1886 Home Rule Bill, 62; sovereignty, 63, 126-27; and 1893 Home Rule Bill, 64; and Government of Ireland Act, 1919, 70; and Irish Free State, 79, 80; claim to legislate for any part of Ireland repudiated, 93; relationship with Northern Ireland Parliament, 126-29; representation of Northern Ireland in, 128
  Irish, in Middle Ages, 39-40; declaration of independence (1460), 41-42; growth of, in sixteenth and seventeenth centuries, 43-45; county and borough representation, 39, 44; septennial and octennial Act, 49-50; under Government of Ireland Act, 1914, 68-69
  Northern Ireland, validity of laws of, 19; survivor of Government of Ireland Act, 1920, 20, 125; constitution of, 73, 125; may consent to Northern Ireland's ceasing to be part of United Kingdom, 93; relationship with United Kingdom Parliament, 127-28; scope of powers, 128-29; extension of powers, 131-33; Select Committee on Statutory Rules and Orders, 189; Speakers of, 191
  Southern Ireland, constitution, 73-74, 125; meetings of, 137
Parnell, Charles Stewart, 60, 66, 268-69
Patriot Parliament, 14, 46, 234
Permanent Court of International Justice, 83
Petition of right, 211
Petty sessions and courts of summary jurisdiction in Ireland, 18; in Northern Ireland, 21; replaced in Irish Free State, 24
Phelan, Edward Joseph, 99
Pim, J., 148
Pitt, William, 53
Pius VII, 166
Plantation of Ulster, 44, 233-34, 246
Plunkett, Sir Horace, 66

Poor Law introduced into Ireland, 56, 241
Porter, L. J., 30
Poynings' Law (10 Hen. 7, c. 4), 42-43, 44-45, 48, 49, 51, 53, 75; (10 Hen. 7, c. 22), 42, 46, 236
Precedent, doctrine of, Ceylon, 27; India, 27; Pakistan, 27; Scotland, 27-28; Northern Ireland, 28-30; Irish Republic, 30-33
President of Executive Council (Irish Free State), 143, 153, 220
President of Irish Republic, accrediting of diplomatic representations to, 98; election, 159; functions, 159-60, 162; reference of bills to Supreme Court, 172-73; mentioned, 25, 160
Privy Council, English: control of Irish legislation, 43, 45, 52; Irish: 7, 39, 43, 52, 62, 64, 69; Northern Ireland: 126, 187. See also Judicial Committee of the Privy Council
Proportional representation, 130
Provisional government and parliament of Irish Free State, 67, 137-38, 182, 218
Public Corporations, 197-200
Public safety, legislation in Irish Free State, 130, 148-50; legislation in Irish Republic, 130

Q

Quarter Sessions in Ireland, 18; in Northern Ireland, 21; replaced in Irish Free State, 24
Queensland, 116
Quekett, Sir Arthur, 182, 186, 263

R

Redmond, John, 72
Referendum, in 1922 Irish Free State Constitution, 144, 147; in Australian Constitution, 145, 154; approving 1937 constitution of Irish Republic, 155; in 1937 constitution, 170
Registration of deeds, 237
Registration of title, 250-51, 256-57
Religious discrimination, prohibition of, 1886 Home Rule Bill, 62; 1893 Home Rule Bill, 64; Irish Council Bill, 1907, 68; 1912 Home Rule Bill, 69; Government of Ireland Act, 1920, 128, 135; Ceylon, 167

Renunciation Act (23 Geo. 3, c. 28), 14, 53, 55
Repeal Arbitration Courts, 58
Repealing Act (22 Geo. 3, c. 53), 14, 52
Republic of Ireland (Eire), proclaimed 1916, 72; republican status, 92; description of State, 93, 157; legal position of Government, 222-23; 1937 constitution: preamble and preliminary provisions, 156-58; area of jurisdiction, 156-57; President, 158-60; legislature, 160-62; executive, 162-63; fundamental rights, 164-68; directive principles of social policy, 168-70; amendment, 170-71; President's power of reference to Supreme Court, 172-73; judicial review, 174; emergency powers, 175-76. *See also* Administrative decisions and tribunals; Attorney-General; Bills; Council of State; Dáil Eireann; Delegated legislation; Diplomatic recognition; Dominion status; External affairs; Land Commission; Land law; Land Purchase Scheme; Ministers and Ministries; Neutrality; Oireachtas; Social Services; Special powers; Treaty practice; Tribunals
Republican loan, 97
Richard II, 9, 38
Richardson, Henry George, 13, 35, 39
Rising, 1641, 44, 46, 233; 1798, 54; 1848, 57, 60, 61; 1867, 57, 60, 61; 1916, 72, 123
Robson, Professor W. A., 203
Roman Catholics, exclusion from Irish Parliament, 44, 54; right to vote, 54
Ronan, L. J., 201
Ross, Sir John, L. C., 20, 29
Royal Ulster Constabulary, 184
Rundale, 230, 265

S

St. John-Stevas, Norman, 196
St. Leonards, Lord (Sir Edward Sugden), 11
Sawer, Professor G., 214
Sayles, Professor G. O., 13, 35, 39
Scotland, doctrine of precedent in, 27-28; Union with England, 14, 45, 54; appeals to House of Lords, 110; movement for devolution in, 136; registration of land, 256

Select Committee on Statutory Instruments (United Kingdom), 189-90; on Statutory Rules and Orders (Northern Ireland), 189-90; on statutory Instruments (Irish Republic), 189-90
Senate
    Irish, under Government of Ireland Act, 1914, 69; proposal by Irish Convention, 72
    Irish Free State, 141-43; constitution, 145; alterations and dissolution, 151-52
    Irish Republic, constitution, 161; time for consideration of Bills, 162; Select Committee on Statutory Instruments, 189
    Southern Ireland, 73-74, 125, 142
    Northern Ireland, 73-74
Settlement, Act of (12 & 13 Will. 3, c. 2), 17
Settlements of Irish land, 46, 230, 232-34
Simnel, Lambert, 43
Sinn Fein, 67, 72, 73, 78, 97, 124, 137, 174
Smith, Professor T. B., 27
Social Policy, Directive Principles of, in 1937 constitution of Irish Republic, 168; in India, 169; in Pakistan, 169-70
Social services, agreement between United Kingdom and Northern Ireland governments, 127, 193-94; National Health Service, 131; reciprocal arrangements, 183-84; administrative procedures in Northern Ireland and Irish Republic, 194-95
Solicitor-General for Ireland, 57
Solicitors, 196
South Africa, provincial councils in, 128; entrenched provisions in South Africa Act, 1909, 154-55; acceptance of advice, 160; Ministers speaking in either House, 163; legal position of Crown, 212; Crown grants of land, 255; registration of land, 256; leases, 267; mentioned, 4, 79, 83, 84, 86, 88, 90, 125, 138, 176
Spain, 100, 105
Special powers, legislation in Northern Ireland, 130-31, 204; tribunals in Irish Free State, 149
Star Chamber, Court of, 9

State succession, 96-97
Statute of Distributions, 237
Statute of Frauds, 237
Statutes, English, application in Ireland, 40-41, 42, 46-47, 49, 230-31, 235-36
Statutory Rules and Orders (Northern Ireland), 183-88; Select Committee on, 189-90; publication of, 190-91
Statutory Instruments
    Irish Republic, 183-88; Select Committee on, 189-90; publication of, 191
    United Kingdom, 185; Select Committee on, 189-90; publication of, 190
Story, J., 226
Strongbow (Earl of Pembroke and Leinster), 5
Sullivan, P. and C. J., 191, 207, 221
Supreme Court
    England, 17
    Ireland, 17
    Irish Free State, 22, 24
    Irish Republic, 24; reference of Bills to, 25, 159, 172-73; setting-up of, 26; determination of President's incapacity, 159; rules of, 185
    Northern Ireland, 19, 20, 111, 127, 131, 185
    Southern Ireland, 19, 111
    United States, 28, 33
Surrender and re-grant, 39, 232

T

Tanaiste (Deputy Prime Minister), 163
Tanistry, Case of, 230
Taoiseach (Prime Minister), advice to President, 159-60; chosen by Dáil, 161; certificate for emergency Bills, 162, functions, 163
Tenant right, 236-37, 246-48, 249-50
Thankerton, Lord, 136
"Three F's," 248-50
Tithe, 240-41
Torrens system of registration of title, 250, 256
Town and country planning, 193
Transport Tribunals in Northern Ireland and Irish Republic, 195
Treaty practice, Irish Free State, 83-84; Irish Republic, 103-4
Tribunals, military and special in Irish

Free State, 23, 207; in Irish Republic, 25; in Ireland, 204
Trinity College, Dublin, 12, 44, 73, 239, 243
Turf Development Board, 199

U

Ulster, proposed exclusion from Government of Ireland Bill, 1912, 70; "county option" proposal, 71; proposed exclusion from Government of Ireland Bill, 1914, 71; inclusion in Government of Ireland Act, 1920, 73, 124. See also Unionist party
Ulster custom, 242, 246-48, 249, 255
Ulster month under Anglo-Irish Agreement, 1921, 129
Ulster Transport Authority, 195, 198
Ulster Volunteer Force, 70
Under Secretary for Ireland, 67
Undertakers, government by, 50
Union, Scotland, and England, 14, 45, 54; Ireland and Great Britain, 15, 54, 55, 110; agitation for repeal of, 58
Unionist party, opposition to Home Rule, 63, 66, 70, 72, 73, 124
United Irish League, 261-62
United Irishmen, 54
United Nations Organization, Eire's membership in, 100-101, 106
United States, Irish Free State and Canadian Ministers to, 83, 97; 1948 co-operation agreement with Eire, 101; attitude to Northern Ireland's position, 102; 1950 Consular Convention with Eire, 103; constitution of, 128, 138, 139-40, 141, 154, 168; Administrative Procedure Act, 183; registration of title, 250, 256
U.S.S.R., 104
Universal Postal Union, 99
University representation, in Irish Parliament, 44; in United Kingdom Parliament, 128; in Irish Free State, 152; in Irish Republic, 161

V

Victoria, State of, 65, 70, 254
Villein, 7
Virginia, 43